PRACTICAL MANAGEMENT
FOR SUPERVISORS

PRACTICAL MANAGEMENT
FOR SUPERVISORS

Second Edition

Lester R. Bittel
Professor of Management Emeritus
and a Virginia Eminent Scholar
James Madison University

Library of Congress Cataloging-in-Publication Data

Bittel, Lester R.
    Practical management for supervisors / Lester R. Bittel. -- 2nd ed.
        p.   cm.
    Rev. ed. of: Essentials of supervisory management. 1981.
    Includes bibliographical references and index.
    ISBN 0-02-802484-2 : $20.00
    1. Supervision of employees. 2. Supervision of employees -- Case studies.
    I. Bittel, Lester R. Essentials of supervisory management. II. Title.
    HF5549.B518 1993   92-36417
    658.3' 02--dc20   CIP

In brief, to Muriel

PRACTICAL MANAGEMENT FOR SUPERVISORS
Second Edition

Imprint 1996

Send all inquiries to:
Glencoe/McGraw-Hill
936 Eastwind Drive
Westerville, Ohio 43081

ISBN: 0-02-802484-2

Printed in the United States of America.

2 3 4 5 6 7 8 9 10 11 12 13 14 15   POH   04 03 02 01 00 99 98 97 96

CONTENTS

CASES IN POINT

PREFACE

Practical Management for Supervisors is intended for the use of all those who wish to learn about or improve their skills in supervisory management. It is especially suitable for men and women already employed in commerce, industry, and government. You will find that its emphasis is on practicality and usefulness. Underlying theories and principles are explained, but optimum coverage is given to real-life, on-the-job applications. The 15 chapters of this text have been distilled from the best of the author's landmark work, *What Every Supervisor Should Know*.

This book is conceived and designed to make reading and learning easy for you. Incorporated in its makeup are the following features to help maximize your own study efforts.

LEARNING OBJECTIVES

These clearly set out the goals you should strive for in terms of what you should know or be able to do after reading the chapter.

KEY CONCEPTS

These should be read first, because they provide a preview, summarized in five succinct statements, of the basic ideas covered in the chapter.

QUESTIONS AND ANSWERS

These constitute the main body of the text. The questions are arranged in a carefully selected sequence to advance one idea at a time, and the answer to each question examines the underlying principle from its fundamental expression to detailed suggestions for applying it in practice. However, you need not read any given chapter from beginning to end. Instead, you may choose to look for and read first those questions and answers that apply most directly to your present interests or work.

REVIEW QUESTIONS

These follow the questions and answers. If you cannot answer them, or are uncertain about your answers, go back to the text and reread the pertinent material. Only by doing this can you be sure that you fully understand the valuable principles and practices covered in the text.

CASES IN POINT

In each chapter, after the Review Questions, there is a real-life supervisory case history. A typical Case in Point tells about a particularly trying on-the-job situation that requires a solution or decision from the supervisor in charge. Read the case. Then study the list of five alternative solutions or conclusions. Choose the one that seems best to you, then the next most appropriate, and so on, down to the one you like least. For each alternative, enter a number from 1 to 5 in the space provided.

ACTION PLANNING CHECKLISTS

In the Appendix you will find 15 checklists (one for each chapter) designed for use on your job. Each checklist contains 15 items, which sum up pivotal action ideas covered in the chapter. Under *Action Needed*, put a check in the "Yes" column for any item that needs action from you. Put a check in the "No" column if you have already taken care of that item or if it doesn't apply to your present work. For each item that you check "Yes" (needs action), make a note of what you intend to do. When you have taken that action, mark under *Date Completed* the date it was done. Of course, just reading through the 15 items in the checklist will provide you with a detailed review and summary of the chapter's main ideas.

SELF-CHECKS

At the end of each major part of the book is a set of questions that will check your understanding of the text in the five chapters in that part of the book. There are 50 questions for each part, 25 true-false and 25 multiple choice. The questions follow the sequence of chapters with five questions in each format for each chapter in the part. For example, for Part 1, questions 1 through 5 relate to Chapter 1, questions 6 through 10 relate to Chapter 2, and so on. After you have answered the questions, turn to the Appendix to find the correct answers. If you have chosen some wrong answers or have been uncertain about your choices, go back to that part of the text where the material was covered. Read it again before trying the Self-Check a second time.

ABOUT THE AUTHOR

Lester R. Bittel has acquired an enormous amount of experience related to the field of supervisory management. He has worked in a number of manufacturing plants and managed more than one. As the training director for a major chemical company, he designed and coordinated the employee and management development programs for 21 plants and six sales offices. As editor in chief of a major business publication, Mr. Bittel visited hundreds of plants and offices and spoke to thousands of first-line supervisors and their bosses. As a management consultant, he has aided dozens of companies in developing and operating their supervisory training programs and also designed the Professional Development Certificate program used by the Commonwealth of Virginia for training supervisors.

Mr. Bittel has written or collaborated on more than three dozen books and 25 educational films on management and supervision. In recent years he has been honored by the American Society of Mechanical Engineers as its Towne Lecturer, granted the Frederick W. Taylor Award for distinguished management writing, and awarded the ASME Centennial Medal.

PRACTICAL MANAGEMENT FOR SUPERVISORS

PART ONE

Taking Hold of
Your Responsibilities

Supervisory management requires the ability to get things done through other people. To master this job, supervisors must first fully understand the nature of managerial work and then learn to set goals and to plan work within an organizational structure. They must also learn to exercise control over the work as it progresses and to use information to solve problems and make decisions.

▶ Chapter 1 describes the nature and scope of managerial work and outlines the role supervisors play in it.

▶ Chapter 2 outlines the principles and procedures for setting goals and developing effective plans.

▶ Chapter 3 shows how to divide up work into effective and manageable organizational structures.

▶ Chapter 4 links the planning process to the controls that are needed to monitor progress and enforce work force standards.

▶ Chapter 5 introduces the techniques by which information is used to solve problems and make decisions.

CHAPTER

1

THE SUPERVISORY MANAGEMENT JOB

LEARNING OBJECTIVES

After studying this chapter, you should be able to:

1. Understand the concept of management and the role and responsibilities of a supervisor.

2. Identify the resources that supervisors must manage and the results that are to be obtained from them.

3. Discuss the major qualifications and competencies that supervisors are expected to bring to the job.

4. Explain the different emphases placed upon technical, administrative, and human relations skills at various levels of management.

5. Discuss the need for balancing a concern for output and a concern for the people who perform the work.

OVERVIEW OF KEY CONCEPTS IN THIS CHAPTER

▶ Supervisors are a vital and legal part of every management group; they add strength to an organization by serving as the keystone (or linking pin) between middle and executive levels of management and the employees who "put their hands on the work."

▶ Supervisors must bring to their work a unique combination of technical competence, individual energy, and ability to get along with and motivate others.

▶ The performance of supervisors will be judged by how well they manage the resources assigned to them (facilities and equipment, power and utilities, material and supplies, information, money, and human resources) and the results they get from the resources in the way of output, quality, and cost control.

▶ The supervisory management job generally requires three skills: technical, administrative, and human relations; of these, the human relations skill is often the most demanding.

▶ It is essential for successful supervisors to balance their skills and efforts equally between that part of the work which is production- or task-oriented and that which is employee- or group-centered. Too much emphasis in a single direction is likely to be self-defeating.

WHAT IS MANAGEMENT?
WHY IS IT SO IMPORTANT?

Management is a unique occupation. **Management** is described as the process of obtaining, deploying, and utilizing a variety of essential resources in support of an organization's objectives. One of the most important resources of an organization is its employees. Managers devote a large portion of their own efforts to planning, organizing, staffing, directing, and controlling the work of these human resources. One clear distinction between managers and other employees, however, is that managers direct the work of others, rather than performing that work themselves.

ARE ALL MANAGERS ALIKE?

No. Managers, and the work they do, differ mainly according to their level in the organization's hierarchy. This difference is illustrated in Figure 1-1. At the top of an organization are its executives. **Executives** are in charge of, and responsible for, a group of other managers. Executives establish broad plans, objectives, and general policies. They motivate, direct, and control the managers who report to them.

Middle managers plan, initiate, and implement programs that are intended to carry out the broader objectives set by executives. Middle managers motivate, direct, and control the supervisors (and any other managers and employees) who report to them.

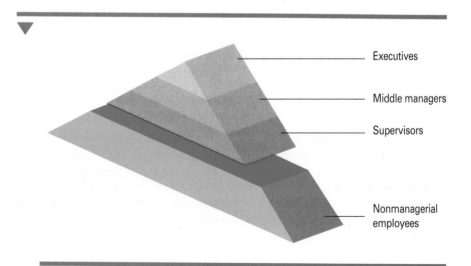

FIGURE 1-1 **Managerial levels**

Supervisors are managers who normally report to middle managers. Supervisors have the responsibility of getting the "hands-on-the-work" employees to carry out the plans and the policies set by executives and middle managers. Supervisors plan, motivate, direct, and control the work of nonmanagerial employees at the operational level of the organization.

WHAT KINDS OF PERSONS BECOME SUPERVISORS?

Just about every kind you can think of. An *average* supervisor, according to statistics describing some 8000 of them, has these characteristics:

Is between 31 and 50 years of age.

Has been with the current employer for five to 15 years.

Has been a supervisor less than five years.

Was promoted from the ranks.

Is a high school graduate, and has probably attended college; one out of three is a college graduate.

Three out of four supervisors are male; about 10 percent are nonwhite. Half of all supervisors are employed in a white-collar environment. One out of three supervisors once belonged to a trade union. About six out of every ten supervisors have only nonmanagerial employees reporting to them. These are called "first-level supervisors." About four out of ten are "second-level supervisors" and are at the fringes of middle management. They supervise other supervisors as well as nonmanagerial employees.[1]

WHY DOES FRONTLINE SUPERVISION GET SO MUCH ATTENTION?

Because it represents just about the most important single force in the American economy. Supervisors, as an occupational classification, form a major segment of the overall labor force. In the United States alone, there is a supervisory management force two million strong. It holds the power to turn on—or turn off—the productivity of most organizations. These supervisors are the men and women who maintain the crucial inter-

[1] Lester R. Bittel and Jackson E. Ramsey, "The Limited, Traditional World of Supervisors," *Harvard Business Review,* July-August 1982, vol. 60, no. 4, p. 26.

face between the management hierarchy and the vast body of employees who put their hands on, or apply their minds to, the real work of enterprise.

Recognition—and acceptance—of supervisors by top management has helped them to emerge finally as essential and integrated members of the management group and to assume all the responsibilities of full-fledged managers. The way hasn't been easy. Too often it has been painfully slow. Even today there are companies where the supervisor's status is shaky. But on the whole, no single group of men and women has achieved and deserved such stature and attention in so short a time after so long a wait as has supervisory management.

LEGALLY, WHAT MAKES A SUPERVISOR A SUPERVISOR?

The federal laws of the United States provide two definitions of a supervisor:

1. The Taft-Hartley Act of 1947 says that a supervisor is

    . . . any individual having authority, in the interest of the employer, to hire, transfer, suspend, lay off, recall, promote, discharge, assign, reward, or discipline other employees, or responsibility to direct them or to adjust their grievances, or effectively to recommend such action, if in connection with the foregoing the exercise of such authority is not merely of a routine or clerical nature, but requires the use of independent judgment.

    This act specifically prohibits supervisors from joining a union of production and clerical workers, although they may form a union composed exclusively of supervisors.

2. The Fair Labor Standards Act of 1938 (or Minimum Wage Law) set the tone for the above by defining a supervisor as

    . . . an executive whose primary duty consists of the management of a customarily recognized department or subdivision; who customarily and regularly directs the work of two or more employees; who has the authority to hire or fire other employees or whose suggestions and recommendations as to the hiring or firing and as to the advancement and promotion or any other change in status will be given particular weight; who customarily and regularly exercises discretionary powers; and who does not devote more than 20 percent of his (or her) hours of work to activities which are not closely related to the (managerial) work described above.

    This law also stipulates that supervisors be paid a salary (regardless of how many hours they work). This latter provision makes some supervisors unhappy, since it makes them exempt from the provision of the law that calls for overtime pay after a certain number of hours have been worked. Many employers, however, voluntarily compensate for supervisory overtime in one way or another.

The thrust of these two laws is to make supervisors, once and for all, a bona fide part of management.

ARE SUPERVISORS PERMITTED TO DO THE SAME WORK AS THE PEOPLE THEY SUPERVISE?

Within the 20 percent stipulation of the Fair Labor Standards Act, there is no law stopping it. Most companies with labor unions, however, often have a contract clause that prohibits the supervisor from performing any work that a union member would ordinarily do (except in clearly defined emergencies, in which the supervisor would do as she or he sees fit).

This is a point on which most managements agree with unions. Few companies want supervisors to do the work their other employees are hired to do. Supervisors are most valuable when they spend 100 percent of their time supervising. It makes little sense for a $500-a-week supervisor, for instance, to do the work of a $300-a-week operator.

HOW DOES A PERSON BECOME A SUPERVISOR?

Three out of four supervisors are promoted from the ranks of the organization in which they serve. Typically, they are long-service employees. They have greater experience, have held more different jobs in the organization, and have significantly more education than the employees they supervise. Usually, it is apparent that supervisors are chosen from among the best and most experienced employees in the organization.[2]

Other than those supervisors who rise from the ranks, 7 percent are hired directly from a college or technical school. Six percent enter through company-sponsored management training programs, and 13 percent are hired into the position from another company or organization.[3]

---

[2] Herbert R. Northrup, Ronald M. Cowin, Lawrence G. Vanden Plas, and William E. Fulmer, "The Objective Selection of Supervisors," *Manpower and Human Resources Studies*, no. 8, The Wharton School, Univ. of Pennsylvania, 1978, pp. 58-69.
[3] Bittel and Ramsey, op. cit.

WHAT PERSONAL CHARACTERISTICS DOES HIGHER MANAGEMENT LOOK FOR IN SELECTING SUPERVISORS?

The job of supervision is so demanding that higher management tends to look for *super* people to fill the role. Most firms, however, do establish a set of criteria against which supervisory candidates are judged. Among the most sought-after qualities in a supervisor are these:

- ▶ Energy and good health
- ▶ Ability to get along with people
- ▶ Job know-how and technical competence
- ▶ Self-control under pressure
- ▶ Dedication and dependability
- ▶ Ability to stay on course
- ▶ Teachability
- ▶ Problem-solving skills
- ▶ Leadership potential
- ▶ A positive attitude toward management[4]

HOW CAN A NEWLY APPOINTED SUPERVISOR MAKE THE JOB OF CROSSING OVER TO THE MANAGERIAL RANKS A LESS TURBULENT ONE?

A person who is made a supervisor crosses over from one style of thought to another. As an employee, an individual's concerns are with self-satisfaction in terms of pay and the work itself. As a manager, this same person is expected to place the organization's goals above all other job-related concerns. This means that a supervisor worries first about meeting quotas, quality, and cost standards; second about the employees who do the work; and last about himself or herself.

To make the task more difficult, the newly appointed supervisor usually has already made the long climb to the top of the employee ranks. Now the person must cross over to a new field of achievement—management, as shown in Figure 1-2. It will take a while to get a toehold at the

---

[4] Lester R. Bittel, *The Complete Guide to Supervisory Training and Development,* Addison-Wesley, Reading, Mass., 1987, chap. 3, "Dimensions of Supervisory Competencies."

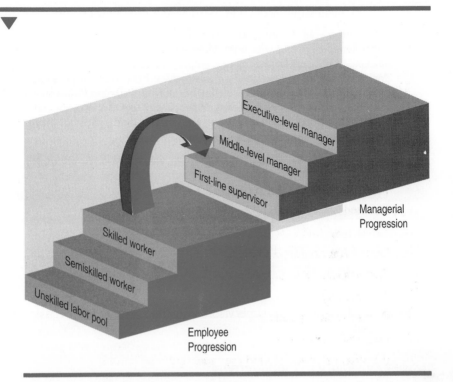

FIGURE 1-2 Crossing over from employee ranks to managerial ranks—from "top of the heap" to "bottom of the heap"

supervisory level. For many, however, it will be the beginning of another long climb—this time to the top of the management heap.[5]

The pressures from managers above and from employees below make some new supervisors very uncomfortable. However, this need not be so, says Professor Keith Davis, one of the most astute observers of organizational relationships. Davis agrees that the supervisor takes pressure from both sides, but he likens the role to a keystone in the organizational arch. Says Davis:

> The keystone takes the pressure from both sides and uses this pressure to build a stronger arch. The sides can be held together only by the keystone, which strengthens, not weakens, the arch. The keystone position is the important role of supervisors in organizations.[6]

---

[5] Carl A. Benson, "New Supervisors: From the Top of the Heap to the Bottom of the Heap," *Personnel Journal,* April 1978, p. 176.

[6] Keith Davis, "The Supervisory Role," in M. Gene Newport (ed.), *Supervisory Management: Tools and Techniques,* West St. Paul, Minn., 1976, p. 5.

Experienced supervisors add this advice for the new person:

Don't throw your weight around. Admit your need for help and seek it from other supervisors and your boss. Make a practice of coming in on time and sticking to your job for the full day; employees despise supervisors who push for productivity but who goof off themselves. Keep yourself physically prepared and mentally alert; the job will be more demanding than you expect. And don't indulge in petty pilfering of supplies or use of shop equipment and time to do personal work; employees may try this themselves but they surely don't respect management people who do.

Working Woman magazine adds this cogent advice for newly appointed supervisors:

Concentrate on cultivating a look of self-assurance. Appearing overworked or harassed is a liability.[7]

WHEN IT COMES TO JOB RESPONSIBILITIES, WHAT IS EXPECTED FROM SUPERVISORS?

Responsibilities for most supervisors encompass four, and occasionally five, broad areas.

Responsibility to Management

Supervisors must, above all, dedicate themselves to the goals, plans, and policies of the organization. These are typically laid down by higher management. It is the primary task of supervisors to serve as a linking pin for management to make sure that these are carried out by the employees they supervise.

Responsibility to Employees

Employees expect their supervisors to provide direction and training; to protect them from unfair treatment; and to see that the workplace is clean, safe, uncluttered, properly equipped, well lighted, and adequately ventilated.

Responsibility to Staff Specialists

The relationship between supervision and staff departments is one of mutual support. Staff people are charged with providing supervisors with

---

[7] Jane Ciabattari, "Crossing the Magic Threshold," *Working Woman*, June 1987, p. 94.

guidance and help as well as prescribing procedures to be followed and forms to be completed. Supervisors, in turn, aid the work of the staff departments by making good use of their advice and service by conforming to their requests.

Responsibility to Other Supervisors

Teamwork is essential in the supervisory ranks. There is a great deal of departmental interdependence. The goals and activities of one department must harmonize with those of other departments. This often requires the sacrifice of an immediate target for the greater good of the organization.

Responsibility to the Union

If there is a labor union in the company, union and management views are often in conflict, and supervisor and shop steward are often at loggerheads. It is the supervisor's responsibility, however, to keep these relationships objective, neither to "give away" the department nor to yield responsibility for the welfare of the organization and its employees.

HOW WILL SUPERVISORY PERFORMANCE BE JUDGED BY HIGHER MANAGEMENT?

It will be judged by two general measures: (1) how well you manage the various resources made available to you to accomplish your assignments and (2) how good your results are. (See Figure 1-3.)

Management of Resources

These are all the things that, in effect, set you up in business as a supervisor. They include the following.

Facilities and Equipment. A certain amount of floor space, desks, benches, tools, computers, and machinery. Your job is to keep these operating productively and to prevent their abuse.

Energy, Power, and Utilities. Heat, light, air conditioning, electricity, steam, water, and compressed air. Conservation is the principal measure of effectiveness here.

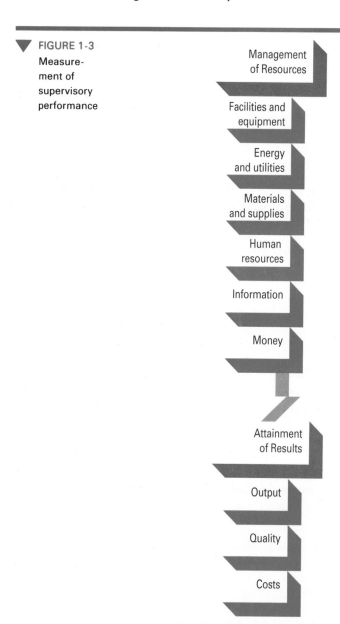

FIGURE 1-3
Measure-
ment of
supervisory
performance

Management
of Resources

Facilities and
equipment

Energy
and utilities

Materials
and supplies

Human
resources

Information

Money

Attainment
of Results

Output

Quality

Costs

Materials and Supplies. Raw materials such as parts and assemblies used to make a product, and operating supplies such as lubricants, stationery, printer ribbons, and wrapping paper. Getting the most from every scrap of material and holding waste to the minimum are prime concerns here.

Human Resources. The work force in general and your employees in particular. Because you do little or nothing with your hands, your biggest job is to see that these people are productively engaged at all times.

Information. Facts made available by staff departments or found in operating manuals, specification sheets, and blueprints. Your success often depends on how well you can use the data and know-how available to you through these sources.

Money. All the above can be measured by how much they cost, although the actual cash will rarely flow through your hands. Nevertheless, supervisors are expected to be prudent in decisions that affect expenditures and may have to justify these in terms of savings or other benefits.

Attainment of Results

It follows that if you manage each of your resources well, you should get the desired results. Whatever your particular area of responsibility and whatever your organization, you can be sure you will be judged in the long run by how well you meet the following three objectives.

Output, or Production. Specifically, your department will be expected to turn out a certain amount of work per day, per week, and per month. It will be expected that this will be done on time and that you will meet delivery schedules and project deadlines.

Quality and Workmanship. Output volume alone is not enough. You will also be judged by the quality of the work your employees perform, measured in terms of the number of product defects, service errors, or customer complaints.

Costs and Budget Control. Your output and quality efforts will always be restricted by the amount of money you can spend to carry them out. Universally, supervisors attest to the difficulty of living up to cost and budget restraints.

WHAT ARE THE MAIN JOB COMPETENCIES REQUIRED OF SUPERVISORS?

No one knows for sure. There are, however, a number of regularly performed duties, or requirements, of the supervisory job that experts can identify. From these duties, the required competencies can be inferred. For example, one major manufacturing company looks for these seven competencies among its supervisors: technical know-how, administrative skill, ability to develop a plan to meet department goals, ability to deal with the manager to whom you report, communications skills, ability to deal with people inside and outside the operating unit, and ability to deal effectively with people who report to you. Other researchers also identify such success-related qualities as creativity, stress tolerance, initiative, independence, problem analysis, decisiveness, tenacity, flexibility, risk taking, and use of delegation.[8]

The American Telephone and Telegraph Company (AT&T) promotes about 12,000 men and women from the ranks into supervisory positions each year (throughout its system and its now-independent constituent companies). To make the choice of these candidates more reliable and to better prepare them for their new jobs, AT&T spent several years studying the "job content" of its master supervisors (those whose performance is the very best). On the basis of this study, AT&T developed a list of skills that supervisors must acquire if they are to be effective at their work. This list is reproduced in Table 1-1. It is generally regarded as applicable to almost any supervisor. The list may seem formidable, but most of the talents it requires can be acquired by supervisors who learn from their experience and take advantage of training and developmental opportunities offered by their employers.[9]

WHERE DO SUPERVISORS FIT INTO THE MANAGEMENT PROCESS?

They are an essential part of it. Supervisors perform exactly the same managerial functions as do all other managers in their organization, up to and including the chief executive. Each specific task, every responsibility, all the various roles that supervisors are called on to perform are carried forward by the managerial process (Figure 1-4). This process, which is repeated over and over daily, weekly, and yearly, consists of five broad functions:

Planning. Setting goals and establishing plans and procedures to attain them.

Organizing. Arranging jobs to be done in such a way as to make them more effective.

---

[8] William C. Byham, "Assessment Center Method," in Lester R. Bittel and Jackson E. Ramsey (eds.), *Handbook for Professional Managers,* McGraw-Hill, New York, 1985, p. 41.

[9] Charles R. Macdonald, *Performance Based Supervisory Development: Adapted from a Major AT&T Study,* Human Resources Development Press, Amherst, Mass., 1982, p. 20.

TABLE 1-1 Principal duties of first-level supervisors (ranked according to time required and frequency of occurrence)

Rank Order	Duties	Percentage of Time Spent*	Frequency of Occurrence
1	Controlling the work	17	Every day
2	Problem solving and decision making	13	Every day
3	Planning the work	12	Every day
4	Informal oral communications	12	Every day
5	Communications, general	12	Every day
6	Providing performance feedback to employees	10	Every day
7	Training, coaching, developing subordinates	10	Every day
8	Providing written communications and documentation	7	Every day
9	Creating and maintaining a motivating atmosphere	6	Every day
10	Personal time management	4	Every day
11	Meetings and conferences	4	Twice monthly
12	Self-development activities	2	Weekly
13	Career counseling of subordinates	2	Bimonthly
14	Representing the company to the community	1	Monthly

*Percentages add up to more than 100 because of overlap of duties. For example: *planning* of the work of a *meeting* called for planning purposes.

Source: Adapted from Charles R. Macdonald, *Performance Based Supervisory Development: Adapted from a Major AT&T Study,* Human Resources Development Press, Amherst, Mass., 1982, p. 20.

Staffing. Selecting and placing just the right number of people in the most appropriate jobs.

Directing. Motivating, communicating, and leading.

Controlling. Regulating the process, its costs, and the people who carry it out.

HOW DO SUPERVISORY JOB ROLES DIFFER FROM THOSE OF OTHER LEVELS OF MANAGEMENT?

They differ only in degree. Higher-level managers spend more time planning and less time directing, for example. Two people who studied this

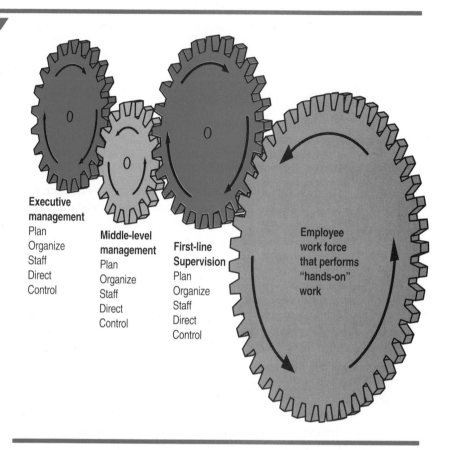

Executive
management
Plan
Organize
Staff
Direct
Control

Middle-level
management
Plan
Organize
Staff
Direct
Control

First-line
Supervision
Plan
Organize
Staff
Direct
Control

Employee
work force
that performs
"hands-on"
work

FIGURE 1-4 All managers take part in the management process: planning,
organizing, staffing, directing, and controlling.

matter came up with three useful guidelines. They first divided all the
tasks and responsibilities we have listed so far in this text into three kinds
of roles. Roles are the parts played by actors on a stage; they are also the
real-life parts played by managers and supervisors in an organization.
These three roles can be classified as those requiring:

Technical skills. Job know-how, knowledge of the industry and its
particular processes, machinery, and problems.

Administrative skills. Knowledge of the entire organization and how
it is coordinated, its information and records system, its ability to plan
and control work.

Human relations skills. Knowledge of human behavior, the ability to work effectively with individuals and groups—peers and superiors as well as subordinates.

The observers then concluded that supervisors' roles emphasize technical and human relations skills most and administrative skills least. This emphasis tends to be reversed for higher-level managers.

SUPERVISORY BALANCE: WHAT DOES IT MEAN?

It is a simplification of a valuable dictum: Pay as much attention to human relations as to technical and administrative matters. Said another way: Be as employee-centered in your interests as job- or task-centered. Said still another way: Spend as much time maintaining group cohesiveness, direction, and morale as you do pushing for productivity or task accomplishment.

This view has been borne out by a number of studies. Its principal basis, however, is in research carried out by Rensis Likert among clerical, sales, and manufacturing employees. He found that, on the average, employees who worked for supervisors who were job- or production-centered produced less than employees who worked for supervisors who were employee-centered.[10]

It would be dangerous to conclude from Likert's studies that being a nice guy is the answer to employee productivity. It isn't. As in sports, nice guys often finish last. The important conclusion the studies lead to is that supervisors who focus on job demands to the exclusion of their interest in the welfare and development of their people don't get the results they are looking for. Conversely, supervisors who bend over backward to make work easy for their employees don't get good results, either. It takes a balance between the two approaches, as shown in Figure 1-5.

HOW PROFESSIONAL IS THE WORK OF SUPERVISION?

It is becoming more professional every day. Two leading management organizations, made up primarily of first-line supervisors, are working hard to make it that way. The International Management Council (IMC), sponsored originally by the Young Men's Christian Association (YMCA), and

---

[10] Rensis Likert, *New Patterns of Management,* McGraw-Hill, New York, 1961.

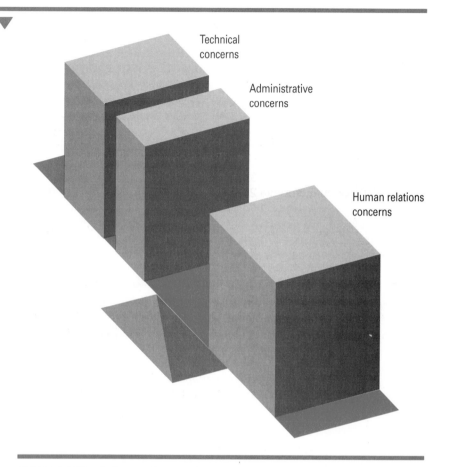

FIGURE 1-5 The balance of supervisory concerns

the National Management Association (NMA) have pooled their resources to form an independent Institute of Certified Professional Managers (ICPM). This institute, working with a qualified licensing-test consultant, has devised and is administering professional certification tests. Certification is based on a combination of experience and examinations in the following three areas: (1) personal skills, such as skills in communications, government regulation, and time management; (2) administrative skills, such as planning, decision making, staffing, and controlling; and (3) human relations skills.

The addresses of the participating organizations are as follows:

International Management Council
430 South 20th Street
Omaha, Nebraska 68102

National Management Association
2210 Arbor Boulevard
Dayton, Ohio 45439

Institute of Certified Professional Managers
James Madison University
Harrisonburg, Virginia 22807

WHY DO SOME SUPERVISORS FAIL?

When a person doesn't succeed as a supervisor, only an examination of the particular situation will pinpoint the real reason. Sometimes, the individual isn't at fault; the boss may not have provided the right kind of training and encouragement. But, if you would avoid failure, guard against these typical pitfalls:

- ▶ Poor interpersonal relations with workers and/or with other management personnel. This cause of failure rates highest on the list.
- ▶ Individual shortcomings, such as lack of initiative and emotional instability.
- ▶ Failure to grasp the management point of view.
- ▶ Unwillingness to spend the necessary amount of time and effort to learn the job and to improve personal performance.
- ▶ Lack of skill in planning and organizing departmental work.
- ▶ Inability to adjust to new and changing conditions.

If success is your target, look ahead to the chapters that follow, and fit the advice to your own job.

REVIEW ▼ 1 ▼ QUESTIONS

1. How many levels of management are there in a typical organization? At which level are supervisors found?

2. Why would a company be likely to object if, as supervisor of the molding department, you spent most of your time setting up and operating the molding machines?

3. Name at least four groups within the organization toward which a supervisor has responsibilities, and briefly describe the nature of the responsibilities to each.

4. Outline (for a new supervisor) nine performance measures grouped into two categories.

5. AT&T's master supervisors have ranked 14 important tasks that supervisors must perform. Sort these out according to the three categories of supervisory skills: (a) technical, (b) administrative, and (c) human relations.

6. How is supervisory management similar to higher-level management? How is it different?

7. When a supervisor is told to achieve supervisory balance, what is it that should be balanced? Why is this balance important?

8. If you had to point to one key area that is most likely to produce failure for a supervisor, what would it be?

A CASE IN POINT

Getting the Act Together

The first month as a supervisor had been very trying for Orpha. As a dispatcher in the mailroom for the Foremost Insurance Company, Orpha had built a reputation second to none. She knew the workings of the mail department inside-out and backwards, and she was respected by the company for her accuracy and diligence. Accordingly, Orpha's promotion to supervisor had seemed like a deserved reward for her. She had not anticipated, however, just how much difference there was between doing a job well herself and getting the people who worked for her to do the same.

Orpha thought about the people who worked *for* her now, rather than *with* her, as before. For example, it turned out that Peter—whom she had thought of as a person who provided a million laughs on the job—rarely got to work on time. Mario—who could be relied upon to know the scores of all of yesterday's ball games—regularly sorted mail into the wrong slots. And Sheila—the buddy she used to share her lunch breaks with—was proving to be an ace at wandering off when on her mail routes. As for the rest of the gang, there wasn't one who didn't appear to have one shortcoming or another.

When Orpha confronted her former associates with the need for better performance, this is what she heard:

Said Peter, "Give me a break. You ought to know how one missed connection in the morning can make you late."

Said Mario, "We're so rushed in the sorting section that you ought to be happy that I don't make more mistakes."

Said Sheila, "Whose side are you on, anyway? The company has the department so understaffed that I have to bust my belt just to make my rounds on time, let alone find time to goof off."

If you were Orpha, what would you do now? Five alternative courses of action are listed below. Rank them in the order in which they appeal to you (1 most effective, 5 least effective). You may add another approach in the space provided, if you wish. In any event, be prepared to justify your ranking.

_____ **A.** Post a notice on the department bulletin board that, in the future, sloppy performance will not be tolerated.

_____ **B.** Speak to each crew member privately and ask for that person's loyalty and cooperation.

_____ **C.** At a department meeting, make exactly clear what you expect in the way of performance—for each operation and for the department as a whole.

_____ **D.** Ask the boss to speak to your crew members at a department meeting, urging them to improve their performance.

_____ **E.** At a department meeting, ask crew members what can be done to get their acts together.

If you have another approach, write it here.

▶ _____

_____

_____

Complete the ACTION PLANNING CHECKLIST
for this chapter, which can be found on page 311.

2

SETTING GOALS AND PLANNING WORK

LEARNING OBJECTIVES

After studying this chapter, you should be able to:

1. Recognize the various terms associated with planning and the planning process.

2. Create a representative set of objectives for a department supervisor.

3. Carry out the planning process and differentiate between long- and short-range plans and between standing and single-use plans.

4. Select appropriate targets for supervisory planning and explain the relationship between plans and controls.

5. Discuss a supervisor's responsibilities for interpreting and implementing an organization's policies.

▶ Planning is the process of systematically working out what you and your work group will do in the future. Plans establish a hierarchy of goals—based on the needs of the organization and on the strengths and weaknesses of the work group—and specific procedures, regulations, and policies designed to achieve the goals.

▶ Objectives, or goals, for a work group should (1) support the goals of the overall organization and (2) be attainable, given the limitations and resources of the group. Objectives should be clearly and concretely stated. Supervisors usually deal with short-term objectives that span a few days, weeks, or months.

▶ Decisions and actions in every enterprise are guided by a body of operating principles that either have been set down in writing or have evolved informally (like common law) as a result of decisions made and actions taken by management under similar circumstances in the past.

▶ Company policies are dynamic, too, in that they are influenced by the decisions and actions of supervisors and managers as they cope daily with ever-changing situations and circumstances.

▶ In the eyes of employees the supervisor is inseparably identified with the policy of the employing organization, because it is at the supervisory level that philosophies and principles are translated into specific actions.

PLANS, PLANNING, POLICIES, GOALS:
WHAT ARE THE DIFFERENCES?

If ever there was an area of management where the terms are mixed up, this is it. *Plans* come out of the *planning* process. Plans or programs are what you intend to do in the future. Before you can develop plans, however, you must set targets, which are called *goals, standards,* or *objectives.*

After you have set these goals (that is the simplest term to use), you establish general guidelines for reaching them. These guidelines are called *policies.* Only after policies have been set should you formulate plans.

Plans typically include operating *procedures, schedules,* and *budgets.*

As a final step, you may choose to lay down some *rules* and *regulations.* These will establish the limits (controls) within which employees are free to do the job their own way.

Take this example. You are thinking ahead—planning—about what your department will do during the annual spring cleaning. You make a list of things that you want to accomplish: filing cabinets cleared of obsolete material, shelving cleaned and rearranged, tools repaired and in tip-top shape. These are your goals. Next you establish some sort of policy. For example, cleaning will be done during normal working hours without overtime; discarding obsolete papers will conform to legal requirements; tool repairs may be done by your own maintenance department or by an outside machine shop. Next you lay out a master plan of how, when, and by whom the housekeeping will be done. If this plan were detailed as to its exact sequence, it would be called a *procedure.* You may want to set time limits for this procedure, which converts it into a *schedule.* If someone sets cost limits for this operation, these costs will form a *budget.* Finally, you set down some firm rules and regulations for your work crew. For example, only file clerks will make judgments about what paperwork will be discarded; before tools are sent outside for repair, employees must check with you; employees who clean shelving must wear protective gloves. Figure 2-1 illustrates common relationships among the terms discussed above.

WHY MUST GOALS COME BEFORE PLANS?

Because plans are the means to an end; goals are ends. Logically, then, you must first decide where it is you want to go and what it is that you want your unit to accomplish. These are, of course, your goals or objectives. You should set them carefully and systematically. This can be done by following these seven steps:

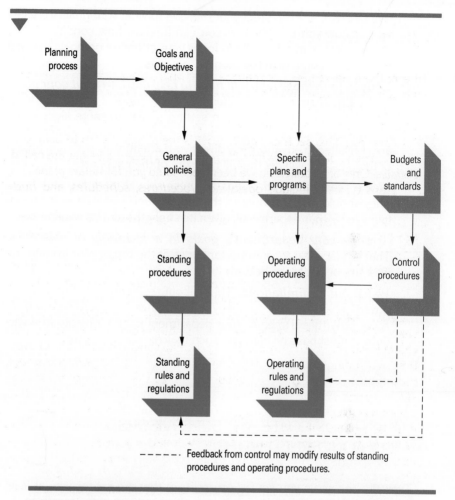

FIGURE 2-1 **Relationships among the various outputs of the planning process**

1. *Consider the goals of the entire organization, not just those of your department.* Think about the needs and wishes of customers— those the company serves as well as those "customers" your department serves internally.

2. *Estimate the strengths and weaknesses of your department.* Ask yourself how they will help or hinder you in trying to meet company goals and in trying to serve external and internal customers.

3. *Don't jump to conclusions at this early stage.* Instead, keep your mind alert to new opportunities—such as ways to improve quality or

reduce costs. Don't restrict your thinking to what your goals were last year or how you met them. If you can forecast how conditions may change next year, this will help focus your attention on goals that will be more meaningful in the months to come.

4. *Consult with those who will have to help you carry out your plans and with those who can offer you their support along the way.* Employees who are involved in setting goals are more likely to be committed to success in reaching those goals. Staff departments that are consulted in advance may direct your attention to potential pitfalls or to goals that will get the full measure of their support.

5. *Pick a reasonable set of goals.* These should meet two standards. They should (a) contribute to the organization's goals and (b) be attainable by your department, given its strengths and its weaknesses.

6. *Arrange your department's goals in a hierarchy of objectives.* That is, place the most important ones at the top of your list and the least important at the bottom.

7. *Watch out for limitations.* Think about restrictions that may be imposed on you by your company or by the need to coordinate with or serve other departments. Your department cannot operate in a vacuum. It must base its plans on such realistic planning premises.

WHAT KINDS OF GOALS ARE SUPERVISORS USUALLY CONCERNED WITH?

Typically, the goals you set for yourself—or that are set for you, at least partially, as part of a company's overall objectives—are targets to be aimed at in the near future. They pin down your department's output, quality of workmanship, and allowable expenditures. Often, they also include goals in such employee-related areas as departmental attendance, labor turnover, and safety, as shown in Table 2-1. These goals may be stated in terms of tomorrow, next week, next month, or as far ahead as a year. More often than not, the goals are quantitative (expressed in terms of numbers of dollars) rather than merely qualitative (described with such words as *improve, maintain, good,* or *better*).

In many companies and organizations, the manner in which you and your department attain your goals becomes the determining factor in what kind of raise you'll get or how good a job you can be groomed for. This is one big reason why it is so important to lay out a detailed set of plans for meeting your goals.

TABLE 2-1 Typical performance goals for a first-line supervisor

▼ Area of Measurement	Last Year's Record	Next Year's Goals
1. Ratio of jobs completed on schedule to total jobs worked	85% average, 92% highest, 65% lowest in June	90% average, minimum acceptable 75%
2. Percentage of job costs held within 3% of standard costs	81% average, 95% highest, 75% lowest in June	90% average, bring up low figure to 87% or better
3. Rejects and rework	Less than 1% rejects Rework averages 7%	Keep rejects to less than 1%, but cut rework to 3%
4. Labor stability	Two quits, one discharge	No quits of employees with over three years of service
5. Absences, latenesses	5% absences, 7% latenesses	5% absences, 2% latenesses
6. Overtime	Only on jobs okayed by sales department	Only on jobs okayed by sales department
7. Accidents	No lost-time accidents; 37 calls to dispensary for minor ailments	No lost-time accidents; reduce number of dispensary visits

HOW CAN GOALS BE MADE MORE COMPELLING?

By making sure that they aren't confused with activity for activity's sake. Professor George Odiorne, author of a dozen books on the setting of objectives, warns that goals should be something to strive for, not just something to do. A few meaningful goals are better than a long "laundry list" to make sure that you look good when reckoning time comes around. Accordingly, Odiorne suggests the following key guidelines for making your objectives more effective. A goal should be:

A statement of output. For example, when you are stating a goal, it's all right to say "100 orders will be handled each day," but it is not all right to say, "We will improve productivity." The former is a statement of output; the latter is a nonspecific, hoped-for result.

Explicit. That is, goals should be clearly stated in terms, or numbers, that make the output measurable.

Time-oriented. The targeted output must always be related to a time period, such as "10 tons per day," "50 shipments by the end of the month," or "5 percent reduction of absenteeism for the year."

ONCE GOALS HAVE BEEN SET, HOW DOES THE PLANNING PROCESS PROCEED?

In six steps. Effective plans flow from clearly stated goals, as illustrated in Figure 2-1. These plans, however, depend upon your following a systematic planning process, just as you did when setting goals. The six steps are:

1. *Develop a master plan.* This should focus on your main objective. If, for example, the company's goal is to have higher-quality products or services, the master plan for your department should give this top priority.

2. *Draw up supporting plans.* This requires that you think about how each activity in your department can contribute to your master plan. Machinists may need more explicit blueprints. Assemblers may need brighter workplace lighting. Clerks may need a different order-entry procedure.

3. *Put numbers and dates on everything you can.* Plans work best when employees know how much or how many are required of them. Since plans are for the future—tomorrow, next week, or next month— times and dates are essential.

4. *Pin down assignments.* Plans are for people. Responsibility for carrying out each part of a plan or procedure should be assigned to a particular individual.

5. *Explain the plan to all concerned.* Plans should be shared. Their rationales should be explained and their goals justified. Employees who know *why* are more likely to cooperate.

6. *Review your plans regularly.* Circumstances and restrictions change. Your plans should be examined periodically to see whether they should be changed, too.

HOW FLEXIBLE MUST A SUPERVISOR'S PLANS BE?

They should be stated firmly and clearly so that everyone concerned can understand them. They should not be so rigid, however, that they prevent your making changes to accommodate unexpected circumstances. A good plan should be flexible enough to anticipate—and allow for—an alternative course of action. Suppose, for example, you planned to start a new order or project on Monday, but the necessary materials are not on hand. Your plans should permit postponement of that project and insertion of a productive alternative without delay.

IN WHAT WAY ARE PLANS OR PROGRAMS USUALLY CLASSIFIED?

They are usually classified according to their duration and purpose.

Long-range plans are typically set by higher management and are expected to be in operation from two to five years.

Short-range plans are those that supervisors are most concerned with and are usually based on operations of one year or less. At the departmental level, short-range plans may be in effect for a day, a week, a month, or a quarter of a year.

Standing plans include just about any activity that goes on without much change from year to year. Standing plans cover general employment practices, health and safety matters, purchasing procedures, routine discipline, and the like.

Single-use plans are used only once before they must be revised. Departmental budgets and operating schedules are examples. They will be good only for a week or a month until new ones are issued.

Generally speaking, then, supervisors will follow short-range, single-use plans for day-to-day operations; but they will also be guided by many standing plans that implement routine, relatively unchanging goals and policies.

WHEN AND HOW OFTEN SHOULD SUPERVISORS PLAN?

Before starting anything new or different. Planning should take place before a new day, a new week, a new product or service, or the introduction of different materials or machinery. As a matter of routine, a supervisor should make new plans each night for the next day, each Friday for the next week, and the last week in the month for the next month.

WHICH AREAS SHOULD BE TARGETS
FOR A SUPERVISOR'S PLANNING PROCESS?

Just about anything qualifies. Any kind of change should trigger new plans. Every area within the supervisor's responsibility is a candidate for planning. For starters, here is a list of a dozen prime candidates:

Use of facilities and equipment—departmental layout and working conditions, equipment utilization and maintenance.

Use and care of materials and supplies—purchases, inventory levels, storage.

Conservation of energy and power—electricity, steam, water, and compressed air usage; waste disposal; fire protection.

Cash and credit management—petty cash, billing, collections.

Human resources management—forecasting requirements, safety and health care, sanitation, communications, absences and turnover, employee training and development.

Information collection and processing—tallies and logbooks, record-keeping, order processing.

Time conservation—startups, shutdowns, personal time.

Schedules—routing, delivery performance, shortages.

Quality benchmarks—inspection and control techniques, rework methods, scrap reduction, employee training and motivation.

Cost reduction and control—cost estimating, correction of variances, work simplifications, and methods improvement.

Productivity—work simplification and methods improvement.

Self-improvement—planning, organization, communicating, public speaking, business writing, leading conferences.

HOW DO CONTROLS RELATE TO PLANS?

Controls are like limit switches that keep plans in line. When a plan is moving directly toward its goal, the track is kept clear and the supervisor need apply no control. But when a plan strays from its target, the supervisor must take corrective action to bring it back in line. When planning a department's goals, the supervisor must also plan its control limits. (See Chapter 4 for details.)

WHAT IS A GOOD WAY TO DOUBLE-CHECK YOUR PLANS AND PROJECTS?

Try using the five-point planning chart illustrated in Figure 2-2.

What spells out objectives in terms of specifications for output, quality, and cost.

Where sets the location for the assignment (its workplace) and the place where the product or service must be delivered (the adjoining department, the shipping dock, the home office).

When records your time estimates for performance of the work and, most important, specifies starting and finishing times and dates.

How verifies short- and long-range methods, procedures, and job sequences.

Who designates the individual responsible for the assignment and specifies that person's authority and extent of control over the resources needed (tools, machinery, additional labor, materials).

Five-Point Planning Check Chart

What	Objectives	Specifications
		Cost/price limits
Where	Locale	Delivery point
When	Time elapsed	Starting date
		Completion date
How	Tactics	Methods
	Strategy	Procedure
		Sequence
Who	Responsibility	Authority
		Control
		Assignment

FIGURE 2-2 Five-point planning check chart

WHAT IS MEANT BY COMPANY POLICY?

Company policies are broad rules or guides for action. At their best, these rules are statements of the company's objectives and its basic principles for doing business. They are intended as guides for supervisors and managers in getting their jobs done. Many policies give supervisors the opportunity to use their own best judgment in carrying them out. Others are supported by firm rules, which supervisors must observe if they are to run their departments in harmony with the rest of the organization.

DOES POLICY APPLY ONLY AT HIGH LEVELS?

Although policy is generally set by managers high up in the company organization, it can be no more than a collection of high-sounding words unless the supervisor translates the words into action on the firing line.

Take an example of a disciplinary policy. Here's how it might sound as it works its way down from the front office to first-line action by the supervisor.

Company president: "Our policy is to exercise fair and reasonable controls to regulate the conduct of our employees."

Vice president: "The policy on attendance in this company is that habitual absenteeism will be penalized."

Department manager: "Here are the rules governing absences. It's up to you supervisors to keep an eye on absences and to discharge any employee absent or late more than three times in three months."

Supervisor: "Sorry. I'm going to have to lay you off for three days. You know the rules. You put me in a bad spot when you take time off on your own without giving warning or getting approval."

Note that no real action takes place until the supervisor puts the words of the policy into effect.

WHAT SORTS OF MATTERS DOES POLICY COVER?

A company may have policies to cover almost every important phase of its business—from regulating its method of purchasing materials to stipulating how employees may submit suggestions. As a supervisor, you will probably be most concerned with policies that affect (1) employees and (2) the operating practices of your department.

Employee policies most commonly formalized are those affecting wages and salaries, holidays and vacations, leaves of absence, termination of employment, safety, medical and health insurance and hospitalization, service awards, and retirement and pensions.

Department practices most often reduced to policy are requisitioning of supplies, preparation of records, timekeeping, safeguarding of classified materials, cost-control measures, quality standards, maintenance and repair, and acquisition of new machinery and equipment.

These listings are not all-inclusive. Some organizations have more policies, whereas others have fewer policies.

IS POLICY ALWAYS IN WRITING?

Far from it. Many rigid policies have never been put down in black and white, and many binding policies have never been stated by an executive. But employees and supervisors alike recognize that matters affected by such policies must be handled in a certain manner, and usually do so.

The existence of so much unwritten policy has led many authorities to the conclusion that all policy is better put into writing so that it may be explained, discussed, and understood. Nevertheless, many companies don't subscribe to this way of thinking, and their policies remain implied rather than spelled out.

IS POLICY JUST A MATTER OF DO'S AND DON'TS?

One of the great misunderstandings about policy is the belief that it's always negative, like "don't do that" or "do it this way or you'll get in trouble."

Policy can also be positive, encouraging, and uplifting. Just examine the written policy of a nationally respected company as expressed in a booklet published by its board of directors:

Importance of the individual. We believe the actions of business should recognize human feelings and the importance of the individual and should ensure each person's treatment as an individual.

Common interest. We believe that employees, their unions, and management are bound together by a common interest—the ability of their unit to operate successfully—and that opportunity and security for the individual depend on this success.

Open communications. We believe that the sharing of ideas, information, and feeling is essential as a means of expression and as the route to better understanding and sounder decisions.

Local decisions. We believe that people closest to the problems affecting themselves develop the most satisfactory solutions when given the authority to solve such matters at the point where they arise.

High ethical standards. We believe that the soundest basis for judging the "rightness" of an action involving people is the test of its effect on basic human rights.

Words? Yes. Policy? Definitely. And as an official guide to action committed to print by the top officers of the organization, these statements are an excellent example of the positive side of policy.

SHOULD A SUPERVISOR CHANGE POLICY?

No. This is a very dangerous thing to do. Policies are set to guide action. It's a supervisor's responsibility to act within policy limits.

Supervisors can influence a policy change, however, by making their thoughts and observations known to the boss, the human resources department, and the top management. After all, supervisors are in the best position to perceive employees' reactions to policy—favorable or otherwise. You do your boss and your company a service when you accurately report employees' reactions, and this is the time to offer your suggestions for improving or modifying the policy.

DO SUPERVISORS EVER SET POLICY?

In a way, supervisors always set policy at the departmental level. Supervisory application of policy is their interpretation of how the broader company policy should be carried out for employees. It's important for you to recognize that company policy usually allows you discretion at your level—even though this discretion may be limited.

Suppose your company has a policy that forbids gambling on the premises. Anyone caught will be fired. You can carry out that policy in many ways. You can bait a trap, hide behind a post, and fire the first person you catch. Or you can quietly size up the most likely violator and warn that there won't be a second chance. You can put a notice on the bulletin board calling employees' attention, generally, to the policy. Or you can hold a group meeting and announce how you will deal with on-site gamblers. You can choose to regard only the taking of horse-racing bets as on-site gambling, or include professionally run baseball, basketball, and football pools. Or you can rule out any kind of gambling. Whatever you decide, so long as you carry out the intentions (and the letter when it's spelled out) of the company policy, you are setting your own policy.

TO WHAT EXTENT WILL EMPLOYEES HOLD YOU RESPONSIBLE FOR COMPANY POLICY?

If you have done a good job of convincing employees that you fully represent the management of their company, your actions and company policy will be one and the same thing in their eyes. Naturally, you will sometimes have to carry out policy that you don't fully agree with—policy that may be unpopular with you or with your employees. Resist the temptation to apologize for your actions or to criticize the policy to employees. When you do, you weaken your position.

If you have to reprimand an employee, don't say, "I'd like to give you a break, but that's company policy." Or when sparking a cleanup campaign, don't say, "The manager wants you to get your area in order." Handle such matters positively. Give the policy your own personal touch, but don't sell the company down the river or you're likely to be caught in the current yourself.

HOW CAN YOU PREVENT YOUR POLICY INTERPRETATIONS FROM BACKFIRING?

Try to protect your actions in policy matters by asking yourself questions before making decisions:

Is policy involved here? What is the procedure? What is the rule?

Am I sure of the facts? Do I know all the circumstances?

How did I handle a similar matter in the past?

Who can give me advice on this problem? Should I ask for it?

Would my boss want to talk this over with me first?

Does this problem involve the union? If so, should I see the union steward or should I check with the labor relations people first?

1. In what way are plans and controls related?
2. Name three characteristics that help to make goals effective.
3. The planning process suggests that you arrange your goals in a hierarchy of objectives. What does this mean?
4. Distinguish between long-range and short-range plans. Which are likely to be more important to a supervisor?
5. Once Mary sets her departmental plans in motion, she rigidly adheres to them. Is this good or bad supervision? Why?
6. Contrast the ways in which policy affects top management decisions and supervisory actions.
7. When would it be wise for a supervisor to check with the boss before carrying out a particular policy?
8. Which do you think is more important to an organization in the long run: the policies it sets or the actions its supervisors take? Why?

A CASE IN POINT

The Forgotten Price Change

The written policy of a major supermarket chain is posted in all its stores. It reads as follows:

Our policy is always to:

Do what is honest, fair, sincere, and in the best interests of every customer.

Extend friendly, satisfying service to everyone.

Give every customer the most good food for the money.

Assure accurate weight every time—16 ounces to each pound.

Give accurate count and full measure.

Charge the correct price.

Refund, cheerfully, customers' money if for any reason any purchase is not satisfactory.

In one of the supermarkets of this chain, located in a low-income neighborhood in a northeastern state, the following was reported to have happened. The store manager received notice from the district superintendent that the price charged for a certain brand of coffee was to be reduced from $2.98 per pound to $2.68 per pound on the Monday preceding Thanksgiving. Routinely (for the manager received dozens of such notices each week), the supermarket manager told the head stock clerk to insert a price change notice in the shelves, to restamp existing stock with the new price, and to make a notation on the registers at the checkout counters. On the Wednesday before Thanksgiving the district office received a telephone call from a customer who complained that this particular store was charging $2.98 for the coffee, although another store had it at a lower price. The district superintendent called the store manager to verify this. The store manager quickly checked the shelves and discovered that the head stock clerk had simply forgotten to carry out instructions. The store manager called back the district superintendent to report what had happened, but commented, "No harm's been done. If customers say they've been overcharged, we'll refund their money. And, besides, not many people down here know the difference anyway."

How would you evaluate the store manager's actions? Five alternative opinions are listed below. Rank them in the order in which they appeal to you (1 most appropriate, 5 least appropriate). You may add another opinion in the space provided, if you wish. In any event, be prepared to justify your ranking.

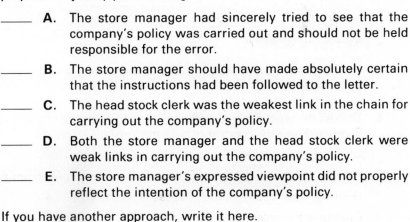

_____ **A.** The store manager had sincerely tried to see that the company's policy was carried out and should not be held responsible for the error.

_____ **B.** The store manager should have made absolutely certain that the instructions had been followed to the letter.

_____ **C.** The head stock clerk was the weakest link in the chain for carrying out the company's policy.

_____ **D.** Both the store manager and the head stock clerk were weak links in carrying out the company's policy.

_____ **E.** The store manager's expressed viewpoint did not properly reflect the intention of the company's policy.

If you have another approach, write it here.

▶ _____

_____

_____

Complete the ACTION PLANNING CHECKLIST
for this chapter, which can be found on page 312.

WORKING WITHIN AN ORGANIZATIONAL SYSTEM

LEARNING OBJECTIVES

After studying this chapter, you should be able to:

1. Describe the organizing process and distinguish between formal and informal organizations.

2. Identify and distinguish among various organizational structures, including functional, line-and-staff, matrix, and centralized and decentralized organizations.

3. Define authority, responsibility, and accountability and explain their relationships.

4. Discuss the unique role of staff personnel, the purpose of the chain of command, and the concept of organizational development.

5. Understand the benefits to be derived from delegation and explain several effective approaches to it.

OVERVIEW OF KEY CONCEPTS
IN THIS CHAPTER

▶ First-line supervisors represent the cutting edge in most organizational structures. They ultimately direct the specific actions that derive from the policies and strategies conceived in the upper echelons
of the organization.

▶ Charts and descriptions of organizational structures, although valuable as starting points, never fully define or stabilize the complexities
of informal relationships at all levels, which may take precedence over
the formally prescribed ones.

▶ Although formal channels for discharging responsibility and authority
must be respected in most instances, it is usually wise for supervisors
to modify their decisions and actions in accordance with the organizational relationships observed by their peers and superiors.

▶ Better-than-average supervisors know how to appeal for, and put to
use, the specialized advice and guidance available from staff departments.

▶ The ability of supervisors to divide their work effectively among subordinates—to delegate—is probably the single most important factor in
managerial success or failure.

WHAT IS AN ORGANIZATION?

An **organization** is the structure derived from grouping people together so that they can work effectively toward a goal that members of the group want to achieve.

The goals of a business organization are primarily profits for stockholders and salaries and wages for managers, supervisors, and employees. There are other important goals, of course, such as supplying goods and services valued by the general population. Although the goals of nonprofit and public organizations do not include profit, members of such organizations expect them to provide compensation in addition to delivering valued services to others.

Members of an organization also look to it as a source of personal satisfactions, such as companionship, accomplishment, and prestige.

WHY ORGANIZE IN THE FIRST PLACE?

Without an organization, we would have nothing but havoc in the workplace. We take organizations for granted because we have lived so long with them at home, in places of worship, and in the educational system. Little that we do together—anywhere—would be effective, however, if we didn't agree among ourselves on who should do what. We need look no further than team sports to see the extent of organizational structure that prevails. What would professional football be, for instance, without its highly organized structure of tasks for offense, defense, special teams, and special situations (that is, first-down run, third-down pass, goal-line defense, etc.)?

The overriding value of an organization, then, is its ability to make more effective use of human resources. Employees working alone and often at cross-purposes require the coordination and direction that an organization can provide. People working together within a sensible organizational structure have a greater sense of purpose and accomplish more than people whose efforts are allowed to run off in any direction they choose.

ARE ALL ORGANIZATIONS FORMAL?

No. In a good many of our activities, even in complex manufacturing plants, some people just naturally take over responsibilities and exercise authority without anyone ever spelling these things out. Chances are that in a group of 15 employees who you might imagine are all at the same level, you'll discover some sort of informal organization. It may be that the person who sweeps the floors actually swings weight in that group. Acting as staff assistant may be the lift-truck driver, who is the informant. The rest of the group may either work hard or stage a slowdown at a nod from a third member of the group, who has authority as surely as if the company president had given it.

So be alert to informal organization—among the employees you supervise, in the supervisory group itself, and in the entire management structure.

HOW DOES THE ORGANIZING PROCESS PROCEED?

Organizing follows planning. The organizational structure must provide the framework for carrying out the plan. Suppose, for example, a supervisor plans to load a boxcar by 5 p.m. The goal will be met if one employee is assigned to remove cartons from the stockroom, another to operate a fork truck, another to stack cartons in the boxcar, and another to verify and prepare the inventory and shipping documents.

Essentially, the organizing process moves from the knowledge of a goal or plan into a systematic *division of labor,* or *division of work.* Typically, the process follows these steps:

1. Making a list of all the tasks that must be performed by the organization to accomplish its objectives.

2. Dividing up these tasks into activities that can be performed by one person. Each person will then have a group of activities to perform, called a job. This in turn allows each person to become more proficient at his or her special job.

3. Grouping together related jobs (such as production jobs or accounting jobs) in a logical and efficient manner. This creates specialized departments or sections of the organization.

4. Establishing relationships among the various jobs and groups of jobs so that all members of the organization will have a clear idea of their responsibilities and of either their dependence on, or their control over, people in other jobs or groups of jobs.

WHAT IS THE PURPOSE OF ORGANIZATION CHARTS?

To help you understand organizational relationships. Such charts are really pictures of how one job or department fits in with others. Each box, or rectangle, encloses an activity or a department. Those boxes on the same horizontal level on the chart tend to have the same degree of authority or power and to have closely related work. Departments in boxes on the next higher level have greater authority; those at lower levels have less authority. Clusters of boxes that enclose departments performing closely related functions (such as shaping, fabricating, assembly, and finishing in a manufacturing plant) are typically connected in a vertical chain to the head manager of that particular function (such as the production manager).

Boxes containing line departments tend to descend from the top of the chart to the bottom (where supervisors' departments typically are located) in vertical chains. Boxes that enclose staff departments tend to branch out to either side of the main flow of authority from top to bottom.

Organization charts can be drawn in any way that shows relationships best, even in circles; but for practical purposes, most charting is done in the manner just described and illustrated in Figure 3-1. One caution: Organizational structures and staffing change constantly; organization charts therefore go out of date very quickly.

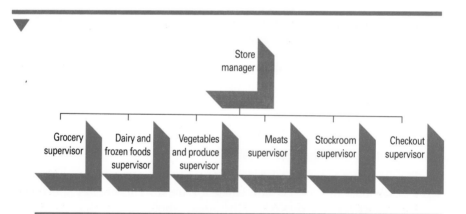

FIGURE 3-1 **Example of a functional organizational structure for a super-market**

WHICH COMES FIRST, THE ORGANIZATION OR THE WORK TO BE DONE?

If there were no job to do, there would be no reason for having an organization. So don't make the mistake of being organization-happy and trying to set up an elaborate organization just for the sake of having one. The best organization is a simple one that puts people together so that the job at hand gets done better, more quickly, and more cheaply than it could in any other way.

WHICH IS THE MOST BASIC OF ALL ORGANIZATIONAL STRUCTURES?

The *functional organization,* in which each group of related activities is collected under one functional head. Thus, the meats supervisor in Figure 3-1 may have under her all the meat cutters, trimmers, and packers; the stockroom supervisor all the receivers, inspectors, and pricing clerks; and so forth. The functional approach to organizing yields the simplest structure. It also provides the basic framework from which other types of structures are built. *It is, essentially, a line organization.*

HOW IS A LINE-AND-STAFF ORGANIZATION FORMED?

A *line-and-staff organization* adds to the basic features of a functional (or line) organization staff groups that either give advice to or perform services for the line functions. A line-and-staff organization is illustrated in Figure 3-2.

WHAT IS THE DIFFERENCE BETWEEN LINE AND STAFF GROUPS?

An organization works best when it gets many related jobs done effectively with the minimum of friction. This requires coordination and determination of what to do and who is to do it. Those managers and supervisors whose main job is to see that products and services are produced are usually considered members of the *line* organization. Other management people who help them decide what to do and how to do it, assist in coordinating the efforts of all, or provide services or special expertise are usually called *staff* people.

In manufacturing plants, line activities are most commonly performed by production departments, sales departments, and, occasionally, purchasing departments. The production supervisor or first-line supervisor is likely to be a member of the line organization.

Departments that help the line departments control quality and maintain adequate records are typically staff departments. Industrial engineering, maintenance, research, MIS, and personnel relations are some examples of typical staff activities.

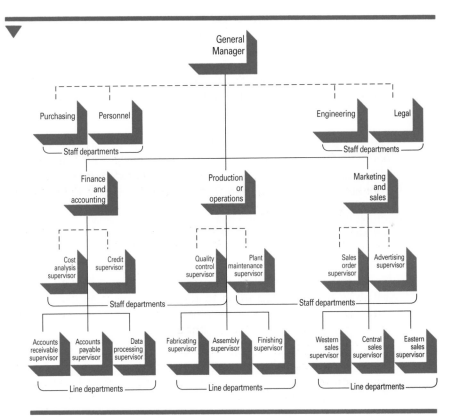

FIGURE 3-2 Example of a line-and-staff organization for a manufacturing company

In service organizations such as banks and insurance firms, the line organization may represent the primary "action" operations (such as deposits, withdrawals, and recordkeeping, or premium collections and claim settlements) whereas the staff organization comprises such support groups as computer departments and actuarial.

In hotels and motels, the line may include everything connected with the operation of a geographic unit, and the staff may include such activities as advertising, accounting, and legal.

In transport companies, the line department may be fleet operations; the staff department, equipment repair and maintenance.

In a hospital, medical and nursing may be the line groups, with laboratory, culinary, and housekeeping constituting the staff groups.

It may help you to think of line people as the doers, and staff people as the advisers. Each function—line or staff—is important in its own way, even though there has often been rivalry between line and staff people for credit and recognition.

IN WHAT OTHER WAYS MAY ORGANIZATIONS BE STRUCTURED?

The great majority of organizations combine some form of functional segmentation along with a line-and-staff format. This allows for a great many variations. Among the most common are these:

Divisional or product. All functions needed to make a particular product, for example, are gathered under one highly placed manager. If a firm manufactures tractors for farmers, road graders for construction contractors, and lawn mowers for home use, it might "divisionalize" to make and sell each major product in its product line.

Geographic. A firm may divide some (such as sales) or all of its activities according to the geographic region where these activities take place.

Customer. A company may also choose to group together some or all of its activities according to the customers it serves, such as farmers, contractors, or homeowners. This kind of organization is closely related to the product organization.

Project or task force. This form is commonly used in research and development organizations and engineering firms for one-of-a-kind projects or contracts. It allows a project manager to call on the time and skills of personnel—for a limited period of time—from various functional specialties. When the project has been completed, the specialized personnel return to their home units to await assignment to another project. Because project managers can exercise their authority horizontally across the basic organization, whereas the specialists receive permanent authority from their functional bosses above them vertically on the chart (Figure 3-3), this form is called a *matrix organization.*

Regardless of organization type, always remember that the purpose of the organizational structure is to make your department's work more nearly fit together with the work of other departments.

WHAT IS THE DISTINCTION BETWEEN A CENTRALIZED AND A DECENTRALIZED ORGANIZATION?

A centralized organization tends to have many levels of management; to concentrate its facilities in one location; to perform certain functions such

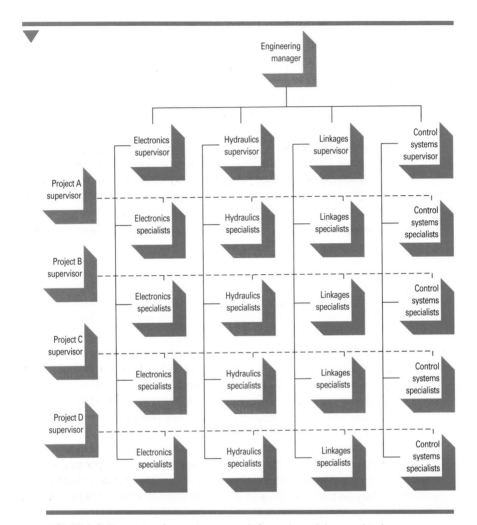

FIGURE 3-3 **Example of a project or task force (matrix) organization**

as engineering, labor negotiations, computer operations, and purchasing from a single source; and to gather together its power and authority at headquarters.

A decentralized organization tends to have the opposite characteristics, especially when the company is divided into distinctly separate units with varying degrees of independence. These units may be set up by product lines, by geography, or by methods of marketing and distribution.

HOW WIDE CAN A SUPERVISOR'S SPAN OF CONTROL BE?

Authorities disagree on this point, but it is a good rule of thumb that no manager or supervisor should have responsibility for more than six separate activities. The more specialized and complex the activities, the shorter the span of control. The more uniform and less complicated the activities (as with many supervisory responsibilities), the greater the span can be. Sometimes the span of control (or of management) is defined by the number of people rather than by the number of activities. If such is the case, it is not unusual for a supervisor to have a span of 30 or more employees, provided they are engaged in only a few simple, related activities. On the other hand, a middle-level manager might have all he or she could do to control the activities managed by the supervisors of six different departments.

ARE AUTHORITY AND RESPONSIBILITY THE SAME THING?

No. Authority should go hand in hand with responsibility, but the two are no more alike than are the two sides of a coin.

Your responsibilities are those things you are held accountable for—such as costs, on-time deliveries, and good housekeeping. Responsibilities are also spoken of as your duties—such as checking time cards, investigating accidents, scheduling employees, or keeping production records.

Authority is the power you need to carry out your responsibilities. A supervisor's authority includes the right to make decisions, to take action to control costs and quality, and to exercise necessary discipline over the employees assigned to help carry out these responsibilities.

It's an axiom that you shouldn't be given a responsibility without enough authority to carry it out. A supervisor who is given responsibility for seeing that quality is up to specifications must also be given authority to stop the production line when the quality falls off or to take any steps considered necessary to correct the problem.

WHERE DOES YOUR ORGANIZATIONAL AUTHORITY COME FROM?

Authority, like responsibility, is usually handed down to supervisors from their immediate bosses. These bosses, in turn, receive their authority and responsibilities from their immediate superiors. And so it goes, on up to the company president, who receives assignments from the board of directors.

The biggest chunk of authority and responsibility rests with the company president, who may split this chunk into as few as three pieces (to the vice presidents of production, sales, and financing) or as many as 20 (to vice presidents in charge of 20 different products). As the responsibilities and authorities come down the line to you, the pieces get smaller and smaller, but they also get much more specific.

For example, a plant superintendent may have the responsibility for producing goods in sufficient quantities to meet sales requirements, whereas the supervisor's responsibility may be to see that ten milling machines are operated at optimum capacity so that 200,000 product units are produced each month. Similarly, the plant superintendent's authority may permit the exercise of broad disciplinary measures, whereas the supervisor's may be limited to recommending disciplinary action for employees who break rules or whose output is not up to production and quality standards.

Most companies try to make the responsibility and the authority at each level of management fairly consistent. For instance, a supervisor in Department A should have the same general responsibilities as a supervisor in Department Z. Their authority would be generally the same even though their specific duties might differ widely.

WHAT OTHER SOURCES CAN YOU DRAW ON FOR YOUR AUTHORITY?

In addition to your organizational imperative to get things done, you may often need to draw from other, more personal sources. Your employer tries to establish your organizational rights by granting you a title or a rank, by depicting your position on an organization chart, or by some visible demonstration of your status such as a desk, an office, or some special privilege. Ordinarily you must reinforce this authority, or power, with one of the following:

Your job knowledge or skills

Your personal influence in the organization (whom you know and can get to help you or your team)

Your personal charm (if you have it)

Your ability to see that things get done (performance)

Your persuasive ability (a communications skill)

Your physical strength (occasionally)

All these sources are important because employees tend to restrict their acknowledgment of organizational rights over them. They expect their supervisors to show a little more real power than that. When employees come to accept your authority as deserved or earned (acceptance theory of authority rather than institutional), you will find that your relationships with people will improve.

SHOULD DISTINCTIONS BE DRAWN AMONG RESPONSIBILITY, AUTHORITY, AND ACCOUNTABILITY?

Yes, although they may appear to you to be only technical ones. As your boss, for example, I might be held accountable to higher management for the way in which operating supplies are conserved in my department. But I have the prerogative to delegate this responsibility to you, if I also grant you the authority to take any steps needed to protect these supplies. If you were to misuse these supplies or to lose track of them, I might discipline you for failing to discharge your responsibility in this matter; but I'd still be held accountable to my boss (and would be subject to discipline) for what happened, no matter which one of us was at fault. Similarly, when you delegate a minor responsibility to one of your employees (together with the necessary authority to carry it out), you will still be held accountable to your boss for the way in which this responsibility is carried out by your subordinate. In other words, you can delegate responsibility, but you cannot delegate accountability.

HOW MUCH LEEWAY DOES A SUPERVISOR HAVE IN TAKING AUTHORITATIVE ACTION?

You can't draw a hard-and-fast rule to follow. Generally speaking, an organization may establish three rough classifications of authority for supervisors, within which they may make decisions:

Class 1: Complete authority. Supervisors can take action without consulting their superiors.

Class 2: Limited authority. Supervisors can take action they deem fit so long as they tell their superiors about it afterward.

Class 3: No authority. Supervisors can take no action until they first check with their superiors.

If many decisions fall into class 3, the supervisor will become little more than a messenger. To improve this situation, first learn more about your company's policy and then spend time finding out how your bosses would act. If you can convince them that you would handle matters as they might, your bosses will be more likely to transfer class 3 decisions to class 2, and as you prove yourself, from class 2 to class 1.

Note that the existing company policy would still prevail. The big change would be in permitting supervisors discretion, and this would be because you have demonstrated that you are qualified to translate front-office policy into front-line action.

WHO CAN DELEGATE AUTHORITY AND RESPONSIBILITY?

Any members of management, including supervisors, can usually delegate some of their responsibility—and their authority. Remember, the two must go together.

A supervisor, for instance, who has responsibility for seeing that proper records are kept in the department may delegate that responsibility to a records clerk. But the clerk must also be given the authority to collect time sheets from the employees and to interview them if the data seem inaccurate. The supervisor wouldn't, however, delegate to the records clerk the authority to discipline an employee. Likewise, a supervisor can't delegate the accountability for seeing that accurate records are kept.

WHAT IS THE CHAIN OF COMMAND?

The term *chain of command* is a military phrase used to imply that orders and information in an organization should originate at the top, then proceed toward the bottom from each management level to the next lower level without skipping any levels or crossing over to another chain of command. The same procedure is followed for information and requests going up the line.

IS IT A BAD PRACTICE TO GO OUT OF CHANNELS?

It's best to conform to the practice of your company. "Channels" is just a word to indicate the normal path that information, orders, or requests should travel when following the chain of command. The channel through which customer orders travel from the sales manager to the production supervisor might be from the sales manager to the production manager, from the production manager to the department superintendent, and from the department superintendent to the supervisor. It would be going out of channels if the sales manager gave the order directly to the supervisor.

The channel used by a supervisor to ask for a raise might be from the supervisor to the department head, from the department head to the production manager, and from the production manager to the vice president. The supervisor who asked the vice president for a raise without having seen each one of the other managers in progression would be going out of channels.

Because authority and responsibility are delegated through the channels of a chain of command, for the most part it's better to handle your affairs (especially decisions) through them, too. It avoids your making changes without letting your boss know what's going on and prevents others from thinking another manager is bypassing the boss.

On the other hand, there are occasions when chain-of-command channels should be circumvented. In emergencies or when time is essential, it makes sense to get a decision or advice from a higher authority other than your boss if your boss is not readily available.

For purposes of keeping people informed and for exchanging information, channels sometimes get in the way. There's really nothing wrong with your discussing matters with people in other departments or on other levels of the company—so long as you don't betray confidences. If you do cross channels, it's a good practice to tell your boss you are doing so, and why. That way, you won't seem to be doing something behind your boss's back, and that is something you should never do.

HOW DO STAFF PEOPLE EXERT INFLUENCE?

Staff departments exert influence, rather than real authority, because their responsibility is to advise and guide, not to take action themselves.

Before the days of staff departments and when companies were smaller, store managers and company superintendents tried to be informed on all kinds of subjects related to their fields. These subjects included personnel management, merchandising, cost control, quality control, etc. As companies grew larger and processes became more complex, many managers found it wiser to employ assistants who could devote their full time and attention to becoming authorities in each of these phases of operations. These assistants have become known as staff assistants, and the departments they manage are called *staff departments.*

It's usually a mistake to assume that a staff department tells you how to do something. More often than not the staff department suggests that you do something differently, or advises that your department is off target (on quality, for instance), or provides information for your guidance. This isn't evasion. It's an honest recognition that the line people must retain the authority to run the company, but that to stand up to today's competition, you need the counsel of specialists in these side areas.

If supervisors are smart, they will make every use they can of the staff department's knowledge. If you were building a house yourself for the first time and someone offered to furnish you free the advice of a first-rate carpenter, a top-notch mason, a heating specialist, and a journeyman painter, you'd jump at the chance. The same holds true in accepting the advice and guidance available from the staff departments and other specialists in your company when you are tackling a management problem.

WHEN SHOULD YOU DELEGATE SOME OF YOUR WORK?

Delegate when you find you can't personally keep up with everything you think you should do. Just giving minor time-consuming tasks to others will save your time for bigger things. Let one employee double-check the production report, for example, and send another employee to see who wants to work overtime.

Plan to have certain jobs taken over when you're absent from your department in an emergency or during vacation. Restrict the arrangement to routine matters, if you will, and to those requiring a minimum of authority. But do try to get rid of the tasks of filling out routine requisitions and reports, making calculations and entries, checking supplies, and running errands.

HOW CAN YOU DO A BETTER JOB OF DELEGATING?

Start by seeing yourself as a manager. Recognize that no matter how capable you might be, you'll always have more responsibilities than you can carry out yourself.

The trick of delegating is to concentrate on the most important matters yourself. Keep a close eye, for instance, on the trend of production costs; that's a big item. But let someone else check the temperature of the quenching oil in the heat treater. That's less important.

Trouble begins when you can't distinguish between the big and the little matters. You may think that you can put off checking the production record—that it can wait until the day of reckoning at the end of the month. You may think that unless the quenching oil temperature is just right, the heat treater will spoil a $500 die today. But in the long run you'll lose your sanity if you don't see that the small jobs must get done by someone else.

Be ready, too, to give up certain work that you enjoy. A supervisor must learn to let go of those tasks that rightfully belong to a subordinate. Otherwise, larger and more demanding assignments may not get done. And don't worry too much about getting blamed by your boss for delegating to an employee work the boss has given to you. Generally speaking, supervisors should be interested only in seeing that the job is done in the right way, not in who carries it out. See Figure 3-4 for an idea on how to decide what jobs to target for delegation.

SHOULD YOU DELEGATE EVERYTHING?

Don't go too far. Some things are yours only. When a duty involves technical knowledge that only you possess, it would be wrong to let someone less able take over. And it's wrong to entrust confidential information to others.

WHAT SHOULD YOU TELL EMPLOYEES ABOUT JOBS DELEGATED TO THEM?

Give them a clear statement of what they are to do, how far they can go, and how much checking you intend to do. Let employees know the rela-

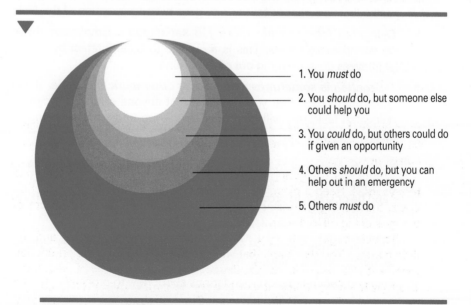

1. You *must* do

2. You *should* do, but someone else could help you

3. You *could* do, but others could do if given an opportunity

4. Others *should* do, but you can help out in an emergency

5. Others *must* do

FIGURE 3-4 **Supervisor's task and delegation chart**

tive importance of the job so that they can judge how much attention it should receive. There's no point in letting an employee think that making a tally will lead to a promotion, if you consider it just a routine task.

Tell workers why you delegated the job to them. If it shows you have confidence in them, they will try that much harder. But if they think you're pushing off all the dirty jobs on them, they may deliberately make mistakes.

Don't mislead employees about their authority; you don't want them trying to crack your whip. But do define the scope of the task and see that others in your department know that this new task isn't something an employee has assumed without authorization. Let the others know that you gave out the assignment and that you expect them to cooperate in carrying it out.

WHY SHOULD EMPLOYEES ACCEPT DELEGATED JOBS?

Employees who accept delegated jobs outside their own job responsibilities are really taking these jobs on speculation. They have a right to know what's in it for them:

▶   *Employees who take on extra duties get a chance to learn.* If they have never seen how the individual records in the department are tabulated, here's a chance for them to get a better perception of this task.

▶   *Delegated jobs provide more job satisfaction.* Employees thrive on varied assignments. This is a chance to build interest by letting employees do something out of the ordinary.

▶   *Delegation is sometimes a reward for other work well done.* If you can truthfully say that you wouldn't trust anyone else with a certain delegated task, this will help build employee pride and a feeling of status.

You may also want to try the concept of "completed staff work." You assign a problem requiring judgment and common sense to a subordinate, and he or she is to provide you with a complete solution according to these specifications:

1.   Consulted other personnel who are affected by, or who can contribute to, the problem's analysis.
2.   Provided concrete recommendations about how to proceed.
3.   Worked out all the details.

4. Avoided overly long and complex explanations.

5. Presented a single, coordinated plan of action in written form.

ARE THERE ANY ORGANIZATIONAL DON'TS?

Yes, but not very many. Once an organization has been set up, pragmatism and practicality ought to prevail. In fact, some odd—and informal—arrangements occasionally work out very well. For example, a highly successful firm operated for years without a visual organization chart. Its president thought the staff would develop the most effective relationships without one; apparently it did. Nevertheless, in the design stages at least, there are a few hazards of organization that ought to be guarded against:

1. *Don't let the chain of command get too long.* Keep the number of responsibility levels at a minimum; otherwise, some information will never trickle all the way to the bottom.

2. *Don't ask one person to report to two bosses.* Anyone caught in this nutcracker knows the dilemma: Which boss's work comes first?

3. *Don't make fuzzy job assignments.* When there is a gray area between two positions, overlap, conflict, and duplication of effort are invited.

4. *Don't be too rigid.* Try to retain flexibility for contingent situations—those problems that inevitably crop up and need to be handled through nonstandard assignments.

WHAT CAN BE DONE TO BUILD A STRONGER ORGANIZATIONAL TEAM IN YOUR DEPARTMENT?

You can apply some of the techniques of *organizational development* (OD). OD is a participative, rather than a purely management-directed, approach to organizing. It assumes that members of an organization (your employees, for instance) are more aware of conflicts and deficiencies caused by organizational constraints than the boss may be. To institute an informal OD program, a supervisor invites employees, singly at first and later when they are all together, to discuss their job roles and relationships. Specifically, employees are asked to comment on the appropriateness of their duties and responsibilities, the extent of their authority, and the way in which their jobs mesh with or abrade other jobs. Inevitably, this brings into the open problems that can be attributed to the division of labor and the organizational structure. At this point, the supervisor and employees try to solve these problems constructively, rather than criticizing and placing blame on one another. For example:

1. *OD strives to achieve clarity of each person's role in the organization.* Group discussions consider such questions as: "What is Bill's role, and what is my role?" "What is the extent of authority that Mary has when working on urgent, red-rush projects?" "What can we expect from the records department, and how much must we do ourselves?"

2. *OD helps set priorities.* It answers such questions as: "When we have six requests from sales for special handling of orders, which gets our attention first? Who decides this?" "In the event of a conflict between a quality standard and a shipping deadline, who makes the decision?" "When it comes to working on my job or helping out with Pete's job, which comes first?"

3. *OD seeks to settle staffing problems.* It encourages employees to find answers to questions such as these: "Which one of us will get the services of temporary help when it arrives?" "If my job gets to be too much for me during the Christmas rush, what kind of assistance can I expect?" "If there is a slowdown this summer, will Adam continue to work with me, or will he be transferred to another operation?"

REVIEW ▼ 3 ▼ QUESTIONS

1. What is the purpose of an organization chart? Is it possible to do without one?
2. Compare the formal organization with the informal organization.
3. Joan is a production supervisor in an electronics components plant. Her department receives maintenance services on its machinery from a plant engineering department. A quality assurance department inspects the output of Joan's department and advises her when it is off grade. What common form of organizational structure do these relationships imply? Identify the kinds of departments represented here.
4. Name three traditional kinds of organizational structures besides the functional and line-and-staff organizations.
5. Which kind of authority are employees most likely to respect most in a supervisor—the authority of his or her position, or that which is earned by the supervisor? Why?
6. Distinguish between authority and responsibility, and explain how the two are related.
7. Which kinds of companies, departments, or groups are most likely to be structured in a matrix organization? What do these groups have in common?
8. What are some of the benefits a subordinate may gain from accepting a delegated task?

A CASE IN POINT

Who's in Charge?

George was about as frustrated as a person can be. As supervisor of production in the finishing room of a furniture plant, he had had his plans upset twice within an hour. First of all, George had assigned Julia, a sanding machine operator, to work on a batch of table tops that were blocking normal production. No sooner had Julia been set up to run the job when the production control manager for the plant insisted that a batch of desk tops be moved ahead of the table tops. Julia lost an hour's production tearing down the setup for the table tops and setting up for the desk tops.

In order to speed up the changeover, George asked Bill, a hand-rubber, to give Julia a hand. "Nothing doing," said Bill, "That job is for sanders, not for finishers. Besides, sanding carries a higher skill classification and a higher rate." When George checked this out with the human resources manager, he learned that Bill's point of view would be supported. "That's the way this department has been organized," said the human resources manager. "If you were to let everyone work anywhere they wanted to, there would be chaos here. Nothing would be accomplished."

"That wasn't my point," replied George, "I was delegating a very simple task to someone who was capable of helping us out." "Too bad," commented the human resources manager, "You should have thought of a way to make that delegated assignment more attractive to Bill."

"It's beginning to look as if I don't have authority to take charge in my own department," declared George.

"No, that's not right," replied the human resources manager. "You do have authority, but only within the established organizational structure."

If you were George, what would you do now? Five alternative courses of action are listed below. Rank them in the order in which they appeal to you (1 most effective, 5 least effective). You may add another approach in the space provided, if you wish. In any event, be prepared to justify your ranking.

_____ **A.** Never delegate a task again.

_____ **B.** Reorganize the department so that sanding and hand-rubbing jobs are interchangeable.

_____ **C.** Work with the human resources manager to redefine jobs within the department so that anyone can be required to fill in on other reasonable assignments in an emergency.

_____ **D.** Establish a delegation policy that invites employees to learn new skills and prepare for advancement by voluntarily accepting temporary assignments outside of their normal jobs.

_____ **E.** Argue that, as a supervisor, you have the authority to make work assignments and that employees must accept them.

If you have another approach, write it here.

_____

_____

_____

Complete the ACTION PLANNING CHECKLIST
for this chapter, which can be found on page 313.

C H A P T E R

4

EXERCISING CONTROL
TO GET RESULTS

LEARNING OBJECTIVES

After studying this chapter, you should be able to:

1. Explain the purpose of controls, define and recognize a control standard, and explain and evaluate the sources of these standards.

2. Apply the four steps of the control process and explain the three major types of controls.

3. Identify the six major areas of organizational control that guide supervisory actions.

4. Explain the techniques of budgetary control and management by exception.

5. Discuss employee resistance to controls, explain some ways to reduce it, and explain the relationship between management by objectives and the control process.

▶ The control function is inseparably linked to planning. It requires that a supervisor keep continual track of progress toward departmental goals so that corrective action can be taken as soon as possible.

▶ Good controls are based on reliable, attainable standards of performance. The best standards are based on systematic analysis.

▶ Budgetary controls place financial restrictions on the actions a supervisor can take in attempting to meet quantity, quality, cost, time, and other interdependent goals.

▶ Because control is only one of several functions that supervisors must perform, they should take maximum advantage of the exception principle to delegate corrective action to qualified employees.

▶ Resistance to controls is a natural human reaction. For this reason, controls should be fair, be specific and numerical where possible, motivate rather than coerce, be consistently applied, and encourage the greatest degree of self-control possible.

WHAT IS THE BASIC PURPOSE OF A SUPERVISOR'S CONTROL FUNCTION?

To keep things in line and to make sure your plans hit their targets. In the restrictive sense, you use controls to make sure that employees are at work on time, that materials aren't wasted or stolen, and that employees don't exceed their authority. These controls tend to be the no-nos of an organization, the rules and regulations that set limits of acceptable behavior. In the more constructive sense, controls help to guide you and your department in reaching production goals and meeting quality standards.

WHAT CAN CONTROLS BE USED FOR?

For just about anything that needs regulation and guidance. Controls, for example, can be used to regulate:

Employee performance of all kinds, such as attendance, rest periods, productivity, and workmanship.

Machine operation and maintenance, such as expected daily output, power consumption, and extent of time for out-of-service repairs.

Materials usage, such as the percentage of expected yield and unexpected waste during handling and processing.

Product or service quality, such as the number of rejects that will be accepted or the number of complaints about service that will be tolerated.

Personal authority, such as the extent of independent action employees can take while carrying out the duties outlined in their job descriptions.

EXACTLY WHAT IS A CONTROL STANDARD?

A control standard, usually called simply a standard, is a specific performance goal that a product, a service, a machine, an individual, or an organization is expected to meet. It is usually expressed numerically: a weight (14 ounces), a rate (200 units per hour), or a flat target (four rejects). The numbers may be expressed in any unit—inches, gallons, dollars, ratios, or percentages.

Many companies also allow a little leeway from standard, which is called a tolerance. This implies that the performance will be considered to be in control if it falls within specific boundaries. A product, for instance, may be said to meet its 14-ounce standard weight if it weighs no less than 13.75 ounces and no more than 14.25 ounces. The control standard would be stated as 14 ounces, ±0.25 ounces. The tolerance is the ±0.25 ounces.

IN WHAT WAY ARE PLANS AND CONTROLS LINKED?

Controls are directly related to the goals that have been set during the planning process. In fact, controls are often identical with these goals. Suppose, for example, that as supervisor of a commercial office of a telephone company, you have planned that your department will handle 100 service calls per day during the next month. The 100 calls per day is your goal. It also becomes your control standard. If your department handles 100 calls per day, you have met your target and need exert no corrective controls. If, however, your department handles fewer than 100 calls and begins to fall behind, it is below its control standard, and you must take some sort of action to correct this performance.

WHERE DO THE CONTROL STANDARDS COME FROM? WHO SETS THEM?

Many standards are set by the organization itself. They may be set by the accounting department for costs or by the industrial engineering department for wage incentive or time standards. They may be issued by the production-control department for schedule quantities or by the quality-control people for inspection specifications. It is typical for control standards in large organizations to be set by staff specialists. In smaller companies, supervisors may set standards themselves. But even in large companies the supervisor may have to take an overall, or department, standard and translate it into standards for each employee or operation.

ON WHAT INFORMATION ARE CONTROL STANDARDS BASED?

Standards are based on information from one, two, or all three of the following sources.

Past Performance. Historical records often provide the basis for controls. If your department has been able to process 150 orders with three clerks in the past, this may be accepted as the standard. The weakness of this historical method is that it presumes that 150 orders constitutes good performance. Perhaps 200 would be a better target. This might be true if improvements have recently been made in the processing machinery and layouts.

High Hopes. In the absence of any other basis, some supervisors ask for the moon. They set unreasonably high standards for their employees to shoot at. Although it is a sound practice to set challenging goals, standards should always be attainable by employees who put forth a reasonable effort. Otherwise, workers will become discouraged, or rebel, and won't try to meet the standards.

Systematic Analysis. The best standards are set by systematically analyzing what a job entails. In this way the standard is based on careful observation and measurement, as with time studies. At the very least, standards should be based on a consideration of all the factors that affect attainment of the standard—such as tooling, equipment, training of the operator, absence of distractions, and clear-cut instructions and specifications.

HOW IS THE CONTROL PROCESS CARRIED OUT?

The control process follows four sequential steps. The first step, setting performance standards, often takes place "off camera." That is, the standards may have been set before the supervisor arrives on the scene. Other times, it is up to the supervisor to set the necessary performance standards for his or her department. Steps 2, 3, and 4 of the control process are illustrated in Figure 4-1. Here are the four process steps in order:

1. *Set performance standards.* Standards of quantity, quality, and time spell out (a) what is expected and (b) how much of a deviation can be tolerated if the person or process fails to come up to the mark. For example, the standard for an airline ticket counter might be that no customer should have to wait in line more than five minutes. The standard could then be modified to say that if only one out of ten customers had to wait more than five minutes, no corrective action need be taken. The standard would be stated as "waiting time of less than five minutes per customer with a tolerance of one out of ten who might have to wait longer." The guideline is that the more specific the standard, the better, especially when it can be stated with numbers as opposed to vague terms such as "good performance" and "minimum waiting time."

2. *Collect data to measure performance.* Accumulation of control data is so routine in most organizations that it is taken for granted.

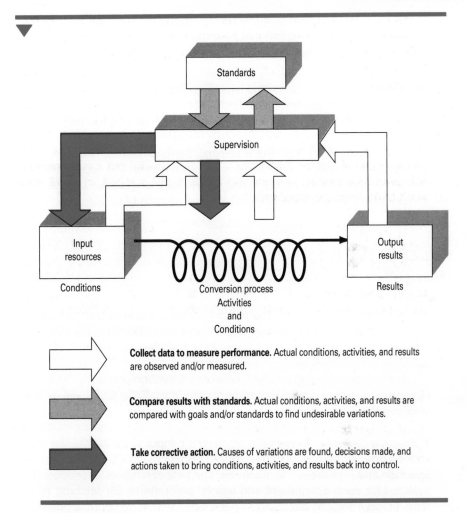

FIGURE 4-1 Steps in the control process, once standards have been set

Every time a supervisor or an employee fills out a time card, prepares a production tally, or files a receiving or inspection report, control data are being collected. Whenever a sales ticket is filled out, a sale rung up on a cash register, or a shipping ticket prepared, control data are being recorded—often with a computer-related terminal. Of course, not all information is collected in written form. Much of what a good supervisor uses for control purposes is gathered by observation—simply watching how well employees are carrying out their work.

3. *Compare results with standards.* From top manager to first-line supervisor, the control system flashes a warning if there is a gap between what was expected (the standard) and what is taking place or has

taken place (the result). If the results are within the tolerance limits, the supervisor's attention can be turned elsewhere. But if the process exceeds the tolerance limits—if the gap is too big—then action is called for.

4. *Take corrective action.* You must first find the cause of the gap (variance or deviation from standard). Then you must take action to remove or minimize this cause. If travelers are waiting too long in the airline's ticket line, for example, the supervisor may see that there is an unusually high degree of travel because of a holiday. The corrective action is to add another ticket clerk. If, however, the supervisor observes that the clerks are taking excessively long coffee breaks, this practice will have to be stopped as soon as possible.

WHERE IN THE PROCESS ARE CONTROLS APPLIED?

There is always a danger of too much control, somewhat like "oversteering" an automobile. Accordingly, supervisors should look for key places—make-or-break points—in their operations and then focus most of their attention on these areas.

The selective timing and/or locale of observation points can also provide three distinct types of control opportunities. Refer to Figure 4-1 as you read their explanations.

Preventive Controls. These take place at the input stage before the conversion process begins. Materials are inspected. Machinery undergoes inspection and preventive maintenance. The proper kinds of employees are selected for each assignment and trained beforehand. By catching problems before they can affect later operations, preventive controls have the greatest potential for savings.

Concurrent Controls. These are controls that take place during the conversion phase of a supervisor's operations. In manufacturing and processing plants, pressures and temperatures are checked and on-line inspections are made as partially converted products flow through the process. In offices and retail shops, supervisors monitor output and quality of employee performance during the workday. Concurrent controls make their biggest contribution by catching and correcting problems before they get out of hand.

Corrective Controls. These controls take place at the output stage after an operation has been completed, a product finished, or a service delivered. Such "final inspections" occur too late to prevent the current problem.

Their value is in alerting supervisors to ongoing performance problems to be avoided in the future.

TO WHAT EXTENT IS CONTROL AUTOMATIC?

Increasingly, operating processes depend upon automatic, or computer-driven, control systems. These try to minimize the human element. We expect "feedback" from a thermostat, for example, to tell the furnace to keep the room warm. In many automobiles, we expect a buzzer to let us know whether or not a seat belt is fastened. Many processes in industry are controlled according to the same principle. A worker feeds a sheet of metal into a press, and the machine takes over. A clerk slips a piece of paper into a copying machine, and the machine automatically reproduces the number of copies the clerk has dialed onto the control mechanism. There will be much more of this in the future.

Computer monitoring of employee performance is the latest in this trend. The computer, by sensing a terminal at which a clerk works—or any mechanism related to an employee's output—automatically counts, times, and records an employee's performance. Such impersonal computer measurement, although viewed as a boon to management, arouses resentment in the minds of many employees. It also raises social issues that are under continuing debate and attack from labor unions.

WHAT SPECIFIC KINDS OF ORGANIZATIONAL CONTROLS ARE MOST LIKELY TO AID OR RESTRICT SUPERVISORY ACTIONS?

These depend largely on the nature of the organization in which the supervisor works. The following controls, however, are most common.

Output Controls. These relate to the demand of almost every organization for some standard of output or production. The quantity of production required is often the basis for all other aspects of control. In other words, a supervisor must first make sure that output quantities measure up. Then the supervisor's attention can turn to controls that specify a certain quality or time, for example.

Quality Controls. If, in meeting the production standard, a department skimps on the quality of its work, there can be trouble. Quantity and quality go hand in hand. The inspection function is intended to make sure the final product or service lives up to its quality standards (specifications). As a supplement to routine inspections, many companies practice statistical quality control, a way of predicting quality deviations in advance so that a supervisor can take corrective action before a product is spoiled.

Time Controls. Almost every organization must also meet certain dead-lines or live within time constraints. A product must be shipped on a certain date. A service must be performed on an agreed-on day. A project must be completed as scheduled. Such time standards point up the fact that it is not enough just to get the job done if it isn't finished on time.

Material Controls. These are related to both quality and quantity standards. A company may wish to limit the amounts of raw or finished materials it keeps on hand; thus it may exercise inventory controls. Or an apparel firm, for instance, may wish to make sure that the maximum number of skirts are cut out of a bolt of cloth so that a minimum amount of cloth is wasted—a material-yield standard.

Cost Controls. The final crunch in exercising controls involves costs. A supervisor may meet the quantity and quality standards, but if in so doing the department has been overstaffed or has been working overtime, it probably won't meet its cost standard.

Employee Performance Controls. These cover a wide spectrum and are often inseparable from all the controls listed above. The difference is that employee performance controls focus on individuals or groups of employees, rather than on a department, a machine, or a process. Such controls may be concerned with employee absences, tardiness, and accidents as well as with performance that is directly related to the quality or quantity of the employees' work.

HOW DO BUDGETS FIT INTO THIS PICTURE?

Budgetary controls are very similar to cost standards. Typically, the accounting or financial department provides a supervisor with a list of allowable expenses for the month. These will be based on the expectation of a certain output—say, 4000 units of production. These allowable expenses become the cost standards to be met for the month. At the end of the month the accounting department may issue the supervisor a cost variance report (Table 4-1). This tells whether the department has met its standards, exceeded them, or fallen below them. Note in Table 4-1 that the department has exceeded its overall budget by $950. It has, however, met a number of its standards while spending more for overtime, temporary hires, operating supplies, maintenance and repairs, and equipment rentals. The supervisor will be expected to do something to bring these cost overruns back into line next month. On the other hand, the department

TABLE 4-1 Cost variance report

▼ COST VARIANCE REPORT

Department: Claims Processing   Month: July

Work unit: Claim forms processed

No. of work units scheduled: 4000

No. of work units actually produced: 4050

Variance in production output: +50 units

Account Title	Actual	Budget	Variance (+over −under)
Regular payroll	$12,000	$12,000	0
Overtime, regular employees	400	0	+400
Temporary hires	900	600	+300
Housekeeping	500	500	0
Operating supplies	500	400	+100
Maintenance and repairs	300	200	+100
Telephone and fax charges	1,100	1,300	−200
Equipment rentals	250	0	+250
Total controllable budget	$15,950	$15,000	+$950

used less than was budgeted for telephone and fax charges. If this keeps up, the accounting department may develop a new standard for these expenses and allow the supervisor less money for them in the future.

MUST SUPERVISORS SPEND ALL THEIR TIME CONTROLLING?

It would appear that way, but by using a simple principle called *management by exception,* supervisors can hold to a minimum the time taken for control activities. Management by exception is a form of delegation in which the supervisor lets things run as they are so long as they fall within prescribed (control) limits of performance. When they get out of line, as in the cost variance report in Table 4-1, the supervisor steps in and takes corrective action.

Figure 4-2 shows how a supervisor can use the management-by-exception principle as a guideline for delegating much of the control work to subordinates.

This example involves a broiler chef in a fast-food restaurant. The boss says that the chef should expect to broil 180 to 200 hamburgers an hour. This is control zone 1. So long as results fall within the prescribed limits, the chef is completely in charge.

If, however, the requests for hamburgers fall below 180 but are above 150, the chef keeps the grill hot and puts fewer hamburgers into the ready position. If requests build up to 225, the chef moves more hamburgers to the completed stage. This is zone 2. The chef takes this action without first checking with the boss, but tells the boss what has been done.

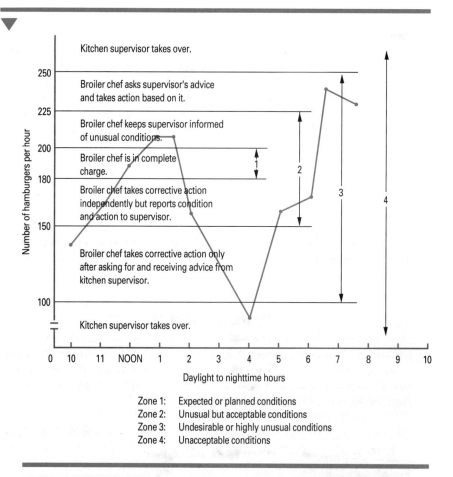

FIGURE 4-2 **Use of a management-by-exception chart for controlling the operation of a hamburger grill**

If business falls from 150 but is more than 100 hamburgers an hour, the chef may ask the boss whether the grill can be turned off for a while. If the requests build up to 250 per hour, the chef may ask if one of the counter clerks can help out. This is zone 3.

If conditions now move to either extreme—hamburger requests drop below 100 or exceed 250—the chef calls this to the supervisor's attention. This is zone 4. The supervisor may in the first instance (below 100) decide to shut down the grill. In the second instance (above 250), the supervisor may decide to start up an auxiliary grill.

WHAT ABOUT THE PEOPLE PROBLEM IN CONTROLS?

Many people do not like to be controlled. They don't like to be told what to do, and they feel boxed in when faced with specific standards. Few persons like to be criticized or corrected. Yet criticism or correction is what control often comes down to. When correction means discipline or termination, controls can seem very harsh indeed. For this reason a supervisor should be realistic about controls. Controls can have a very negative effect on employees, to say nothing to what they may do to the supervisor.

The negative aspects of controls, however, can be minimized. Supervisors should consider any of these more positive approaches.

Emphasize the Value of Controls to Employees. Standards provide employees with feedback that tells them whether or not they are doing well. Standards minimize the need for the supervisor to interfere and often allow the employee to choose the way of doing the job so long as standards are met. The supervisor says, "You do the job, and I will stay out of your hair."

Avoid Arbitrary or Punitive Standards. Employees respond better to standards that can be justified and supported by past records. "Our records show that 150 per day is a standard that other operators have consistently met." Standards based on analysis, especially time studies, are even more acceptable. "Let's time this job for an hour or two so that we can be sure the standard is reasonable." Compare this with: "We'll just have to step up our production rate to 175 units each day."

Be Specific; Use Numbers if Possible. Avoid expressions such as "improve quality" or "show us better attendance." Instead, use numbers that set specific targets, such as "fewer than two days' absence in the next six months," or "decrease your scrap percentage from 7 out of 100 to 3 out of 100."

Aim for Improvement Rather than Punishment. Capitalize on instances of missed standards to try to help employees learn how to improve their work. "Your output was below standards again last month. Perhaps you and I ought to start all over again to see what it is that is preventing you from meeting them. There may be something that I haven't shown you about this particular operation."

Resort to Punishment as the Last Step. A supervisor must balance rewards with punishment. Most employees respond to positive motivation; many do not. All employees, however, good and poor alike, want to know what the "or else" is about their jobs. The guiding rule is to hold off punishment if you can, but to make it clear to everyone that standards must be met. Specify in advance what the penalty will be for those who don't meet them.

Avoid Threats that You Can't or Won't Back Up. If an employee is to be disciplined for failing to meet a quota or a standard of workmanship, be specific about the nature of timing of the discipline. "If you don't get your production up to 150 per day by the first of April, I will recommend that you be laid off for good." Don't say, "If you don't shape up soon, your head will be in a noose." If you do make the specific threat, it is good to make certain in advance that the company will help you make it stick.

Be Consistent in Application of Controls. If you have set standards that apply to the work of several employees, it should go without saying that you will be expected to make everyone measure up to them. If you think that exceptions can be made, be prepared to defend that position. In the main, however, standards should be the same for everyone doing the same work. Similarly, rewards or punishment should be the same for all those who meet, or fail to meet, these standards.

WHAT ABOUT ENCOURAGING SELF-CONTROL?

Self-control is beautiful for those who can exert it. Douglas McGregor insisted that many people need only be given the targets for their work—the standards. After that, he said, they wish to be left alone and to be judged on the basis of their results in meeting or not meeting these targets. Employees will, McGregor said, provide their own control and do not need a supervisor to threaten them or cajole them into meeting standards. For more about McGregor's views, see questions regarding Theory X and Theory Y in Chapter 10.

My advice is to give an employee the benefit of the doubt. Give a free hand to those who take charge of themselves. Keep the reins on those who soon show that they need, or expect, the control to come from the supervisor.

WHEN DO MANAGEMENT GOALS BECOME CONTROL STANDARDS?

Very often, as was shown when the link between planning and controlling was explained. More specifically, however, many companies convert their organizational goals into control programs by using a system of *Management by Objectives* (MBO). Management by Objectives is a planning and control process that provides managers at each organizational control point a set of goals, or standards, to be attained. This process is usually repeated every 12 months. These MBO goals are similar to the list of supervisory performance goals illustrated in Table 2-1 in Chapter 2. It is presumed that if all supervisors reach their goals, the organization also will reach its goals. In companies where MBO is practiced to its full extent, the supervisors' goals literally become the standards of performance that must be met. The assumption is that the supervisors are capable of exerting, and will exert, their own controls in striving to meet these objectives. The MBO system also presumes that the supervisors have been given enough freedom of action so that they can meet these goals within the resources provided by staff and budget. In essence, MBO is simply a formalization at managerial levels of the principle of self-control.

REVIEW ▼**4**▼ QUESTIONS

1. What is the ultimate purpose of the control process?
2. How are control standards related to the goals established in plans?
3. Of the three chief ways of setting standards, which is the best? Why? What's wrong with the other two?
4. If a supervisor has been given the standards for the department, what three other steps in the control process will that supervisor have to deal with?
5. How is a departmental budget used to control costs?
6. In what way are management by exception and control-standard tolerance related?
7. What are some of the benefits employees may derive from the presence of control standards for their work?
8. How should a supervisor approach the issue of self-control among employees? What technique is sometimes applied to supervisors for controlling their own performance?

A CASE IN POINT

A Constant Watch

Charley breathed a sigh of relief. He had just caught a potentially big problem before it could cause trouble in his department. Charley supervises the assembly room of the Ace Electric Clock Company. He was "walking around" his department today when he spotted a palletload of clock motors that did not look quite right. "What voltage ratings are these?" he asked his receiving clerk. "I don't know," the clerk replied, "but these motors came along with the other batch of parts for the clocks we are assembling now." Charley checked the bill of materials that had accompanied the order. There, he found the problem. The motors that were specified were 220-volt motors that conformed to the requirements of an overseas customer. The ones on the pallet were 110-volt motors for domestic use only.

"'This almost got away from you," Charley charged the receiving clerk. "If we had assembled them to this order, the entire shipment would have been sent back to us for rework. That would have cost the company a bundle!"

"Nobody ever told me there was a difference in motor voltages," the receiving clerk said.

"You should have checked the parts numbers," said Charley.

"I've got more than enough to do," said the clerk, "counting to be sure there are enough motors for the order without worrying about whether the guys over in the stock room have their heads on straight."

If you were Charley, what would you do to prevent the repeat of such an occurrence? Five alternative courses of action are listed below. Rank them in the order in which they appeal to you (1 most effective, 5 least effective). You may add another approach in the space provided, if you wish. In any event, be prepared to justify your ranking.

_____ **A.** Spend more time in the office instead of "walking around" the shop.

_____ **B.** Make sure that each employee has a clear and specific set of control standards for his or her operation.

_____ **C.** Agree with the receiving clerk, and others who excuse their mistakes, on the grounds that they have too much to do.

_____ **D.** Check with the company's engineer to see if there isn't some way to automate the inspection of incoming parts instead of relying on the clerk to spot errors.

_____ **E.** Advise the receiving clerk that the next error he makes will result in disciplinary action.

If you have another approach, write it here.

▶ _____

_____

_____

Complete the ACTION PLANNING CHECKLIST
for this chapter, which can be found on page 314.

C H A P T E R

5

USING INFORMATION TO SOLVE PROBLEMS AND MAKE DECISIONS

LEARNING OBJECTIVES

After studying this chapter, you should be able to:

1. Recognize and define a problem or a potential problem.

2. Explain how problems are solved and the relationship between problem solving and decision making.

3. List and apply the eight steps in problem solving and decision making.

4. Discuss the rational and intuitive approaches to decision making and explain cost-benefit analysis and ABC analysis.

5. Describe a management information system and its purpose.

OVERVIEW OF KEY CONCEPTS IN THIS CHAPTER

▶ Important marks of effective supervision are (1) the ability to recognize the existence of a problem or the need for a decision and (2) the ability to identify opportunities for improvement as well as anticipate potential trouble spots.

▶ Problems are characterized by a gap between what is expected to happen and what actually occurs. Gaps are usually caused by changes in procedures or conditions. Problems are solved by removing or correcting the cause of the change, which in turn closes the gap.

▶ Decision making, an inseparable part of the problem-solving process, is the phase in which solutions, ideas, and new courses of action are examined critically and then chosen on the basis of their chances for success or failure in meeting related objectives.

▶ Problem solving should always be approached systematically. Decision making utilizes intuition and creativity as well as logic, but is always more effective when based on firm objectives and adequate information.

▶ Problem solving and decision making are greatly aided by the use of mathematical techniques, which arrange and analyze numerical data in ways that maximize a supervisor's mental abilities and minimize personal bias.

WHAT, SPECIFICALLY, IS A PROBLEM?

A problem is a puzzle looking for an answer. When it occurs within an organization, a *problem* can be described as a disturbance or unsettled matter that demands a solution if the organization is to function productively. In many instances, the solution requires a decision that is arrived at only after (1) an extensive review of relevant information and (2) application of considerable thought and skill. A supervisor's work is full of such problems. For convenience in analysis, problems can be classified into three groups:

> *Problems that have already occurred or are occurring now.* Examples include merchandise that has spoiled, a valued employee who has quit, costs that are running out of line, and shipments that are not meeting delivery dates. These need immediate solutions to correct what has taken place or is taking place.
>
> *Identified problems that lie ahead.* Examples are how to finish a specific project on time, when to put on a second shift, where to place the new press, and whether or not to tell employees of an impending change in their work. These, too, require immediate solutions to set effective plans and procedures.
>
> *Problems that you want to detect and forestall.* These lurk in the future. You'd like to take preventive action now so that they will never arise and thus never require solutions.

Problems and their solutions are, of course, inseparably related to the management process. Problems arise all along the way. Supervisors must solve them when they plan, organize, staff, direct, and control. Otherwise, problems will stand in the way of the attainment of the department's goals.

WHAT CAUSES A PROBLEM?

Change. If everything remained exactly as it should be, problems would not occur. Unfortunately, change, especially unwanted change, is always with us. Changes occur in materials, tools and equipment, employee attitudes, specifications received from customers, the work space itself, and just about anything else you can imagine. The trick to problem solving is often the ability to spot the unwanted and unexpected change that has slipped into an otherwise normal situation.

HOW CAN YOU RECOGNIZE A
PROBLEM OR A POTENTIAL PROBLEM?

A problem exists when there is a gap between what you expect to happen and what actually happens. Your budget, for example, calls for 2200 insurance policies to be processed this week; the count at 5 p.m. on Friday shows that you completed only 1975, a gap of 225 policies (Figure 5-1). Or you expected to hold the total of employee absences in your department to 300 days this year; the total is 410, a gap of 110 days.

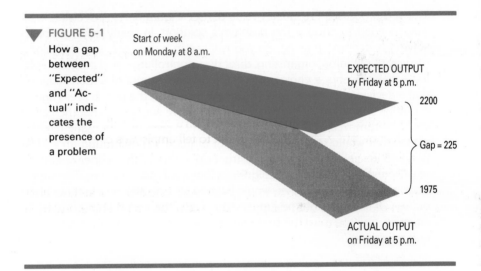

▼ FIGURE 5-1
How a gap between "Expected" and "Actual" indicates the presence of a problem

Start of week on Monday at 8 a.m.

EXPECTED OUTPUT by Friday at 5 p.m.

2200

Gap = 225

1975

ACTUAL OUTPUT on Friday at 5 p.m.

It is almost the same with potential problems. You know what you would like to have happen in the future: a project completed, a perfect safety record, fewer than ten customer complaints. These are your goals. But when you look ahead at your procedures and the potential for mishaps, you think that your department will fall short of its target—that there will be a gap.

HOW ARE PROBLEMS SOLVED?

By removing whatever has caused, or will cause, a gap between the expected or desired condition and the actual condition. That's the main idea, at least. Suppose, for example, that your hoped-for safety record of zero accidents is spoiled by three accidents on the punch press machine. You will want to find their cause (bypassing of the safety guard by the operators) and remove it (by designing a foolproof guard).

Finding and removing the cause or causes, however, is usually difficult and requires considerable examination and thought. There will be more discussion about the problem-solving process later.

WHAT IS THE CONNECTION BETWEEN PROBLEM SOLVING AND DECISION MAKING?

The two processes are closely related. (See Figure 5-2.) A decision is always needed to choose the problem's solution. In many ways, problem solving *is* decision making. As you will see in a moment, any step along the way of planning, organizing, directing, controlling—and problem solving—that presents a choice of more than one course of action requires that a decision be made. Take the safety record on the punch press again. A complete analysis of the problem might have suggested that the cause could be removed in three different ways: (1) using an automatic feeding device that would remove the need for a guard, (2) instituting an education and discipline program to instruct operators in the proper operation of the present guard, or (3) designing a foolproof guard system. The supervisor, as the decision maker, would have to choose among the three alternatives. The first might be judged too costly, the second not completely effective, and the third the best choice because it is relatively inexpensive and reliable.

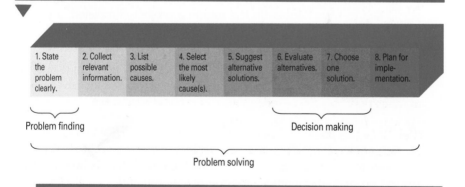

FIGURE 5-2 The problem-solving process: how problem solving and decision making overlap

HOW CAN YOU RECOGNIZE
THE NEED FOR A DECISION?

Whenever there is more than one way of doing things, a decision is needed. Any kind of choice, alternative, or option calls for a decision. You might ask: If this is so, why are so many decision opportunities overlooked? The answer is that managers and supervisors alike get preoccupied with the status quo. In effect, they say: "The way we are doing this is the only way." Such supervisors miss the point that there are always alternatives. There is always the choice to do something or not to do it, to speak or to remain silent, to correct or to let well enough alone. All too often a supervisor's decision is made by default. The supervisor does nothing. The tide of events carries the department along until a crisis occurs. In reality, however, doing nothing represented a choice. It was a decision not to change, not to plan for improvement, not to anticipate a potential problem.

MUST THE APPROACH TO
PROBLEM SOLVING BE SYSTEMATIC?

Yes. There are few exceptions to the rule that the best results come from a systematic approach. Here is a fundamental procedure.

Step 1. State the Problem Clearly and Specifically. Stay away from general statements such as "We have a problem with quality." Instead, narrow it down and put figures on it if you can, as in "Between the first of the month and today, the number of rejects found at final inspection has totaled 32, compared with our standard of 15."

Step 2. Collect All Information Relevant to the Problem. Don't go too far afield, but do find data that may shed light on process changes, materials used, equipment function, design specifications, or employee performance and assignments. Much of the data will not tell you anything except where the source of the problem is not. If your information shows, for example, that there has been no change in the way materials have arrived or machinery has been used, good! You can look elsewhere.

Step 3. List as Many Possible Causes for the Problem as You Can Think of. Remember, a problem is a gap between expected and actual conditions. Something must have occurred to cause that gap. Most particularly, something must have been changed. Was a different operator used? Was a power source less regular than before? Was there a change, however slight, in the specifications?

Step 4. Select the Cause or Causes that Seem Most Likely. Do this by a process of elimination. To test a cause to see if it is a probable one, try seeing or thinking through what difference it would make if that factor were returned to its original state. For example, suppose a possible cause of rejects is that compressed air power is now only 75 psi instead of 90 psi. Try making the product with the pressure restored to 90 psi. If it makes no difference, then power irregularity is not a likely cause. Or perhaps you think that the new operator has misunderstood your instructions. Check this out. See if the operator is, in fact, following the instructions exactly. If not, what happens when your instructions are followed? If the rejects stop, then this is a likely cause. If the rejects persist, this is not a likely cause.

Step 5. Suggest as Many Solutions for Removing Causes as You Can. This is a good time for brainstorming. There is rarely only one way to solve a problem. If the cause of an employee's excessive absenteeism, for instance, is difficulty in getting up in the morning, this cause might be removed in a number of ways. You might change the employee's shift, insist on the purchase of an alarm clock, telephone a wake-up call your-self, or show where failure to get to work will threaten the job. The point is to make your list of alternative solutions as long as possible.

Step 6. Evaluate the Pros and Cons of Each Proposed Solution. Some solutions will be better than others. But what does better mean? Cheaper? Faster? Surer? More participative? More in line with company policy? To judge which solution is best, you'll have to have a set of criteria like the ones just listed. Evaluation requires you to make judgments based on facts. Consult the information gathered in step 2. Also consult anyone who can offer specialized opinions about the criteria you have chosen.

Step 7. Choose the Solution that You Think Is Best. Yes, this—like what you did in step 6— is the decision phase of problem solving. In effect, you will have weighed all the chances of success against the risks of failure. The strengths of your solution should exceed its weaknesses.

Step 8. Spell Out a Plan of Action To Carry Out Your Solution. Decisions require action and follow-up. Pin down exactly what will be done and how, who will do it, where, and when. How much money can be spent? What resources can be used? What is the deadline?

HOW SYSTEMATIC MUST THE DECISION-MAKING PROCESS BE?

Unlike problem solving, there are good reasons to believe that decision making need not always be systematic or even logical. A systematic approach helps up to a point, but when you are dealing with the future, hunches and intuition often pay off.

The systematic, or rational, approach to decision making takes place during steps 6 and 7 of problem solving: evaluating alternative solutions and selecting the best one based on the facts available. You can make this approach even more rational and more reliable by first setting goals that the decision must satisfy. For example, a problem-solving decision about cost cutting must be effective for at least six months and not involve employee separations. Or, if you are developing future plans, the decision may be required to fulfill the goal of ensuring that production schedules are met without overtime.

This rational step of first setting a goal tends to make the quality of decisions better, even when they are ultimately made by hunches, because you know what your target is and what limitations will be placed on your choice of plans for implementation.

WHAT IS MEANT BY MATHEMATICAL DECISION MAKING?

Mathematical decision making refers to the use of certain mathematical, statistical, or quantitative techniques to aid the decision maker. These are very valuable aids in many instances, but they are only aids. They do not make decisions. Numerical information is arranged so that it can be analyzed mathematically, but the executive, manager, or supervisor must make the final decision, based on interpretation of the results.

WHAT IS MEANT BY COST-BENEFIT ANALYSIS?

It is not unlike the closing steps in problem solving and decision making. This is the phase when you examine the pros and cons of each proposed solution. Cost-benefit analysis has become a popular technique for evaluating proposals in the public sector. Take a proposal for a local government to offer a child-care service to its residents. Cost-benefit analysis adds all the implementation costs and equates them with the value of the services to the community. Typically, the benefits of such nonprofit services are hard to quantify; that is, it is hard to place a dollar value on them. Accordingly, many cost-benefit analyses include quality judgments of benefits as well as dollar estimates.

Cost-benefit analysis is similar to *input-output analysis,* which tries to make sure that the cost and effort expended in carrying out a decision will at least be balanced by its outputs or results. In business, when outputs exceed inputs, the result is a *profit.* If there is an excess of benefits over costs in nonprofit organizations, the excess is called a *surplus.*

ARE DECISIONS BASED ON INTUITION AS GOOD AS THOSE BASED ON LOGIC?

If it works out well, it won't make any difference how a decision was reached. Many decisions based on hunches have proved to be correct. They are harder to defend, however, when they go wrong. More important, any decision is likely to be better if its goals are clearly understood. The logical approach helps to strip away distractions and irrelevancies. Intuition often adds a valuable dimension by calling on some inner sense we don't clearly understand. Many authorities believe that the best decisions come from the dual approach—a combination of logic and hunch.

WHAT CAN BE DONE TO MAKE YOUR DECISIONS MORE EFFECTIVE?

Besides starting with a specific goal in mind and laying a foundation of facts and systematic analysis, you can turn to a couple of other kinds of insurance.

Pick Your Spots. First, avoid decision making, if you can, where risks are high. Second, try to make decisions only where the potential for payoff is great. You can identify the second kind of opportunity by using ABC analysis. The ABC concept is based on an established economic fact: A vital few problems or opportunities for action account for the greatest loss or greatest gain. The majority of problems and opportunities are basically of little consequence. Economists call this the 20/80 syndrome. It means that 20 percent of your problems will account for 80 percent of your losses or profits. Then, to turn the idea around, 80 percent of your problems will account for only 20 percent of your losses or profits. In ABC analysis, the vital few are called "A" items; the inconsequential many are "C" items; and those that fall somewhere in between are "B" items (Figure 5-3). If you were to take an inventory of items in your stockroom, for example, it is a sure bet that only a relatively few items would account for most of its value. A great many items, however, such as paper clips and erasers, would account for only a small portion of the inventory's total worth. Astute purchasing managers concentrate on the vital few items, not the trivial many. You should apply the same principle to your problems and decisions selection.

Maintain Your Perspective. Statistically, problems fall in what is called a normal distribution, and so do the results of most decisions. We say, "You win some and you lose some." That's really what a normal distribution tells us. If you make ten decisions, one or two will work out fine. One or two

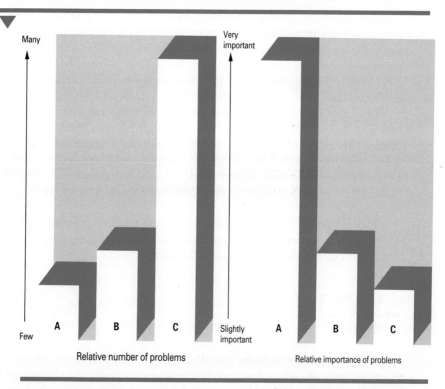

FIGURE 5-3 Distribution of problems: from vital few (A) to trivial many (B)

are likely to be bombs. The rest will fall somewhere in between. Knowing this, you should keep the following guidelines in mind when making decisions:

1. Don't reach too high. Don't set your objectives at the very top; allow some room for mistakes.

2. Don't overcommit or overextend your resources on one problem; you may need them later for an unanticipated problem.

3. Always prepare a fallback position, a way to alter plans and attain at least part of the objective.

IN SEEKING INFORMATION TO SOLVE A PROBLEM OR MAKE A DECISION, WHAT SHOULD BE THE CUTOFF POINT?

Stop looking when the trouble and cost of obtaining the extra information exceeds its value. *The rule is:* The more critical and lasting the effect of a decision, the more you can afford to look for the last scrap of vital information. Don't spend two days hunting for background data on a purchasing decision, for example, if the item plays only an insignificant part in your process and will be used only once or twice. On the other hand, it might pay to defer a decision to hire a full-time employee until you have made a reference check.

Do guard against using the absence of information as an excuse for procrastination. Some decisions are especially hard to arrive at and unpleasant to carry out. When you are faced with these situations, there is a temptation to put off an answer (yes, answers are decisions—or should be) by asking for more information. Rarely is the questioner fooled by this tactic, and rarely does the additional information add much to the quality of the decision.

The burden of information collection and analysis has now become so enormous, however, that most organizations provide support with some form of management information system.

WHAT, REALLY, IS A MANAGEMENT INFORMATION SYSTEM? WHY IS IT SO IMPORTANT?

At its root, a *management information system* (MIS) is plain old accounting, but with a much broader base and an electronic twist. An MIS is important because it can provide an informed basis for all management decisions. When the system is a good one, decisions are likely to be good. When the system is skimpy or overdone or misleading, decisions will suffer.

A modern management information system tries to keep track of everything that may help to make a manager's decisions effective. In a manufacturing company, for example, the MIS collects and analyzes information about product development, production, marketing, and finance. In a service company such as a commercial airline, the MIS may encompass other functions, such as aircraft operation, maintenance, scheduling, and customer sales and ticketing.

The ultimate objective of an MIS is to tie together all a company's past and present data into a great big library with instant electronic recall. Managers at all levels draw from this library (called a data bank) any kind of information that aids short-range or long-term decisions. Few organizations reach this ideal. Most management information systems operate in functional pockets with separate systems for each important activity. Production and inventory control may form one system, for example, and payroll and accounting another. These functional systems are only loosely tied into the overall company MIS, with little cross-referencing between them. The goal, however, is gradually to link all separate MISs into a fully integrated system.

REVIEW ▼ 5 ▼ QUESTIONS

1. Think of the last time something happened to you that you did not expect. What was the gap, or difference, between the "actual" and the "expected"? What sort of a problem did it cause?

2. If a furniture factory failed to produce as many finished chairs as were scheduled for the month, what possible causes would you look for?

3. What is the relationship between problem solving and decision making? If you must choose among three problems to try to solve, does that require a decision? Why?

4. If a fast-food restaurant kitchen ran out of hamburger patties several times a month, what are several things the supervisor might do to ensure that there are enough on hand in the future? What are the pros and cons of each alternative action?

5. If you were asked to decide which of five projects might be chosen for a public health-care program under your supervision, what technique might you use? Why?

6. What are some of the weaknesses of depending entirely on your hunches for a decision?

7. In a normal day you make dozens of decisions, some very important and others that are of little significance. List at least three vital decisions and at least ten trivial ones that you make daily.

8. What is the ultimate objective of a management information system (MIS)? Do most organizations reach this ideal? What is a supervisor more likely to encounter?

A CASE IN POINT

The "No Hardship" Problem

Donny Ghandel is the supervisor of a keypunch operation in a data processing section of a state agency. He has ten operators reporting to him. Yesterday, Donny and other supervisors received a directive from the agency's commissioner. The directive read: "Effective the 1st of next month, due to a reduction in federal funding, all departments will be expected to reduce their staff by 10 percent. This should provide no hardship since it is expected that the data processing work load will be reduced by the same percentage. Please make plans accordingly." Donny complied with the directive by sending the last operator who had been hired over to the state's human resources center for separation or transfer.

Prior to the reduction in staff, Donny's department had punched about 10,000 documents per month, or an average of 1000 per operator. True to the commissioner's expectations, Donny's department received only 9000 documents for processing during the month following the reduction in staff. Donny was dismayed, however, to discover that his operators were able to punch only 8100. When Donny confronted his staff with the problem, several explanations for the deficiency were offered: (1) there had been an increase in the number of items to be punched per document, (2) the format of data on the documents was more complex than it previously had been, (3) the employee who had been separated had been the most productive operator in the department, (4) the 1000 documents-per-operator rate had been obtained under unusual circumstances, (5) the operators were responding to pressures for greater accuracy in punching, and (6) absences due to illness had been higher than normal.

If you were Donny, how would you go about solving this problem? Five alternative courses of action are listed below. Rank them in the order in which they appeal to you (1 most effective, 5 least effective). You may add another approach in the space provided, if you wish. In any event, be prepared to justify your ranking.

_5_   **A.**   Dismiss the operators' explanations as excuses and insist that in the future they must match their previous rate of 1000 documents per month.

_2_   **B.**   See what can be done to simplify the format of incoming documents so as to allow faster keypunching.

_4_   **C.**   Set new production standards. Based on what appear to have been changed conditions, the operators will now be expected to punch only an average of 900 documents each per month.

_3_   **D.**   Place a request with the human resources center for an additional keypunch operator.

_1_   **E.**   Study all of the explanations offered to see if any, or all, represent the true cause or causes of the problem.

If you have another approach, write it here.

▶ _____

_____

_____

Complete the ACTION PLANNING CHECKLIST
for this chapter, which can be found on page 315.

Test your comprehension of the material in Chapters 1, 2, 3, 4, and 5. Correct answers are in the Appendix.

True-False

By writing T or F in the space provided, indicate whether each statement is true or false.

1. Under the Fair Labor Standards Act, supervisors are required to be paid under the same wage plan and given the same overtime benefits as the people they supervise.

    1. _F_____

2. Unlike middle-level managers and executives, supervisors do not become involved in the management process.

    2. _F_____

3. Supervisors perform the same functions as managers at other levels of the organization, but to differing degrees.

    3. _T_____

4. Research by Rensis Likert has shown that supervisors who place greatest emphasis on the technical demands of their jobs are sure to be more effective.

    4. _F_____

5. Although much is expected of supervisors, individuals who apply themselves to the job and to their self-development can become very effective.

    5. _T_____

6. Policies are generally guidelines for achieving important goals.

    6. _T_____

7. Supervisors should not consider their departments' current weaknesses when setting objectives; to do so leads to lowered performance.

    7. _F_____

8. The most common plans followed by supervisors in day-to-day operations are standing plans.

    8. _F_____

9. "Improve the department's attendance record" is a well-stated goal because it is precise and quantitative.

9. _F_

10. In enforcing policies, it is not a good idea to apologize or criticize the policy to employees, even if you disagree with the policy.

10. _T_

11. An organization chart shows the relationship of different positions, functions, and levels of an organization.

11. _T_

12. A supervisor who is asked by higher management to reduce costs must also be given the authority to do so if the supervisor is to reach that goal.

12. _T_

13. Delegation involves entrusting others with power as well as charging them with obligations.

13. _T_

14. Members of staff departments use expert advice and skill to help improve overall performance in the organization.

14. _T_

15. When a company has carefully prescribed its structured organizational relationships it is unlikely that significant informal organizational relationships will arise.

15. _F_

16. Control standards are ineffective if they include a tolerance, which is an allowable deviation from the absolute standard.

16. _F_

17. Management by exception is a time-saving technique for delegating control responsibilities according to the degree of deviation from the prescribed standard.

17. _T_

18. An inspection of incoming raw materials received for a manufacturing operation is a form of preventive control.

18. _T_

19. The corrective phase of the control process takes place when steps are taken to remove the cause of an observed deviation from a standard after it has occurred.

19. _T_

20. Management by Objectives (MBO) is a form of automatic control in that it removes the responsibility for control from the supervisor or manager involved.

20. _F_

21. One good way to identify a problem is to see if there is a difference between what was expected to happen and what actually did happen.

21. _T_

22. Because in major decisions so much relevant information is unknown, a systematic approach to problem solving has no advantage over an unsystematic approach.

22. _F_

23. Decision making takes place at the phase in the problem-solving process where a choice must be made as to which solution is most appropriate.

23. _T_

24. Cost-benefit analysis is similar to input-output analysis in that they both try to balance the effort expended to attain certain results with the value of those results.

24. _T_

25. A management information system (MIS) is intended mainly for high-level planning and is of little help to supervisors who must deal with down-to-earth problems and decisions.

25. _F_

Multiple Choice

For each item below, choose the response that best answers the question or completes the statement. Write the letter of the response in the space provided.

1. Which of these is the best example of a good supervisor?

   a. Julia is a great technician and spends much of her time doing actual production work.
   b. Mike aspires to be an executive-level manager, so he spends very little time on the shop floor.
   c. Jane concentrates on the welfare and productivity of her employees and on linking her department with the goals and policies of higher management.
   d. Tony stresses only the output his department is able to achieve.

1. _____

2. According to the AT&T study, the three highest-ranking competencies expected of supervisors are:

   a. time management, career counseling, and meetings and conferences.
   b. controlling work, problem solving and decision making, and planning work.
   c. planning, communications, and motivating.
   d. communications, training, and motivating.   2. _____

3. The management process consists of the functions of planning, organizing, and:

   a. staffing, directing, and controlling.
   b. budgeting, scheduling, and controlling.
   c. recruiting, placement, and training.
   d. staffing, directing, and motivating.   3. _____

4. Supervisors are judged by how well they manage the resources available to them and by the results they get from them in terms of:

   a. productivity and morale.
   b. productivity and cost control.
   c. employee satisfaction.
   d. output, quality, and costs.   4. _____

5. Mary, a supervisor of a word-processing department, wants to obtain the highest productivity possible from her employees. To do so, she should:

   a. concentrate on pushing for more productivity.
   b. focus her supervisory efforts on human relations; productivity will naturally follow.
   c. try to balance her productivity concerns with her concern for the human relations needs of her employees.
   d. concentrate on getting her employees to like her, because that is the best way to get results.   5. _____

6. Which of the following would normally be established first when planning?

   a. Goals and objectives.
   b. Procedures.
   c. Policies.
   d. Rules and regulations.   6. _____

7. In most organizations, general employment practices would follow a:

   a. single-use plan.
   b. short-term plan.
   c. standing plan.
   d. long-term plan.   7. _____

8. Which of the following is the best example of an effective statement of a goal?

   a. Employees will maintain and sharpen their cutting tools during regular work hours.
   b. Our company will exercise fair and reasonable controls to regulate the conduct of employees.
   c. The department will produce 8500 units by the end of next month.
   d. No materials may be set down inside the areas of the plant marked by yellow striping.   8. _____

9. To be effective, plans should be:

   a. unchanging; otherwise operations get out of control.
   b. freely changed whenever even slight obstacles arise.
   c. limited to periods of less than three months; it is not realistic to plan beyond that point.
   d. reviewed regularly to determine whether adjustments should be made to respond to changed conditions.   9. _____

10. Roberto has to suspend an employee who has been caught gambling on the job. Which of the following statements would be the best way for Roberto to approach this problem?

    a. "I think this is an unrealistic policy, but I have no choice in the matter."

    b. "You know the rules; anyone found gambling here draws an automatic suspension."

    c. "I'd like to look the other way, but if the boss found out it would be my job."

    d. "Guys like you set a bad example and you should be ashamed of yourself; suspension is too good for you."

                                                  10. _____

11. Making a list of all the tasks that must be performed by the organization to accomplish its objectives is the first step in:

    a. planning.

    b. organizing.

    c. division of labor.

    d. organizational development.   11. _____

12. Responsibility without _____ tends to make a supervisor powerless.

    a. chain of command.

    b. span of control.

    c. authority.

    d. accountability.   12. _____

13. _____ is defined by the number of activities for which a manager or supervisor can effectively assume responsibility or by the number of employees he or she can effectively supervise.

    a. Span of control.

    b. Delegation.

    c. Authority.

    d. Accountability.   13. A____

14. An organization's overriding value is its ability to make more effective use of its:

    a. authority.
    b. responsibility.
    c. human resources.
    d. span of control.   14. _____

15. The organizational structure that is particularly well suited to one-of-a-kind projects and for research and development is a:

    a. functional organization.
    b. matrix organization.
    c. line-and-staff format.
    d. centralized authority unit.   15. _____

16. When the standards for a department's results are set by engineers or planners outside the department,

    a. this relieves the department supervisor from control responsibilities.
    b. the outside planners assume the responsibility for seeing that standards are met.
    c. the department supervisor usually must take these overall standards and translate them into standards for each employee and operation.
    d. the department supervisor should view these standards as general guidelines only.   16. _____

17. Polly instructs her copy-machine operators to order a new supply of paper when there are still two boxes of paper on hand. Polly is using:

    a. preventive control.
    b. concurrent control.
    c. corrective control.
    d. automatic control.   17. _____

18. A cost variance report is a form of:

    a. budgetary control.
    b. corrective control.
    c. cost control.
    d. all of the above.   18. _____

19. Of the following, the key term associated with management by objectives (MBO) is:

   a. exceptions.
   b. variances.
   c. self-control.
   d. automatic control.   19. _____

20. Supervisors who establish explicit controls that are well understood by employees will:

   a. never have to give precise instructions to employees.
   b. have no further need for disciplinary action.
   c. eliminate the need for performance feedback to employees.
   d. minimize the need to interfere with the way employees do their jobs.   20. _____

21. Which of the following problem statements is the best?

   a. The boss says that the 3.0 percent reject figure reported in June is too high; we've got to get that percentage down by the end of July.
   b. Products rejected during testing increased from 1.5 percent in May to 3.0 percent in June.
   c. Producing products with a failure rate at testing of less than 3.0 percent is the highest goal of this department.
   d. Our employees are so careless that they are producing products now with a failure rate of 3.0 percent.   21. _____

22. The final phases of problem solving and decision making are most similar to:

   a. planning.
   b. organizing.
   c. staffing.
   d. directing.   22. _____

23. Problems are usually caused by planned and un-
    planned changes. Problems are solved, however, by:

    a. identifying their causes and proposing possible ways
       to remove these causes.
    b. evaluating possible solutions and choosing from
       among them.
    c. following a plan of action to carry out the chosen
       solution.
    d. all of the above.   23. _____

24. ABC analysis leads supervisors to devote maximum at-
    tention to:

    a. quality-related problems.
    b. quantity-related problems.
    c. the greatest number of problems that occur.
    d. the fewest, but largest, problems that occur.   24. _____

25. According to the text, many authorities believe that the
    best decisions are made by:

    a. intuition alone.
    b. logic alone.
    c. both intuition and logic.
    d. mathematical analysis.   25. _____

PART
TWO

Building an Effective Work Team

O nce goals and plans have been set and an organizational structure created, the most difficult—and rewarding—part of a supervisor's job begins. Success for supervisors depends largely on how well they staff their departments, the effectiveness of the training they provide their employees, the degree to which they motivate their work force, the clarity with which they communicate, and the intelligence of the leadership they exert.

▶ Chapter 6 outlines the many facets of employment interviewing and staff selection, with special emphasis on compliance with equal employment opportunity guidelines.

▶ Chapter 7 emphasizes the supervisor's role in applying a variety of useful techniques for breaking in new employees and training all employees to be more skillful in their work.

▶ Chapter 8 explains why individuals and groups act the way they do and suggests a number of approaches that supervisors can use to provide positive direction, or motivation, for their work force.

▶ Chapter 9 describes the communication process and shows how to use it effectively in spoken, written, and nonverbal form to issue orders and instructions.

▶ Chapter 10 presents a variety of leadership approaches and offers concrete suggestions for their use.

CHAPTER

6

EMPLOYMENT STAFFING AND INTERVIEWING

LEARNING OBJECTIVES

After studying this chapter, you should be able to:

1. Identify the five steps of the staffing process and explain the extent of a supervisor's participation in each.

2. Distinguish among a job analysis, a job description, and a job specification, and explain the factors that affect work-force size, forecasting, and balancing.

3. Be aware of the main features of an employment interview and identify those questions that are most suitable and those that are prohibited by equal employment opportunity legislation.

4. Point out the critical aspects of the selection process and explain the roles of tests, physical examinations, and reference checks.

5. Explain how careful selection can reduce employee turnover and absences and calculate specified turnover and absenteeism rates.

OVERVIEW OF KEY CONCEPTS
IN THIS CHAPTER

▶ Effective staffing is accomplished by a five-step process that places the right numbers—and kinds—of people on the right jobs at the right time.

▶ Worker output, work schedules, vacations and holidays, and anticipated absences determine the size of the work force, which should be neither too large nor too small.

▶ Employment interviewing should focus on job-related education, experience, and skills; all questions must be free of any implication of bias.

▶ Employee selection should be based on finding the persons whose qualifications best match the requirements of the jobs to be filled.

▶ The selection process also seeks to minimize the employment of people whose unsuitability would result in excessive absences and/or high turnover rates.

WHAT DOES IT TAKE TO PUT A
DEPARTMENT'S WORK FORCE TOGETHER?

The staffing of an organization usually follows a five-step procedure:

1. *Specifying the kinds of jobs needed to "flesh out" the boxes of an organization's structure.* Supervisors are greatly involved in this step.

2. *Estimating the total number of employees needed to complete a given work schedule.* This, too, is a vital responsibility of supervisors.

3. *Recruiting applicants to be screened for unfilled job openings.* Candidates can come from either inside or outside the organization. Recruiting, including the initial review of completed application forms and preliminary screening of candidates, is largely the responsibility of the personnel or human resources department.

4. *Interviewing job candidates.* Supervisors participate actively in the interviewing process.

5. *Selecting the most appropriate individuals from among the candidates.* Supervisors play a prime role in selection decisions.

HOW ARE JOBS CREATED AND SPECIFIED?

Most organizations practice what has been described as a "division of labor." That is, the tasks to be performed in a particular department are broken up into several different kinds, or classes, of work. The simplest jobs are called "unskilled"; the most complex are called "skilled." In between, there are "semiskilled" jobs. Many organizations go much further. They identify dozens of different jobs, and classes of jobs, ranging from unskilled to highly skilled.

In order to describe and specify each of the resulting jobs, the human resources department—working with the department supervisor—conducts a job analysis and prepares a job description and job specification. A brief explanation of each follows.

Job analysis is the process of collecting and studying information about the operations and responsibilities of a particular job. This information typically includes: a list of all duties performed; identification of the most important aspects of the job; equipment and materials used on the job; products or services produced; people with whom the employee has significant contact; and required technical knowledge.

A *job description* translates the information gathered during the job analysis into "an organized, factual statement of the duties and responsibilities of the job." A good job description, like the one in Table 6-1, tells *what* is to be done on the job, *how* it is to be done, and *why* it is to be done.

A *job specification* differs from a job description in that the emphasis is put on specifying the kinds of knowledge, skills, and experience that *a person* needs in order to carry out that job satisfactorily. The job specification is especially useful in recruiting, screening, and selecting applicants to fill open jobs. Typically, the job specification spells out exactly what the requirements are, such as, for example: experience (three years); education (high school graduate or equivalent); skills (typing—accurate, 40 wpm); knowledge (of Lotus 1-2-3 program); physical requirements (occasionally lift 75 pounds, vision corrected to 20/20); and special requirements (driver's license).

TABLE 6-1 Example of a job description

▼ **Position:** Shipping Clerk
Department: Shipping and Receiving
Location: "C" Building Warehouse

Job Summary

Under general supervision of warehouse manager, processes shipments to customers in accordance with shipment authorization forms forwarded by the sales department. Together with other clerks and packers, removes goods from shelves by hand or by powered equipment and packs in containers for shipment by truck, rail, air, or parcel service. Prepares and processes appropriate paperwork and maintains related files.

Duties Performed

1. The following duties represent 70 percent of working time:
   a. Removes stock from shelves and racks and packs into proper shipping containers.
   b. Weighs and labels cartons for shipment by carrier designated on the shipping order.
   c. Assists in loading carriers.
2. The following duties represent 15 percent of working time:
   a. Prepares and/or processes authorization forms including packing lists, shipping orders, and bills of lading.
   b. Maintains shipment records by tally sheets or keypunch.
   c. Does miscellaneous typing of forms and labels.
   d. Maintains appropriate files.
3. The following duties represent the balance of working time:
   a. Drives company truck to post office or for an occasional local delivery.
   b. Assists in taking inventory.
   c. Acts as checker for other shipping or receiving clerks.
   d. Keeps workplace clean and orderly.

(continued)

TABLE 6-1 *(continued)*

Supervision Received

Except for general instructions and special problems, works independently.

Relationships

Works in close contact with packers, material handlers, and other clerks. Has contact with truck drivers when loading. Has occasional contact with order department personnel.

Equipment

Operates mechanized stockpicker, powered conveyor belts, carton sealing machinery, keypunch terminals, and typewriter.

Working Conditions

Clean, well-lighted, heated. Requires normal standing, walking, climbing, lifting. Subject to drafts when shipping doors are open.

HOW DO YOU ARRIVE AT AN ESTIMATE OF WORK-FORCE SIZE?

The number of employees a supervisor needs to run a department depends on two factors: (1) the scheduled output of the department, and (2) the productivity expected from each employee. Two simple formulas combine these factors to provide you with a rough estimate of work-force size.

Staffing Formula No. 1

$$\text{Total number of worker-hours required during the period} = \frac{\text{Scheduled number of units of output for the period}}{\text{Productivity rate (units of output per worker-hour)}}$$

Using symbols, the formula becomes:

$$\text{Total worker-hours (TWH)} = \frac{\text{Scheduled units of output (SUO)}}{\text{Units per worker-hour (U/WH)}}$$

For example, a word processing supervisor is given a schedule calling for an output of 64,000 label entries (or units) for next month. Her records show that an employee on this kind of work averages an output of 40 labels per hour. Substitute these figures in the formula:

$$\text{TWH} = \frac{\text{SUO}}{\text{U/WH}} = \frac{64{,}000 \text{ units}}{40 \text{ units/worker-hour}} = 1600 \text{ worker-hours required}$$

To convert the total number of worker-hours required to the number of employees needed, the second formula is used.

Staffing Formula No. 2

$$\frac{\text{Number of employees needed}}{\text{during the period}} = \frac{\text{Total number of worker-hours required}}{\substack{\text{Number of hours scheduled per} \\ \text{employee during the period}}}$$

Expressed symbolically, this becomes:

$$E = \frac{\text{TWH}}{\text{EH}}$$

In the example above, if the month is to consist of 20 workdays of eight hours each, then the number of hours each employee is scheduled to work for the month is 160. Substituting this information (EH = 160) and the result for Formula No. 1 (TWH = 1600) into Formula No. 2 provides the answer:

$$E = \frac{1600 \text{ worker-hours required}}{160 \text{ hours per employee}} = 10 \text{ employees}$$

IS THAT ALL THERE IS TO IT?

Not quite. Long-term estimates must also consider the effects of absences, holidays and vacations, and turnover. If, for example, a department has ten employees, each of whom is entitled to ten vacation days and eight paid holidays a year, then over a year's time, the supervisor must allow for 1440 nonproductive hours per year (10 employees × 18 days × 8 hours per day = 1440 hours).

Absences have a similar effect. If the department's annual absence rate averages 5 percent, the supervisor must allow for another 1000 nonproductive hours (0.05 × 2000 possible worker-hours per year per employee × 10 employees).

Employee turnover (quits and hires) also cuts down on expected output. Newly hired employees are rarely as quick as the incumbents they replace.

Even without considering turnover, you can see that in a ten-employee work force, absences, holidays, and vacations can account for upwards of 2000 hours annually, or the equivalent of at least another employee.

SHOULD YOU OVERSTAFF OR UNDERSTAFF?

That depends. If you plan for too many employees, department costs will go up unless your schedule and equipment availability will permit you to assign them to productive jobs. It's bad, too, to have idle people in the shop or to use them on make-work jobs. Overstaffing, however, does allow you to handle production emergencies and to cover peak loads.

Understaffing can be just as bad. It can get you behind on schedules and in trouble on deliveries. It can also give employees the feeling of being overworked. And it doesn't give you much flexibility.

Your company can minimize both overstaffing and understaffing by pooling the work-force estimates of each supervisor and maintaining an optimum-size labor pool as a cushion against unpredictables—such as unusual absences or sharp upward adjustments in schedules.

WHAT IS MEANT BY BALANCING THE WORK FORCE?

Making sure that the number of employees on hand just matches the work load. Most departments have peaks and valleys that last an hour or a day. This is to be expected and is ordinarily accepted. Mismatches between work force and work load that extend as long as a week, however, are costly and should be avoided.

WHAT IS THE TABLE OF ORGANIZATION?

The expression *table of organization* (TO) is derived from military staffing practices. It implies that, for each department or unit, (1) staffing is limited to certain specified positions and (2) a specified number of people are prescribed for each position. When a department is "not up to its TO," either vacancies exist as positions with no incumbents or the number of incumbents in one or more position classes is less than that prescribed—

or some combination of the two exists. The TO principle can be applied to business beneficially if the specific TO capacity (or productivity) is carefully related to the organization's responsibilities and goals.

HOW SHOULD YOU BEGIN AN INTERVIEW WITH A JOB CANDIDATE?

Preview the job for the applicant. This is a great time-saver to tell the applicant what the fixed requirements of the job are. Mention such things as job title, relationships to other jobs, and the main activities involved in the job, such as walking, standing, sitting, or performing heavy work. Tell the applicant what kind of materials and machines are used and describe the working conditions.

It's especially wise to forewarn an applicant about any undesirable conditions, such as fumes, dampness, and night work. Don't scare the applicant, but be sure the facts are known ahead of time. Better that the applicant turn down the job than walk off it after three days.

You can also describe the good aspects of the job—opportunities for advancement, the company's benefit programs, and so forth. This is the time to do some sound, factual selling, but don't make promises about raises or promotions. These can come back to haunt you later on.

WHAT KINDS OF QUESTIONS SHOULD YOU ASK THE APPLICANT?

Don't turn the interview into a "third degree" by asking too many point-blank questions—especially those that can be answered with a simple yes or no. The job seeker is likely to be on guard during the interview, anyway. For example, the answer will ordinarily be "yes" to a question such as "Did you get along well with your boss in the last place you worked?"

Ask "open-ended" questions that begin with *what, where, why, when,* or *who.* This gives the applicant a chance to talk and, while talking, to show you the kind of person she or he really is. If the applicant does most of the talking and you do most of the listening, you'll have lots of time to form an opinion. And that's the purpose of an interview.

Ask open-ended questions such as:

▶   What about your education? How do you feel that it would help you do the kind of work we do here?

▶   Where did you get your most valuable experience? Suppose you tell me about your working experience, starting with your first job.

▶   Whom did you report to in your last job? Can you describe that supervisor?

▶   When did you first decide you liked to do this sort of work? What have you found most difficult about it? Most pleasant?

▶   How would you describe your health? What kind of attendance record have you maintained during the last year?

WHAT KINDS OF QUESTIONS ARE YOU FORBIDDEN TO ASK A JOB APPLICANT?

Be careful. Listen to whatever your human resources department advises. Otherwise, you as well as your company may get into trouble over some unintended equal employment opportunity infringement. The following is just a partial list of prohibitions:

▶   *Race or color.* Don't ask. Don't comment.

▶   *Religion.* Don't ask. Don't say, "This is a (Catholic, Protestant, Jewish, or other) organization."

▶   *Citizenship.* You may ask, "Are you a citizen of the United States?" If the answer is "No," don't comment or ask further questions related to this issue.

▶   *National origin.* Don't ask. Don't comment.

▶   *Sex.* Don't ask. Don't comment. Don't indicate prejudgment about physical capabilities.

▶   *Age.* Don't ask, "How old are you?" Don't ask for a birth date. You *may* ask if the applicant is over the age of 18.

▶   *Marital status.* Don't ask for this, or for ages of children, or where a spouse works.

▶   *Disability.* You may ask if the person has a present disability that will interfere with the job to be performed, but you may *not* ask about past disabilities or illnesses.

▶   *Address.* You may ask for the applicant's address and how long he or she has lived there. You may ask if the applicant is an American citizen and, if not, whether the person has the legal right to remain permanently in the United States. It is generally unlawful to press for answers beyond this point.

▶   *Criminal record.* You may ask if the person has ever been convicted of a crime and, if so, when and where it took place. You may *not* ask if a person has ever been arrested, nor can you deny employment on this basis unless it can be proved that it would damage the employer's business.

▶ *Physical capabilities.* Don't ask how tall or how strong an applicant is. This may indicate a sexist prejudice. You may explain physical aspects of the job, such as lifting, pulling, and so forth, and show how it must be performed. And you may require a physical examination. The hope is that if the applicant has a clear chance to estimate the job's physical requirements, the application will be withdrawn if the job appears too demanding or beyond the person's capabilities. Legally, however, you may not make that decision during an interview.

Questions about *education* and *experience* are pretty much unrestricted. The main point to be sure about in any interviewing area is that the question's relevance to the job for which the individual is applying can undeniably be shown. This legal requirement is called a bona fide occupational qualification (BFOQ).

WHAT DO YOU LOOK FOR WHILE INTERVIEWING AN APPLICANT?

Besides the factual things you obviously need to know about an applicant's skills and know-how, you'll want to be alert to what the interview tells you about the applicant's background and personal characteristics.

Suitable Background. Do the applicant's education and experience, and even residence and off-the-job associates, indicate that the person will be happy working with the people in your company? If education isn't a strong point and hobbies are bowling and baseball, the applicant won't find many friends among employees who take their education seriously and spend their spare time discussing opera and stamp collecting.

Desirable Characteristics. Are the applicant's achievements outstanding? Did the person work five years at the XYZ Company without missing a day?

How about personal interests? If the jobs liked best in the past have been outdoor ones, such as truck driving, why is the applicant now looking for a confining job in an office?

Try to spot attitude. Does the person act mature or sound as if given to childish boasting? Does the person listen to what you say? An example of an attitude you'll want to steer clear of is one where an individual goes out of the way to criticize the last company worked for, the people worked with, or the quality of the product. You'll probably be making no mistake in concluding that this individual is the kind of person who'd find everything wrong at your company, too.

You can tell a lot about physical condition, too, from the interview. The person applying for a job who appears slow-moving and lethargic may put no energy into the job either. Remember, most people looking for work are trying to put their best foot forward. If an interviewee can't show you a very good side during the interview, there's a chance that you won't see anything better on the job.

WHAT SHOULD YOU AVOID IN CONDUCTING A JOB INTERVIEW?

James Menzies Black, an old friend who used to be a director of personnel for a major railroad, cautioned:

1. ***Don't be overly formal.*** The more you do to help the applicant relax, the more effective the interview will be.

2. ***Don't take notes.*** A busy pencil writes off a productive interview. Train your memory so that you can make your notes after the interview has been completed.

3. ***Don't high-pressure applicants.*** If you paint a glowing picture to job seekers that quickly fades after they are on the payroll, you will have disappointed employees on your hands. Worst of all, you will have employees who don't trust your word.

4. ***Don't hire a chief when you really need a worker.*** If an applicant is too intelligent or experienced to be happy in the job and there is little opportunity for quick promotion, say so. You want employee and job to match. That's why you conduct an interview.

5. ***Don't tell applicants you are rejecting them for personality reasons.*** If you think the experience or the knowledge to hold a job is lacking, be frank and say so. If you are reluctant to hire for intangible reasons such as a poor personality, uncertainty about reliability, or a dislike of general attitude, keep your reasons to yourself. Frankness may offend applicants and will certainly discourage them for no good reason.

6 ***Don't make moral judgments or give advice.*** The applicant's personal life is no concern of yours.

7. ***Don't ask trick questions that may embarrass.*** If you see that there is conflict in the applicant's statements, you should certainly explore the matter, but do so discreetly. Your job is not to "catch" the prospect. It is to find out what you can about the individual.

8. *Don't let your facial expression, tone of voice, or gestures reveal your feelings.* You give applicants confidence by showing interest and sympathy. If they think you disapprove of what they are telling you, they will become silent or try to shift ideas around so that they will please you.

9. *Don't be impatient.* Try not to let the applicant know you're in a hurry, even if you are. A look at a watch has killed many an interview.

10. *Don't be misled by your prejudices.* Keep an open mind. Good inter-viewers never allow their biases to cloud their judgment.

WHAT CAN A SUPERVISOR DO TO IMPROVE THE SELECTION PROCESS?

Whenever a supervisor is given a chance to interview a prospective job candidate, that's a golden opportunity to help make sure the department gets a first-rate employee. Interviewing points that apply most directly to selecting employees are reviewed here.

Know What Kind of Employee You Want. Don't describe the person vaguely as a good worker who will stay on the job. That doesn't tell you much about the qualities you are looking for to suit the job that is open. Try making a checklist of necessary or desirable qualifications, such as:

▶ *Experience.* The applicant should have worked a couple of years with computer graphics or spreadsheets, for example, even though the computer system used by the applicant wasn't exactly like yours.

▶ *Blueprint reading.* The person has to be able to work directly from blueprints.

▶ *Speed.* This job doesn't require a quick worker as much as it requires a steady, consistent worker.

▶ *Initiative.* Does the applicant's previous experience show work with-out close supervision?

▶ *Attendance.* Has the applicant a good record of attendance (because this job needs someone who's going to be here every day)?

See Enough Candidates. Your human resources department will probably screen out the obvious misfits before an applicant is sent to you for ap-proval. But if you do the hiring directly, make a point of interviewing at least three candidates before making up your mind. That way you get a chance to make comparisons and to get the feel of the prevailing labor market. For some hard-to-fill jobs requiring special skills, you may have to see as many as 20 or 30 persons.

WILL TESTS HELP YOU SELECT BETTER EMPLOYEES?

Over 50,000 firms think so. Properly selected, administered, and evaluated, so-called performance tests can be a big help in picking better workers. Tests may be simple and direct, such as those that show whether an applicant can read and write or perform the simple arithmetic that recordkeeping on the job may demand. Other, highly specific tests may enable an applicant to demonstrate the ability to perform the special skills your job demands. For instance, any person looking for a job can claim competence in operating a multiple-spindle automatic or a calculator. A ten-minute tryout will prove whether the claim is valid. These "can do?" tests, called *performance* (or *skill*) *tests,* are widely used.

WHICH TESTS ARE MOST SENSITIVE TO RESTRICTIONS OF THE EQUAL EMPLOYMENT OPPORTUNITY LAWS?

Psychological tests that attempt to find out whether a person has the ability to learn a particular kind of job (aptitude tests) can also be fairly reliable, but under present U.S. laws these are often open to challenge by the applicant. For this reason your company may or may not choose to use them.

Personality, intelligence, and job or career *interest* tests are widely used for applicants seeking higher-level management positions. But these, too, must be fully validated and their reliability proved before they can pass the civil rights hurdle. *Validity* simply means that the test really measures what it is supposed to measure. *Reliability* means that if an applicant were to take a test several times, the score would always be the same. See also *content validity* and *construct validity* on page 286 in Chapter 15.

Underlying the challenges of validity and reliability is the requirement that any test given to applicants (1) should be directly related to the job's content and (2) should not discriminate unfairly against the person taking it. In other words, it would not be right to require that an applicant for a typist's job pass a test designed for an administrative secretary. Nor should the test be worded in such a way that it favors a person with a particular background over another who does not have it—unless it can be shown that the job requires that background.

WHOM SHOULD YOU HIRE?

Deciding which applicant to hire isn't easy. But you can make a better decision if you separate facts from hunches—not that you should ignore your intuition or inferences. It's a good idea to take five minutes after you've interviewed an applicant to jot down what you think are the significant facts, and list your hunches, too.

Facts may show that the job seeker has had ten years of experience on a milling machine, has good health, and can read blueprints. But your conversation may have brought out the feeling that the individual is stubborn and boastful and might be hard to supervise. Only you can tell to which items you'll give the most weight. Some supervisors don't mind having a prima donna on their staff as long as that individual can produce. Others fear that a prima donna is likely to upset teamwork. And, of course, your hunches can be wrong.

You can be sure, however, that your choice will be better than flipping a coin if you've gone about your interview in a systematic way and if you've kept personal prejudices pertaining to race, religion, age, sex, or nationality out of your figuring.

HOW DO YOU PICK THE BEST FROM A LIST OF QUALIFIED APPLICANTS?

First, be sure that you have dropped no one from the list of possibilities because of discrimination or prejudice; in other words, be sure that all things are equal according to the law. Then, pick the applicant who fits your sense of what kind of person will do the job best. This is where your experience and intuition can help. For example, Bobby Knight, the highly successful Indiana University basketball coach, lists three things he looks for when recruiting basketball players:

> (1) *Strength.* Wiry strength to hold onto the ball, to maintain a position on the boards or a defensive stance. (2) *Quickness.* The slow, plodding team will have trouble over the long season. (3) *Concentration.* There isn't a right way to play the game, but there are a lot of poor ways. You have to play in a way that utilizes the abilities of your team. Concentrate, and you will be successful.

Your department won't be playing basketball. But you can look for such things as (1) *perseverance,* as demonstrated by a work record that shows the applicant can stay with a difficult situation; (2) *alertness,* as indicated by the applicant's ability to follow your description of the work to be done—because many jobs require a person who can sense when a deviation from rigid procedures is desirable; and (3) *cooperation,* as illustrated by the applicant's willingness to go through the red tape and employment interviewing and processing without quibbling about it. Other jobs, of course, may need another set of personal qualities. Initiative in a salesclerk, for example, may be more important than cooperation. Single-mindedness may be more valuable than alertness in a chemical processing plant that requires rigid conformance to prescribed sequence.

WHAT GOOD ARE PHYSICAL EXAMINATIONS?

As a supervisor, you'll want to know whether a person assigned to your department has any physical limitations. There's no way of actually finding out about poor eyesight, a hernia, or a heart condition, for instance, without a complete physical examination. A physical defect doesn't necessarily rule out an applicant, but knowledge of it does ensure that person's being put on a job where the best work can be done and where the disability is not aggravated.

SHOULD YOU CHECK EMPLOYEE REFERENCES?

Absolutely yes! It's foolhardy to hire anyone without checking with the last employer to find out the actual job the applicant held and to verify dates of employment. Most former employers will not tell you much more for fear of illegally prejudicing the applicant's chances. For this reason, it's wise also to tell the job candidate that you will be checking his or her education and employment statements. One good way to obtain the applicant's own views about his or her employment record is to ask, "What do you think your last employer would say about your performance, work habits, and attendance?"

Personal references, on the other hand, are usually not of much value. Few people will supply you with names of others who will say something bad about them.

WHAT'S THE CONNECTION BETWEEN THE STAFFING PROCESS AND HIGH TURNOVER AND ABSENTEEISM AMONG EMPLOYEES?

A high incidence of turnover and absenteeism among employees is a major indicator of an ineffective staffing and selection process. Other signs of ineffective staffing include excessive tardiness, poor quality of work, low productivity, and missed deadlines. Experts also identify low creativity and poor teamwork as other symptoms.

It costs upwards of $5000 to add an unskilled person to the payroll and as much as $15,000 to add an engineer or a computer programmer. A conservative estimate of the cost of keeping a semiskilled factory or office worker on the payroll for a year is $20,000. Figure it this way: Wages for a good employee run more than $12,000 a year. It costs an average of $2000 a year to train a new employee or keep an experienced employee up to production standards. Add another $3500 in fringe benefits that don't show up in salary. And cap this off with another $2500—the cost of depreciation on the capital investment that makes the job possible. Consequently, each employee who works for you must return about $20,000 or more in productive efforts before his or her employment can break even.

When the cost of hiring employees to replace those who quit or are discharged (turnover) is added to the losses of their costly services through absenteeism, you can readily see why it is so important to hire people most suitable for the work in the first place.

HOW DO YOU MEASURE EMPLOYEE TURNOVER?

Turnover is the name given to the measure of how many people come to work for you and don't stay for one reason or another. Turnover includes employees who are hired or rehired and employees who are laid off, who quit, or who are discharged. It also includes those who retire or die.

For consistency's sake, the U.S. Department of Labor suggests that the rate of turnover compare only the total number of separations (quits, fires, deaths, and so on) with the average number of employees on your payroll during a particular period. The *rate of turnover* is calculated as follows:

$$\frac{\text{Number of separations} \times 100}{\text{Average size of work force}} = \text{Turnover percentage}$$

For instance, if you had an average of 50 employees during the month, but you laid off three, the turnover would be 3. Your turnover rate would be $(3 \times 100)/50 = 6$ percent a month. If that rate persisted, your turnover rate for the year would be 72 percent (6×12).

Turnover rates vary from department to department, from company to company, and from industry to industry. The national average for all businesses in the United States is about 7 percent a month, or 84 percent a year!

Decisions as to what kind of separations and hires to include in turnover computations vary from organization to organization. Obviously, if certain kinds of separations or hires are excluded, the turnover rates will be lower. So it's good to know exactly what the specifications are when comparing turnover rates.

WHAT'S SO BAD ABOUT ABSENTEEISM?

Absences (like turnover) are costly—to the organization as well as to the employee. If it costs about $20,000 a year to keep a person on the payroll, then each day that person is absent can cost your department something like $80 (based on 240 working days a year) in lost effort. Don't be misled, either, by the hourly worker who says, "I don't get paid when I'm not here, so what do you lose?" Absences frequently create a need for hiring temporary employees or for overtime caused by delays in getting an operation started or a machine running. And every supervisor can testify to the aggravation absence and lateness cause. Absenteeism is the biggest obstacle you have in your work-force planning—from day to day or from month to month.

There are two popular ways to compute absenteeism rates:

1. Absenteeism rate $= \dfrac{\text{Total days absent}}{\text{Average size of work force}}$

    $=$ Average days absent per employee

2. Absenteeism rate $= \dfrac{\text{Total days absent} \times 100}{\text{Worker-days worked plus worker-days lost}}$

    $=$ Percentage of scheduled worker-days lost

For example, suppose that at the end of six months a supervisor found that the schedule showed a crew of 25 employees working for 120 days. Examining the record, the supervisor found that ten employees had worked every day for 1200 (10 $\times$ 120) worker-days; ten employees worked 116 days for 1160 (10 $\times$ 116) worker-days; three employees had worked only 110 days for 330 (3 $\times$ 110) worker-days; and two employees had worked only 100 days for 200 (2 $\times$ 100) worker-days. The total of worker-days worked is 2890. If all 25 employees had worked every day for 120 days, the total worker-days would have amounted to 3000. Therefore, 110 worker-days were lost (3000 $-$ 2890). The department's absenteeism rate would be:

$\dfrac{110 \text{ days absent}}{25 \text{ employees}} = 4.4$ days lost per employee in 6 months, or 8.8 days a year

The percentage of scheduled worker-days lost each year would be calculated as follows:

$\dfrac{110 \text{ days absent} \times 100}{2890 + 110} = \dfrac{110 \times 100}{3000}$

$= 3.7$ percent of scheduled worker-days lost

National averages for days lost per employee range from nine days a year to as high as three days a month (36 days a year). Absence and lateness, like turnover, can be controlled by good supervision. But it's better to avoid this demand on your supervisory time and skill if you can. And you can, by screening out applicants who have displayed these undesirable characteristics in the past or are likely to develop them on the job in your company—simply because they are unsuited for the work they were hired to do.

HOW CAN BETTER HIRING REDUCE TURNOVER AND ABSENTEEISM?

 Selecting the proper person to fit first the company and then the available job opening attacks the turnover and absenteeism problem at its source. There are hundreds of thousands of people looking for work who would be misfits almost anywhere. But there are millions who would probably be out of place in your company. Sue doesn't like close work. Pete can't stand heavy work. Joe wants a job with lots of room for initiative. Alma wants a job where she doesn't have to think. And so on. Turnover and absences show up when people such as Sue, Pete, Joe, and Alma find work that doesn't suit them.

To complicate the matter further, Joe may want a job that allows for initiative, but maybe he doesn't have the native ability to produce without close supervision. Alma wants a job where she doesn't have to think, but maybe all those jobs call for someone who can work rapidly, and Alma is slow as can be.

A third complication, and perhaps the most serious, is that the ability to handle the human side of the job varies widely among different people. And, of course, the human relations requirements of jobs vary, too. If you put an employee who likes to be one of the gang back in the corner working alone, that employee won't be happy no matter how much he or she likes the work or how skillfully he or she can perform it. Similarly, a person who has never been able to get along well with superiors won't be much of a help on a job that demands a lot of close supervision.

Keep in mind that employees, too, are continually assessing the suitability of their employment after being hired. They ask themselves: "Is this the right job for me? Is this an organization I want to continue working for?" An effective staffing procedure is more likely to find these employees answering "yes" to such questions.

REVIEW ▼ 6 QUESTIONS

1. In which aspect of the staffing process are supervisors *not* likely to play a major part? Which organizational unit usually handles this aspect?

2. What factors affect the determination of the size of a department's work force?

3. Gerry expects that his sales order department will have to handle peak loads during the spring and fall seasons. Should he plan to staff a year-round work force large enough to handle these peak loads when they occur? Why, or why not?

4. What is meant by an "open-ended" question, as used during an employment interview? Provide some examples.

5. What kinds of information can generally be obtained from a job candidate without infringing upon rights guaranteed by equal employment opportunity legislation?

6. Would it be wise to hire a college graduate for a job that requires only a high school education, as long as the applicant was willing to take the job at the prevailing wage rate? Why, or why not?

7. Explain the difference between an aptitude test and a performance test.

8. What are the main differences between the two ways of computing absenteeism rates?

A CASE IN POINT

Who Stuck Me with This Lemon?

Matt was more than Helen had bargained for. Matt was a night clerk at the convenience store at which Helen was the manager. Matt had made a good impression on Helen when she spoke with him during the employment interview. In fact, the impression had been so good that Helen had hired Matt on the spot and had seen no more job applicants. The good impression, however, was fading fast. Matt's seemingly pleasant manner and cooperative attitude during the employment interview was not borne out in practice. He could be surly with customers and downright defiant about accepting instructions from Helen. Matt was also careless in ringing up sales, and his inventory tallies were unreliable. This was at odds with Matt's claim during the employment interview that he had good arithmetic skills. To top it off, Matt could pick the most difficult times to be absent. Although his excuses always seemed reasonable, the number of Matt's absences kept mounting.

The situation came to a head when Matt called in sick at the last minute on a Friday afternoon before the Fourth of July. This left the store short-handed during one of the busiest weekends of the year. As Helen placed the receiver down, she rolled her eyes to the ceiling and—with expletive deleted—exclaimed, "Who ever stuck me with this lemon!"

What could Helen have done to avoid this dilemma? Five alternative courses of action are listed below. Rank them in the order in which they appeal to you (1 most effective, 5 least effective). You may add another approach in the space provided, if you wish. In any event, be prepared to justify your ranking.

_____ **A.** Checked with Matt's previous employers to find out about his performance.

_____ **B.** Asked Matt to make some simple computations to demonstrate his ability with figures.

_____ **C.** Requested that he take a lie-detector test.

_____ **D.** Extended the employment interview by asking open-ended questions so as to get a better picture of Matt's personality.

_____ **E.** Interviewed more job candidates.

If you have another approach, write it here.

▶ _____

_____

_____

Complete the ACTION PLANNING CHECKLIST
for this chapter, which can be found on page 316.

ORIENTING, TRAINING, AND DEVELOPING EMPLOYEES

LEARNING OBJECTIVES

After studying this chapter, you should be able to:

1. Explain the concept of the teachable moment and how this is implemented during orientation training.

2. Apply the four-step training method, make a job breakdown, and identify key points.

3. Understand the training roles of supervisors and those of human resources development specialists.

4. Explain the importance of the training sequence, employee motivation to learn, and the transfer of training.

5. Choose from among a variety of training techniques.

▶ In the absence of a sound training effort, employees learn haphazardly and often inaccurately. Only by careful planning, systematic instruction, and responsible follow-up can a supervisor be certain that employees will learn how to perform their work accurately and in the most effective manner.

▶ Learning rarely can begin until trainees are properly prepared to learn. They must first be made aware of the value of the information they are expected to absorb—made aware in a way that arouses their interest and motivates them to provide their own initiative in making the training process productive.

▶ The process of instruction should use many techniques and appeal to many senses. Demonstration of a skill should (1) feature exercise and repetition, (2) include showing as well as telling how a job is correctly performed, and (3) make an impact on the eyes, the ears, and the senses of smell, touch, and motion.

▶ Trainees can absorb only a little information at a time. This information ideally should be arranged in a sequence that advances the learning from the familiar to the unfamiliar, from the easy to the difficult, from the simple to the complex.

▶ Learning is accelerated to the degree that training provides the learner with insights—intellectual, sensory, and procedural—into the essentials that are required for the successful performance of a task.

WHEN CAN YOU TELL THAT
TRAINING IS NEEDED?

Training needs are often the underlying causes of other problems. Be on the alert whenever you observe any of these conditions: too much rework, subpar production rates, operating costs that are out of line, high accident rates, excessive overtime, and even a general state of poor morale. Any of these symptoms may respond better to a training program than to a crackdown on discipline, for example.

WHAT ARE THE SPECIAL REWARDS
FOR A SUPERVISOR WHO DOES A
GOOD JOB OF TRAINING WORKERS?

In addition to making a better showing for your department in terms of better quality and quantity of output, training puts you in a favorable light in other ways. Effective employee instruction:

Improves your handling of intradepartmental transfers.

Allows you more time for planning and scheduling your work.

Provides a reserve of trained personnel in your department for emergencies.

Wins the confidence and cooperation of your workers.

Perhaps most important of all for a supervisor who wants to get ahead, training your employees makes you "available" for your own advancement.

WHEN DOES A GOOD SUPERVISOR BEGIN
TRAINING AN EMPLOYEE?

When a new employee is hired. There are two reasons for this. First, new workers who get off on the right foot by knowing what to do and how to do it are like a baseball team that builds a ten-run lead in the first inning. With a head start like that, there's a good chance of eventual success. The second reason revolves around the idea of the *teachable moment.* This is the time when new employees are most receptive to instruction, because they want to learn and succeed. Good supervisors respond to this need and begin training almost immediately.

Training recently hired workers, which is called *induction training* or *orientation training,* is a little like introducing friends at a club meeting where they are strangers. You want to introduce them to others and try to make them feel at home. You show them where to hang their hats and coats and where the rest rooms are. If you want to have them think well of your club, you might tell them something about its history and the good people who belong to it. If you have to leave them for a time to attend to some duty, you come back occasionally to see how they are getting along. It's the same way with new employees who report to you. You want them to think well of you and to feel at home in your department from the beginning, so treat them accordingly.

WHAT SHOULD BE INCLUDED IN ORIENTATION TRAINING FOR NEW EMPLOYEES?

Orientation sessions should cover the major topics of probable interest to employees, as well as the items that you feel are important to their success. These include:

▶   Pay rates, pay periods, when pay is first received, deductions from pay, and how pay increases may be earned.

▶   Hours of work, such as reporting and quitting times, lunch periods, breaks, and cleanup time.

▶   Availability of overtime and overtime pay, and premium pay for working on second or third shifts.

▶   Time-reporting systems, including location of time cards and how to punch in and out.

▶   Employee options under the company's benefit plans, such as group life, health, and dental insurance.

▶   Procedure to follow when sick.

▶   Procedure to follow when late.

▶   Basic safety rules, the procedure for reporting accidents, and the joint employee-company responsibility for identifying hazards under the Occupational Safety and Health Administration (OSHA) law.

Induction activities should also include:

▶   Tour of the department and other areas of the company.

▶   Introduction to coworkers.

▶   Assignment to a work area and identification of necessary resources.

▶   Location of cafeteria, lockers, and rest rooms.

▶   Location of first-aid facilities.

This basic information is a lot for new employees to swallow at once. So don't be afraid to ask questions to gauge their understanding or to repeat what you tell them several times. Better still, give them some of the more detailed information in small doses. Give them some today, a little more tomorrow, and as much as they can take a week from now.

Note that in many companies new employees receive orientation talks from the personnel or training department. As valuable as such talks may be, they won't help new employees half as much as informal, one-on-one chats with their supervisors. You are an important person in the eyes of a new employee, and you also want to begin developing a healthy work relationship with that employee. Grab the opportunity to do so!

HOW DO YOU GET DOWN TO THE REAL BUSINESS OF TRAINING EMPLOYEES TO DO THEIR JOBS THE WAY YOU WANT THEM TO?

Training can be either the simplest or the most difficult job in the world. If you can grasp just four fundamentals, you can be a superior trainer. If you don't learn and practice this approach, you'll spend the rest of your life complaining that employees are stupid, willful, or not like workers used to be in "the good old days."

The foundation of systematic, structured job training (also called Job Instruction Training, or JIT) has four cornerstones, as follows.

Step 1. Get the Worker Ready To Learn. People who want to learn are the easiest to teach. Let trainees know why their jobs are important and why they must be done right. Find out something about the employees as individuals. Not only does this give them more confidence in you, but it also reveals to you how much they already know about their jobs, the amount and quality of their experience, and what attitudes they have toward learning. This familiarization period helps the trainees to get the feel of the job you want them to do.

Step 2. Demonstrate How the Job Should Be Done. Don't just tell the trainees how to go about it or say, "Watch how I do it." Do both—tell *and* show the correct procedure. Do this a little at a time, step by step. There's no point in going on to something new until the trainee has grasped the preceding step.

Step 3. Try the Workers Out by Letting Them Do the Job. Let the employees try the job—under your guidance. Stay with the trainees now to encourage them when they are doing right and to correct them when they are wrong. The mistakes made while you're watching are invaluable, because they show you where the trainee hasn't learned.

Step 4. Put the Trainees on Their Own, Gradually. Persons doing new jobs have to fly alone sooner or later. So after the trainees have shown you they can do the work reasonably well while you're standing by, turn them loose for a while. Don't abandon them completely, though. Make a point of checking on their progress and workmanship regularly—perhaps three or four times the first day they are on their own, then once or twice a day for a week or two. But never think they are completely trained. There's always something an employee can learn to do, or learn to do better.

HOW MUCH SHOULD YOU TEACH AT A TIME?

This depends on (1) the speed with which a trainee can learn and (2) how difficult the job is. Each learner is different. Some catch on fast, others more slowly. It's better, therefore, to gauge your speed to the slow person. Try to find out why the person has trouble learning. With new employees it may simply be that they are nervous and trying so hard that they don't concentrate. So be patient. Give them a chance to relax, and when they complete even a small part of the task successfully, be sure to praise them.

Going ahead slowly is especially important at the start, because learning is like getting a stick-shift car into motion. You first warm up the engine, then start slowly in low gear. You shift into second only as the car picks up speed, and finally into high when it's rolling along under its own momentum.

WHAT CAN YOU DO TO MAKE THE JOB EASIER TO LEARN AND TO TEACH?

Jobs that seem simple to you because you're familiar with them may appear almost impossible to persons who have never performed them before. You may have heard the advice given to the diner faced with the overwhelming task of eating an elephant: "Just take one bite at a time!" Similarly, experience has shown that the trick to making jobs easier to learn is to break them down into simple (bite-size) steps. That way, employees need to learn only one step at a time, adding steps systematically, rather than trying to grasp the whole job in a single piece. At an early stage, however, it is useful to portray the entire task to the trainees so that they can see how each step fits into the larger picture.

Breaking a job down for training purposes (a *job breakdown*) involves two elements:

1. You must observe the job as it is done and divide it into its logical steps. For instance, if the job is to provide written responses to customer complaints, the first step would be to read the letter. The next

two steps would be to identify all issues raised and to select the specific nature of the problem to be solved. The fourth step would be to consult a company policy manual, and the fifth would be to determine the acceptable type of response. The sixth step would be to select appropriate standard paragraphs from a computer-based inventory of prepared statements, and so on until the job is finished. (See Table 7-1.)

2. For each step in a job breakdown, you must now consider the second element—called the *key point*. A key point is anything at a particular step that might make or break a job or injure the worker. Essentially, it's the knack or special know-how of experienced workers that makes

TABLE 7-1 Example of a job instruction breakdown

▼ JOB BREAKDOWN SHEET FOR TRAINING

Task: Responding to customer complaints	Operation: Preparing written letter using word processor
Important Steps in the Operation	**Key Points**
Step: A logical segment of the operation during which something happens to advance the work.	Key point: Anything in a step that might make or break the job, injure the worker, make the work easier to do (i.e., knack, trick, special timing, bit of special information)
1. Read the customer's letter.	Knack—avoid defensive reactions.
2. Identify all issues raised.	Take notes using only key words.
3. Select a specific problem to be solved.	Identify the real complaint among a variety of frustrations expressed.
4. Consult the company policy manual.	Use table of contents or index to find relevant material.
5. Determine acceptable response.	Knack—ask yourself how you would feel if you received that reply.
6. Pick appropriate standard paragraphs from computer files.	Refer to list of key words, and match with those in file paragraphs.
7. Tailor the letter to fit the individual.	Personalize letter by frequent use of customer's name and specific problem.
8. Proofread the product for errors.	Review letter once now; set it aside a while; return to it when you are "fresh."

the job go easier or faster for them. The key point for the third step in the customer relations representative's job in the previous paragraph would be to know the knack of sorting out the real complaint from a variety of frustrations expressed by the customer. For the seventh step it would be the capacity to personalize a standard solution to fit the unique problem and individual.

Table 7-1 shows how this customer relations job might be broken down into several steps with their appropriate key points for training purposes. Table 7-2 lists 16 factors, and sample questions for each, that will help you identify key points in product- and machine-oriented jobs for training purposes. In professional and service-related jobs, key points often will revolve around factors such as logic, courtesy, timeliness, and accuracy.

WHERE WILL THE KEY POINTS FOR A JOB BE FOUND?

They may be found in several places: in an operating or maintenance manual prepared by the manufacturer of equipment; in a record of "bugs" or peculiarities that has been gathered on a particular operation, procedure, or piece of equipment; or in the mind and/or know-how of an experienced operator. One of the reasons that training results are often poor when an experienced employee has been asked to break in a new one is that the older employee may "conveniently" forget or, more likely, not be aware of key points that she or he has come to take for granted through years of experience. Because experienced employees have "internalized" these key points, they may no longer be conscious of what they are doing. Their descriptions of their jobs may be either incomplete (missing key points such as "Speed up the engine if you feel that the auto is about to stall while shifting gears") or altogether wrong (such as "Depress the clutch pedal after you have moved the gearshift").

As you (or a trained observer) break down a job for training purposes, you'll want to check all three sources of key points—manuals, records, and current employees. Table 7-2 also lists questions that help to identify key points for training purposes.

IN WHAT SEQUENCE MUST THE PARTS OF A JOB BE TAUGHT?

The best way to teach a job is to present its elements in a logical order, or start with the easiest part and proceed to the most difficult. This isn't always possible, of course. But if you can arrange your employee training

TABLE 7-2 Key-point checklist

▼ Key points are those things that should happen, or could happen, at each step of a job which make it either go right or go wrong. Key points include any of the following:

1. Feel. Is there a special smoothness or roughness? Absence of vibration?

2. Alignment. Should the part be up or down? Which face forward? Label in which position?

3. Fit. Should it be loose or tight? How loose? How tight? Can you show the trainee? When can you tell that a part is jammed?

4. Safety. What can happen to injure a worker? How are the safety guards operated? What special glasses, gloves, switches, or shoes are needed?

5. Speed. How fast must the operation proceed? Is speed critical? How can you tell if it's going too fast or too slow?

6. Timing. What must be synchronized with something else? How long must an operation remain idle—as with waiting for an adhesive to set?

7. Smell. Is there a right or wrong smell about anything—the material, the cooking or curing during the process, the overheating of a machine?

8. Temperature. Is temperature critical? How can you tell whether it is too hot or too cold? What can you do to change the temperature, if necessary?

9. Sequence. Is the specified order critical? Must one operation be performed before another, or doesn't it make any difference? How can the worker tell if he or she has gotten something out of order?

10. Appearance. Should surfaces be glossy or dull? Should the part be straight or bent? How can you correct an unsatisfactory condition?

11. Heft. Is weight important? Can you demonstrate how heavy or light a part or package should be?

12. Noise. Are certain noises expected (purring of a motor)? Unacceptable (grinding of gears)?

13. Materials. What is critical about their condition? How can the worker recognize this? When should the material be rejected? What should be done with rejected material?

14. Tools. What is critical about their condition? Sharpness? Absence of nicks or burrs? Positioning? Handling?

15. Machinery. What is critical about its operation? How is it shut down in emergencies? What will damage it? How can this be avoided?

16. Trouble. What should be done in the case of injury to persons or damage to materials, parts, products, tools, or machinery? How can damage be recognized?

in a systematic sequence, learning will go more smoothly and teaching will also be easier. Figure 7-1 shows how you can arrange your training sequence so that the learner works up to the difficult parts gradually from sequence 1 to sequence 4.

HOW SOON SHOULD YOU EXPECT AN EMPLOYEE TO ACQUIRE JOB SKILLS?

This depends on the employee and on the job. It's wise, however, to set a timetable for learning. This can be very simple, as shown in Figure 7-2, or

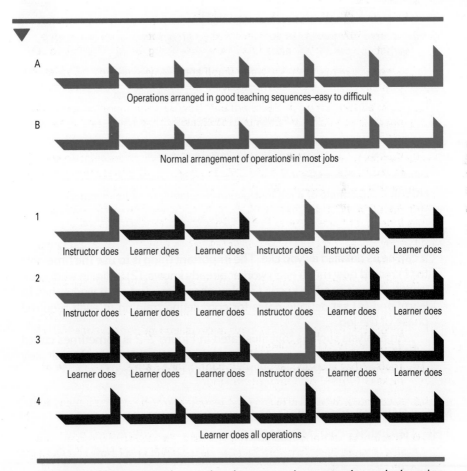

A

Operations arranged in good teaching sequences–easy to difficult

B

Normal arrangement of operations in most jobs

1

Instructor does   Learner does   Learner does   Instructor does   Instructor does   Learner does

2

Instructor does   Learner does   Learner does   Instructor does   Learner does   Learner does

3

Learner does   Learner does   Learner does   Instructor does   Learner does   Learner does

4

Learner does all operations

FIGURE 7-1 How a normal operational sequence is arranged to make learning easier and more effective

	Answer telephone calls	File correspondence	File reports	Make logbook entries	File sales order forms	Prepare day-end report	Etc.	Etc.	Etc.
Garcia	√	√	√	√	√	√			
Nolan	√	√	√	11-10	–	–			
Smith	11-1	11-20	–	√	√	12-1			
Chan	–	–	√	11-15	12-1	12-8			
Etc.									

A checkmark (√) means the worker can already do the job.

A dash (–) means the worker doesn't need to know the job.

A date (11-1, 11-15, etc.) indicates the date the supervisor has set to have the worker *trained* to do the job required.

FIGURE 7-2 Example of a job instruction timetable, or skills inventory

it can be as detailed as you like. The important thing is to use the timetable to (1) record how much each worker already knows; (2) indicate what each worker doesn't need to know; (3) plan ahead for what each worker has to learn; and (4) set definite dates for completing training in each required phase of the job.

An analysis such as that illustrated in Figure 7-2 is sometimes called a "skills inventory" because it tells you what skills each worker has already acquired as well as the total skills capability of your department.

MUST SUPERVISORS DO ALL THE TRAINING THEMSELVES?

No. Instruction is a job that can be delegated—provided that the employee who is to conduct the training is a qualified trainer and that a job breakdown sheet with key points has been prepared. Just as you must know the ins and outs of teaching a job, any employees you appoint as instructors must also know how to train others. This means that they should have completed a course in Job Instruction Training (JIT) or have been thoroughly indoctrinated by you or by the company's training director in how to train. Nothing is worse than bringing a new employee over to an older employee and just turning that person loose. If the older worker doesn't know how to train, chances are 1000 to 1 that the new employee will never learn the job correctly, and the training process itself will be slow and costly. So never depend on an older employee to show a new one the ropes.

Caution: Even if you have a qualified job instructor in your department, you can never completely delegate your training responsibility. It's up to you to show a personal interest in every trainee's progress and to supervise the training just as you supervise any of your other responsibilities.

IF SUPERVISORS ARE RESPONSIBLE FOR TRAINING, WHAT'S THE PURPOSE OF A COMPANY TRAINING DEPARTMENT?

The function of a company training (or human resources development) department is to identify training needs, specify and/or provide training programs and methods, and assist or supplement supervisors and other managers in discharging their training responsibilities.

Generally, the training department people are experts in teaching methods. For example, training specialists can be of real help in determining specific training needs. They can help you recognize and interpret the training symptoms mentioned previously. You'll want their help, too, in learning how to be a good instructor and in training some of your key employees to be trainers. And the training department is invaluable in getting you started in making job breakdowns, lesson plans, and training timetables.

Certain employee training is best done by a central training group. Such general subjects as company history and products, economics, and human relations are naturals for centralized training. Other classroom-type instruction (for instance, in basic literacy skills or statistical quality control) lends itself to centralized training, too. But when the training department does these jobs for you, you must still assume the responsibility for requesting this training for your employees and for making sure they apply what they learn to their work.

CAN YOU DEPEND ON AN EMPLOYEE TO LEARN A JOB BY READING AN EQUIPMENT MANUFACTURER'S INSTRUCTION MANUAL?

Absolutely not. It's a very exceptional person who can solely on the basis of an instruction manual learn how to operate equipment. Instruction manuals are valuable training aids, however, and they will help you draw up job breakdown sheets. But they are not substitutes for personal instruction.

HOW MUCH TRAINING CAN BE ACCOMPLISHED THROUGH OUTSIDE READING AND BY CORRESPONDENCE INSTRUCTION?

If employees are ambitious to learn and to improve themselves—and if they are the rare persons who can absorb knowledge and skills through reading and self-help—they can learn much through reading or through correspondence courses. But make no mistake about it, this is the hard way! Few employees are up to it. And despite the claims of many advocates of correspondence courses, the percentage of workers who have learned their jobs this way is very small.

This is not to say, however, that outside reading combined with personalized instruction by the supervisor is not effective. It is, but the two must go hand in hand.

HOW DO YOU GET EMPLOYEES TO WANT TO LEARN?

Employees must see how training will pay off before they pitch into training with a will. So show the younger employees how training helped others to get ahead—how it built job security for them and increased their incomes. For older workers, stress the prestige that skill gives them with other workers. Show them how learning new jobs or better methods makes the work more interesting.

Telling workers why a job is done a certain way is often the key to securing their interest. To see the necessity for training, an employee needs to know not only *what* to do and *how* to do it, but *why* it needs to be done. This process may be compared to a technical problem in transmitting color television. As you may know, the picture is broken down into three separate channels, one of which carries the red, another the green, and the third the blue part of the picture. Unless all three are transmitted in harmony, the picture is blurred and distorted. So, too, unless all three requisites of training (what, how, and why) are transmitted to the employees, it will make little sense to them.

HOW SMOOTHLY SHOULD THE TRAINING PROCESS PROCEED?

The learning process doesn't go smoothly for most people. We all have our ups and downs. Expect trainees to learn quickly for a while, then taper off on a plateau temporarily. They may even backslide a little. That's the time to reassure them that their halt in progress is normal. Don't let them become discouraged. If necessary, go through the demonstration again so that they can get a fresh start. And pile on the encouragement.

CAN YOU TEACH OLD DOGS NEW TRICKS?

Yes. Older workers can and do learn new methods and new jobs. And although they may learn more slowly than younger workers, this is mainly because older workers frequently have to unlearn what was taught to them in the past. Older workers often don't have the same incentive to learn that younger ones do. They tend to feel more secure in their jobs and have less interest in advancement. For these reasons, Step 1—getting the worker ready to learn—is of prime importance when you are teaching older workers.

WHAT IS VESTIBULE TRAINING?

When employees are trained by the company in the kinds of work they have been hired to perform but are separated from the actual job site and the related pressures of performance, the training is called *vestibule training.* It gets its name from the fact that such training is often done away from the noise, activity, and peer pressure associated with the trainees' future workstation—as if it were performed in the vestibule of the company before actual entry into the working area. Then, when the trainees gain competence and self-confidence in their new skills, they can be moved into the regular job site.

HOW VALUABLE IS APPRENTICE TRAINING?

Traditionally, the top-notch, all-around skilled artisans were schooled through *apprenticeship* programs. These programs are based on a long, thorough, and costly training process that blends classroom instruction with hands-on skill practice under the guidance of experienced coaches. Apprenticeships may last from one to four years. They have two disadvantages, however. They prepare trainees for a wide variety of job skills, even though new employees may use only a small number of them in their first job. Also, such programs may fail to be tailored to your organization, requiring you to retrain apprentices immediately. The use of apprenticeship programs has declined somewhat, and today more emphasis is placed on providing employees with just enough competency to perform a single job. As a result, the training is more focused, is done faster, and costs less.

HOW GOOD ARE OFF-THE-JOB TRAINING METHODS?

Although individualized training is effective for developing job skills, it can still be expensive and time-consuming for the supervisor. Some training can be conducted in small groups at less cost per person with equal success. This is particularly true when new policies or procedures need to be explained to all workers or when employees need to know the theory and background behind an operation. Value is also gained from the comments that experienced employees make to others in support of the ideas being presented.

Another alternative that relieves the supervisor of direct training responsibility is the use of self-paced instructional methods. *Programmed learning,* for example, exposes a trainee to a small block of information and then tests the trainee immediately to see if the material has been grasped. If the trainee answers the questions correctly, another block is provided. If the trainee cannot respond correctly, the block is repeated or rephrased and then the trainee is questioned again. This is a "small-bite" approach that allows trainees to move ahead at their own pace as they master the material. It also uses regular feedback to reinforce learning.

Many such training programs are now presented by mechanical and visual devices that add further stimulation and efficiency to the learning process. When programmed-learning materials are linked to a computer and a television screen, they are called *computer-assisted instruction* (CAI). Newer technologies involve the use of interactive videodiscs, which use exciting graphics displays, realistic experiences, and even touch-screen responses. They are expensive to produce but highly appealing to trainees, who suddenly become active participants. As a result, the chances of learning and retention are sharply improved.

WHAT IS THE PURPOSE OF VISUAL AIDS?

The classic Chinese proverb still tells the story best: One picture is worth 1000 words. Any device that helps trainees visualize what you're telling them speeds up the learning process. After all, most of us use our eyes to pick up 80 percent of what we know. So it's only natural for training that utilizes the visual sense to be more effective.

Visual aids may include a variety of devices, such as transparencies, slides and filmstrips, and motion pictures. Visual aids may also be simple and obvious, such as writing on a blackboard or demonstrating a point on a machine. Practically nothing beats making the demonstration right on the equipment a worker will use.

In the last few years, audiovisual instruction has increasingly invaded the training field. Tape cassettes linked to programmed texts, audio-TV cassettes with capsulated instructions, and closed-circuit television demonstrations and lectures—live or on tape—have demonstrated their ability to ensure consistent instruction. In the main, however, such methods are prohibitively expensive and are used only selectively where their costs can be justified.

HOW CAN A SUPERVISOR INCREASE THE PROBABILITY THAT TRAINING WILL TRANSFER TO THE JOB?

Many supervisors are effective trainers. Many employees want to learn new skills. Yet evidence suggests that much training (especially training of the classroom variety) doesn't result in improved job performance. Training has failed if it has not been transferred to the job. The reasons are diverse—lack of supervisory reinforcement, impractical training, or even peer-group norms that create barriers to the use of training.

What can you do to aid the transfer of training? Discuss the objectives of training in advance with your new employees so that they will know what to expect. Point out effective workers to them so that they can have successful role models. Visibly monitor trainee performance; this lets the trainees know what you think is important. Praise successful behaviors regularly so that your new workers will feel good about their developing skills. Above all, consider training to be an important supervisory function and give it the attention it deserves.

REVIEW ▼ 7 ▲ QUESTIONS

1. In what ways can a human resources development (or training) specialist supplement the efforts made by supervisors to train their employees?
2. Contrast vestibule training with induction or orientation training.
3. What is the significance of the teachable moment?
4. Would it be wise for a supervisor to let an employee try a new job before showing the employee how it is done? Why?
5. Compare the preparing-to-learn phase of job training with the identification of key points.
6. Why might a supervisor not want to teach a job's sequence of steps in the exact order in which they are performed?
7. In what ways should the training of older workers differ from that of younger workers?
8. Ed, a telephone clerk for a mail-order house, attended a workshop conducted by the company's training department on proper telephone techniques. Ed's boss, Ms. Calla, is disappointed because Ed uses little of what he learned at the workshop on his job. What can Ms. Calla do to improve this situation?

A CASE IN POINT

Wrong Worker or Wrong Start?

Steven, who is supervisor of food services at St. Vincent's Hospital, is justifiably concerned about the job performance of Max, his newest employee. Max was hired three months ago as a food-service assistant. His three-month probationary period is about to conclude, and his work still leaves a lot to be desired. At times Max is confused about exactly what he should be doing next. He constantly interrupts Steven throughout the shift to ask a variety of questions about equipment. Then, too, on a number of occasions Max has made simple mistakes, resulting in wasted supplies or leftover food items. Steven wonders, "Is it possible that I hired the wrong person?"

Thinking back, Steven reviews the major events of Max's employment. On his first day, Steven welcomed Max and asked him if he wanted a tour of the kitchen. Max replied that he didn't think it was necessary because he had just finished a training course in food preparation at a vocational school. He said, "I assume that most kitchens are similar to the layout there." Steven then handed Max a set of manuals provided by the manufacturers of the ovens, grills, and cookers. He sat Max at a table in the kitchen and told him to read the manuals during the rest of the morning.

After lunch that day, Steven was too busy to spend time with Max. He did, however, set up the VCR in the training room so that Max could watch an instructional videotape that was on hand. The video was entitled "Successful Customer Service," and although it was not particularly aimed at hospital food service, it did contain a few useful tips for food-service personnel in general. When Max finished watching the tape, Steven asked him if he had any questions. Max had none. Accordingly, Steven told Max to go home early and to start his regular shift the next day.

Because it is the end of Max's probationary period, Steven must decide whether to keep Max or recommend his release. When Steven speaks to the human resources director about his dilemma, the director asks, "Are you sure that you started Max off on the right foot?" Steven replies, "If I had it to do over again, I'd do it differently."

If you were Steven, how would you have gone about starting Max off on the right foot? Five alternative courses of action are listed below. Rank them in the order in which they appeal to you (1 most effective, 5 least effective). You may add another approach in the space provided, if you wish. In any event, be prepared to justify your ranking.

_____ **A.** Assigned Max to begin work right away so that he could learn the ropes from an experienced food server.

_____ **B.** Insisted that Max tour the kitchen so that he could see where and how it differed from the one at his school.

_____ **C.** Made Max feel comfortable by introducing him to the people he would be working with on his shift.

_____ **D.** Picked out a more appropriate training video for Max.

_____ **E.** Given Max the operating manuals to read at home rather than at work, where there were too many distractions.

If you have another approach, write it here.

▶ _____

_____

_____

Complete the ACTION PLANNING CHECKLIST
for this chapter, which can be found on page 317.

8

MOTIVATING INDIVIDUALS AND GROUPS

LEARNING OBJECTIVES

After studying this chapter, you should be able to:

1. Recognize some of the factors that shape the development of each person's unique personality.

2. Describe the five factors that make up Maslow's hierarchy of needs and explain how they influence an individual's motivation and performance.

3. Explain the differences between satisfaction and dissatisfaction, according to Herzberg, and discuss how they affect a supervisor's ability to motivate employees.

4. Identify various forms of people-centered job design and explain how, when incorporated in the work itself, they can provide motivation and satisfaction.

5. Anticipate the presence and power of informal work groups and apply participative methods to set goals and solve problems with them.

▶ There is no one best way to handle interpersonal relationships. They depend on the particular situation (its urgencies and its technical, social, or economic pressures) and on who is involved in it. All human relationships are complex, with many influencing elements often hidden deep beneath the surface evidence.

▶ Individual behavior depends on a vast heritage of genealogical characteristics and is shaped by the forces of home environment, education, and work experience. This individuality causes people to behave the way they do, even though their behavior often appears illogical to others.

▶ Although it may appear that most people work mainly to satisfy their needs for food, shelter, and clothing, it is a fact that today most people expect much more from their work in the way of social relationships, self-esteem, and meaningful endeavor. This awareness has led to today's great emphasis on the potential for motivation in the work itself, which—when released—creates "empowered employees."

▶ Because supervision is involved with organized human effort, group relations are present in every situation; the characteristics of a particular group's behavior must be weighed just as carefully as the behavioral characteristics of an individual. Work groups may be either formal, established consciously by management, or informal, created spontaneously by members because of mutual interests and enthusiasms.

▶ With groups especially, the principle of participation presents an effective approach. By recognizing the force a group exerts in attaining (or in blocking) goals, a supervisor who invites participation encourages the group to direct its influence in a productive manner.

WHY DO PEOPLE ACT THE WAY THEY DO?

If you mean, "Why don't employees act the way I wish they would?", the answer will take a long time. But if you are really asking, "Why do people act in such unpredictable ways?", the answer is simple: People do as they must. Their actions, which may look irrational to someone who doesn't understand them, are in reality very logical. If you could peer into people's backgrounds and into their emotional makeup, you'd be able to predict with startling accuracy how one person would react to criticism or how another person would act when told to change over to the second shift.

The dog who's been scratched by a cat steers clear of all cats. Workers who have learned from one boss that the only time they are treated as human beings is when the work load is going to be increased, will go on the defensive when a new boss tries to be friendly. To the new boss, such employee actions look absurd. But to the workers, it's the only logical thing to do.

So it goes—each person is the product of parents, home, education, social life, and work experience. Consequently, when supervisors deal with employees, they are dealing with persons who have brought all their previous experiences to the job.

THEN ARE ALL PEOPLE DIFFERENT?

Each person *is* a distinct individual. In detail, his or her reactions will be different from anyone else's. But to understand human relations, you must first know *why* people do things before you can predict *what* they will do. If you know that Bill dislikes his job because it requires concentration, you can make a good guess that Bill will make it hard for you to change the job by increasing its complexity. If Mary works at your company because of the socializing she has with her associates, you can predict that Mary will be hard to get along with if she's assigned to a spot in an isolated area.

The important tool in dealing with people is the recognition that, although what they do is likely to differ, the underlying reasons for their doing anything are very similar. These reasons, incidentally, are called **motives,** or **needs.**

As a consequence of the increasing recognition of these differences, the term "diversity" has become important in supervisory management. **Diversity** reflects the dramatic changes by which it is anticipated that nonwhites, women, and immigrants will make up more than 80 percent of the net additions to the work force by the year 2000. Management of such diversity requires that stereotypes be set aside while differences in perception, behavior, and style be accommodated.

WHAT DETERMINES AN
INDIVIDUAL'S PERSONALITY?

Just about everything. An individual's personality cannot be neatly pigeon-holed (as we so often try to do) as pleasant or outgoing or friendly or ill-tempered or unpleasant or suspicious or defensive. An individual's personality is the sum total of what the person is today: the clothing worn, the food preferred, the conversation enjoyed or avoided, the manners and gestures used, the methods of thought practiced, the way situations are handled. Each person's personality is uniquely different from anyone else's. It results from heredity and upbringing, schooling or lack of it, neighborhoods, work and play experiences, parents' influence, religion—all the social forces around us. From all these influences people learn to shape their individuality in a way that enables them to cope with life's encounters, with work, with living together, with age, with success and failure. As a result, personality is the total expression of the unique way in which each individual deals with life.

WHAT DO EMPLOYEES WANT
FROM LIFE—AND FROM THEIR WORK?

Most of us, including employees, seek satisfaction from life in relation to what a very famous psychologist, A. H. Maslow, called the "five basic needs" (see Figure 8-1), and we seek a good part of this satisfaction at our work. Dr. Maslow outlined the basic needs as explained below and conceived of them as a sort of hierarchy, with the most compelling ones coming first and the more sophisticated ones last.

We Need To Be Alive and To Stay Alive. We need to breathe, eat, sleep, reproduce, see, hear, and feel. But in today's world these needs rarely dominate us. Real hunger, for example, is rare. All in all, our first-level needs are satisfied. Only an occasional experience—a couple of days without sleep, a day on a diet without food, a frantic 30 seconds under water—reminds us that these basic needs are still with us.

We Need To Feel Safe. We like to feel that we are safe from accident or pain, from competitors or criminals, from an uncertain future or a changing present. Not one of us ever feels completely safe. Yet most of us feel reasonably safe. After all, we have laws, police, insurance, social security, union contracts, and the like, to protect us.

We Need To Be Social. From the beginning of time we have lived together in tribes and family groups. Today these group ties are stronger than ever.

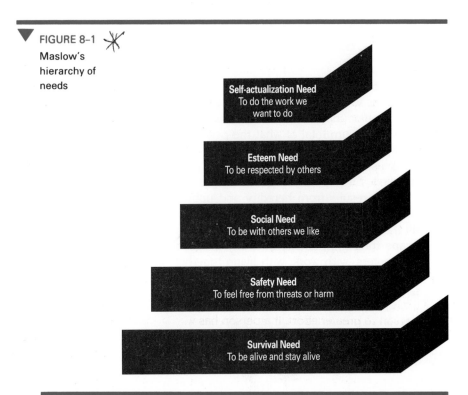

FIGURE 8–1
Maslow's hierarchy of needs

Self-actualization Need
To do the work we
want to do

Esteem Need
To be respected by others

Social Need
To be with others we like

Safety Need
To feel free from threats or harm

Survival Need
To be alive and stay alive

We marry, join lodges, and even do our praying in groups. Social need varies widely from person to person—just as other needs do. Few of us want to be hermits. Not everyone, of course, is capable of frank and deep relationships—even with a wife or husband or with close friends. But, to a greater or lesser degree, this social need operates in all of us.

We Need To Feel Worthy and Respected. When we talk about our self-respect or our dignity, this is the need we are expressing. When a person isn't completely adjusted to life, this need may show itself as undue pride in achievements, self-importance, boastfulness—a bloated ego.

But so many of our other needs are so easily satisfied in the modern world that this need often becomes one of the most demanding. Look what we go through to satisfy the need to think well of ourselves—and have others do likewise. When a wife insists her husband wear a jacket to a party, she's expressing this need. When we buy a new car even though the old one is in good shape, we're giving way to our desire to show ourselves off.

We even modify our personalities to get the esteem of others. No doubt you've put on your company manners when out visiting. It's natural, we say, to act more refined in public than at home—or to cover up our less acceptable traits.

We Need To Do the Work We Like. This is why many people who don't like their jobs turn to hobbies for expression, and why so many people get wrapped up in their work. We all know men and women who enjoy the hard burden of laboring work, or machinists who hurry home from work to run their own lathes, or bored terminal operators who stay up late in their own homes playing with their own microcomputers. This need rarely is the be-all and end-all of our lives. But there are very few of us who aren't influenced by it.

WHICH OF THESE NEEDS IS THE MOST POWERFUL?

The one or ones that have not yet been satisfied. Maslow's greatest insight was the realization that once a need is satisfied, it will no longer motivate a person to greater effort. If a person has what is required in the way of job security, for example, offering more of it—such as guaranteeing employment for the next five years—normally will not cause a person to work any harder. The supervisor who wishes to see greater effort generated will have to address an unsatisfied need, such as the desire to be with other people on the job, if this employee is to be expected to work harder as a result.

It should also be noted that people tend to move up and down the hierarchy as one of their needs is threatened. For example, rumors of layoff can shift attention quickly back to "safety and security."

IN WHAT WAY CAN A JOB SATISFY A PERSON'S NEEDS?

It's a fact: Many people are happier at work than at home! Why? Because a satisfying job with a good supervisor goes such a long way toward making life worth living. Whereas all of us may complain about our jobs (or our bosses) from time to time, most of us respond favorably to the stability of the work situation. At home, Jane may have a nagging husband, sick children, and a stack of bills to greet her at the end of the month. At work, Jane can have an appreciative supervisor, a neat job with a quota she can meet each day, and assurance of a paycheck (and other benefits) at week's end. No wonder Jane enjoys herself more at work than at home.

Or look at it this way: A rewarding job with a decent company and a straight-shooting boss easily provides the first two basic needs: (1) a livelihood that keeps the wolf away from the door and (2) a sense of safety from the fears of layoff, old age, and accidents. Satisfaction from the other three basic needs—to be social, to be respected, and to do the work we like—is often more a function of a person's supervisor than of the job itself.

A good supervisor can ensure that a person's job satisfies the *social need* by demonstrating to the rest of the work group the desirability of taking in a new worker. For instance: "This is Paula Brown, our new computer clerk. We're glad to have her with the agency. I've told her what a great gang of people you all are. So how about taking Paula along to the vending area during the rest break and showing her where she can get a cup of coffee."

To satisfy the *esteem need,* a good supervisor will make sure workers know when their work is appreciated. For example: "Paula, here's your locker. I think you'll agree that this is a pretty clean washroom. We feel that when we hire a first-rate person, we should provide first-rate conditions so that you can do the best possible work."

To satisfy the *desire to do worthwhile work,* a good supervisor gives thought to placing employees on jobs for which they have the most aptitude and training. The supervisor might say to Paula: "Since you've worked at this type of terminal before, suppose you start here. When you've got the hang of things, we'll give you a chance to broaden your experience on some more challenging assignments."

IN WHAT IMPORTANT WAYS DOES SATISFACTION DIFFER FROM DISSATISFACTION?

One noted behavioral scientist, Frederick Herzberg, made these distinctions between satisfaction and dissatisfaction:

* **Satisfaction** for an employee comes from truly motivating factors such as interesting and challenging work, utilization of one's capabilities, opportunity to do something meaningful, recognition of achievement, and responsibility for one's own work.

  Dissatisfaction occurs when the following factors are *not* present on the job: good pay, adequate holidays, long-enough vacations, paid insurance and pensions, good working conditions, and congenial co-workers.

Herzberg bases these definitions on his *two-factor theory.* He says that every human being has two motivational tracks: (1) a lower-level one, animal in nature and bent only on surviving, and (2) a higher-level one, uniquely human and directed toward adjusting to oneself. Herzberg labels the first set of motivations "hygiene," or "maintenance," factors. We need to satisfy them, he reasons, to keep alive. People try to avoid pain and unpleasantness in life; they do the same on the job. Satisfaction of these needs provides only hygiene for people. These factors physically maintain the status quo, but they do not motivate. If they are not present in the workplace, an employee will be dissatisfied and may look elsewhere for a job that provides these factors. But the employee will not work harder just because these factors are given to him or her. Said another way, a general pay increase may keep employees from quitting, but it will rarely motivate an employee to work harder.

WHAT HAPPENS WHEN EMPLOYEES DON'T GET SATISFACTION FROM THEIR JOBS?

Their morale drops, absences and lateness increase, and it becomes increasingly difficult to obtain their cooperation or to introduce necessary changes.

SHOULDN'T JOB SATISFACTION BE PRIMARILY THE COMPANY'S RESPONSIBILITY—NOT THE SUPERVISOR'S?

The company's stake in good human relations is, of course, just as big as a supervisor's. And when a company helps a supervisor establish the right climate for employee job satisfaction, the supervisor's work with people becomes a lot easier. But a supervisor's relationship with his or her employees is—ultimately—a very personal one. No amount of policies and procedures, fancy cafeterias, generous fringe benefits, or sparkling rest rooms can take the place of a concerned supervisor who treats his or her employees wisely and well. From your point of view, responsibility for employees' job satisfaction is one you must share with the company or parent organization.

HOW CAN WORK BE TAILORED TO PROVIDE THE GREATEST MOTIVATION FOR THE PERSONS WHO PERFORM IT?

By redesigning jobs according to *people-centered* considerations. Most work is first designed according to process-centered constraints. That is, emphasis is given to the dictates of (1) product specifications, (2) tool and machine requirements, (3) process-flow sequences, (4) computer-assisted controls, and (5) work-space layout. Only by a subsequent redesign will most work be made more satisfying and convenient to human beings.

Most present-day efforts at job redesign stress an accommodation of the psychological, as well as the physiological, needs of workers. And that is where supervisors enter the picture most actively.

HOW DOES THE PEOPLE-CENTERED APPROACH TO JOB DESIGN DIFFER FROM THE PROCESS-CENTERED APPROACH?

It strives for maximum employee involvement in the design of each individual's job. It does not ignore process considerations. Instead, it encourages employees to view demands and restrictions as problems they are invited to help solve. The way in which this involvement takes place has led to its having many names: job enlargement, job enrichment, work design or, sometimes, work redesign. The big difference is that the people-centered approach stresses genuine participation by employees, singly or in groups, in making their work effective and their jobs more attractive.

The boon to supervisors in the people approach is that it focuses everyone's attention on the "work itself" (another term sometimes used, defined on the next page). Supervisors aren't expected to be part-time psychologists or extraordinary leaders in seeking cooperation from their employees. It is the work that is examined, criticized, and restructured rather than human beings. The responsibility for these changes is no longer the sole burden of the supervisor; it is shared by all those employees who are able to, and wish to, get involved.

SHOULD DISTINCTIONS BE MADE AMONG THE VARIOUS KINDS OF PEOPLE-CENTERED JOB DESIGN?

Not necessarily, but such distinctions help add perspective to the ways that job design can be accomplished.

Job enlargement, for example, extends the boundaries of a job by adding different tasks at the same level of expertise. First tried at IBM, the concept is to let manufacturing employees be responsible for the production step just before or just after the one they currently are doing. Thus punch press operators might fill their own tote boxes and carry the punched parts to the next operation. This provides an opportunity to get away from a fixed place all day and a chance to converse for a minute or two with adjoining operators and to feel that the job isn't limited to the second or two it takes to load the press and wait for the die to stamp out a part.

Job enrichment is an outgrowth of the job-enlargement concept. It expands a job vertically by adding higher-skill activities and by delegating greater authority. For example, the punch press operators might set up their presses with the die required for each new job, inspect their own work with gauges typically used by roving inspectors, and maintain their own output tallies.

Goal-oriented management is the approach developed by M. Scott Myers while at Texas Instruments Company in Dallas. Like "work itself," it emphasizes the need for supervisors to shift their thinking from "I am the boss who must think of everything" to "These are the goals we must reach together." Under the Myers system the supervisor leads (by "facilitating") and controls when necessary; employees are responsible for planning tasks and accomplishing them. Conversely, authority-oriented supervisors typically plan, lead, and control the doers, who have little say in planning how their work is to be accomplished. (See Figure 8-2.)

Associated with goal-oriented management are the technique of Quality Circles and the concept of employee empowerment. *Quality Circles* involve the formation of voluntary departmental and interdepartmental teams charged with the responsibility for investigating and offering suggestions for improvement of methods, quality, and productivity. *Employee empowerment* is a more general term used to describe an attitude, approach, or program used by the organization to provide employees with greater opportunities to plan and control their own work.

Work itself was the term initially used by AT&T for a program it now labels *work design.* It typifies people-centered job design because it strives for a balance among process demands, organizational goals, and employee abilities and interests.

WHY ARE GROUP RELATIONS MORE IMPORTANT TODAY THAN THEY WERE IN YEARS PAST?

Business, industrial, service, and government enterprises are larger and more complex. As a result, they depend more on the effectiveness of group effort. At the turn of the nineteenth into the twentieth century, employees worked more by themselves, and their productivity often depended on their efforts alone. Then, too, many of the jobs were unskilled. People were hired to do routine work or to perform specific tasks that machines perform today. Automation, computers, and modern technology have made those jobs scarce. Instead, modern jobs involve great interdependence among individuals and among departments and demand close cooperation among all parties.

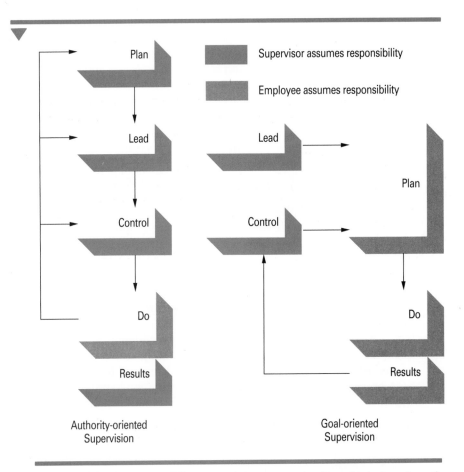

FIGURE 8-2 Job design differences between authority-oriented and goal-oriented supervision.

Adopted from a concept in M. Scott Myers, *Every Employee a Manager,* McGraw-Hill, New York, 1970, p. 99.

As Casey Stengel, the eccentric but immensely successful manager of baseball's Dodgers, Yankees, and Mets, once observed: "It's easy to get the players. Gettin' 'em to play together, that's the hard part."

WHICH GROUPS TAKE PRIORITY—THE FORMAL OR THE INFORMAL ONES?

Formal groups do, such as your own department or assigned work teams within your department. They have been set up routinely to carry out the work in the best fashion. But informal groups require your attention and consideration, too. A supervisor must be realistic about formation of informal groups within the department:

1. *Informal groups are inevitable.* They'll form at the water fountain and in the locker room. They will be made up of carpoolers and those with common interests in sports or politics. You will find them everywhere. There is no way to blot them out.

2. *Informal groups can be very powerful.* They influence your employees strongly. To enforce compliance among group members, such groups often establish sanctions that run counter to a supervisor's formal authority. Most informal groups, however, can be assumed to work either for you or against you, depending on your relationships with them.

3. *Informal leaders tend to emerge within these groups and to guide opinion within them.* Supervisors should be aware of such leaders and be prepared to contend with their influence.

WHAT CAUSES EMPLOYEES TO CREATE THEIR OWN INFORMAL GROUPS?

There are a number of causes. Most powerful is a common specialty or skill. For example, the keyboard operators in a data processing office are naturally going to find things in common to talk about. Other common experiences, backgrounds, or interests will also serve to pull parts of a formal group of employees into "cliques." Proximity plays a role, too. Workers who are physically close together tend to form close relationships to the exclusion of others in the department who are in more remote locations.

Membership in informal groups is developed gradually. Over a period of time, an individual begins to feel that he or she is accepted by the others. In return, the individual begins to accept—and carry out—the interests and behavior of the group. The bonds are tighter when the attraction is fostered by a desire for protection or support (often with regard to the company or management). Groups are less cohesive when based on common bonds that are more casual, such as hobbies and sports.

A supervisor must be careful in his or her relationships with informal groups. They can't be ignored, and sometimes they can be helpful. On the other hand, giving these groups too much attention, especially to the exclusion of those outside of them, will surely bring about dissension and lack of cooperation.

HOW DOES A GROUP OF EMPLOYEES DIFFER FROM ANY SINGLE EMPLOYEE IN THE GROUP?

Take a group of ten employees who work in a small can-filling line in a food-packing plant. This group is respected and feared by its supervisor as one of the most productive, most-likely-to-strike groups in the plant. Yet in the group are three people who, polled separately, are strongly against a walkout. And there are another three who, when working with other groups, are low producers. This is typical. Each person in a group may be a fairly strong individualist when working alone. But when people work in a group, the personality of the group becomes stronger than that of any single individual in the group. The group's personality will reflect the outlook and work habits of the various individuals, but it will bring out the best (or worst) in some and will submerge many individual tendencies of which the group does not approve.

Furthermore, each group sets the standards of conduct—or *norms*—for its members. Norms are accepted ways of doing things—the accepted way of life within the group. The group's ways may not be the best ways. Often, group norms stand in the way of things being done in the manner in which the company and the supervisor want them done. But the group will support the group standards. Individuals who don't conform will be cut off from the group's gossip sessions and social activities. It's not uncommon for the group to ridicule those who don't "play ball" or to purposely make it difficult for "outsiders" to get their own work done.

WHAT ARE WORK GROUPS LIKELY TO DO BEST?

Solve work problems. Groups, formal or informal, seem to have an uncanny knack for unsnarling complex work situations. In a few minutes they can straighten out crossover procedures between employees. They often know causes of difficulty hidden from the supervisor. Typically, they are acutely aware of personality conflicts among their members. Thus a group's ability to put together jointly held know-how in a constructive manner is one that experienced supervisors like to tap. This technique of securing group aid in solving departmental problems is called *participation.*

IN WHAT WAYS ARE GROUPS MOST LIKELY TO CAUSE PROBLEMS?

By ganging up to present mass resistance (spoken or silent) and by pressuring individual members to conform to the group's standards. Strong work groups stick together. They will protect one of their loyal members, and they will force a nonconformist to go along with the majority. The pressure can be so strong that even an eager beaver or a loner can be made to fall in line—or to quit. Groups are powerful. Their support is to be cherished. Their enmity can be awesome. For these reasons, prudent supervisors seek a group's help in establishing attainable work goals.

WHICH COMES FIRST, THE INDIVIDUAL OR THE GROUP?

It's almost impossible to say. We do know that the group is not just the sum of the individuals in it. Individually, each of your employees may be loyal and honest. But as a group, they may be more loyal to the group's interest than to yours. As a result, the individual may cheat a little on output or quality if this is the standard the group respects.

It seems unavoidable that you must place your bets on the group's being collectively stronger than any of its individuals. Hardly any one person can stand up to group pressures for long. The person who does so may keep on working in your area but is no longer a member of the group. Such persons become oddballs who are difficult for you to deal with fairly and intelligently because you're never sure what standards of performance to impose on them—theirs or the department's. For this reason, don't press individuals to support you in favor of the work group. Accept the fact that they will be loyal to you when this loyalty doesn't put them at odds with their peers.

By and large the supervisor's charge is to treat each person as individually as possible without challenging the prerogatives of the group to which that individual belongs. The work group is an organization for which you are expected to provide direction and inspiration, not moral judgments.

HOW CAN A SUPERVISOR SET GOALS WITH THE WORK GROUP WITHOUT SACRIFICING AUTHORITY?

Unless the people you supervise believe that what you want them to do is to their advantage as well as to yours, you'll have little success as a supervisor. The solution lies in permitting the members of the work group to set their goals along with you and in showing them that these goals can be attained only through group action—teamwork.

It may be only natural for you to feel that to permit the group to get into the decision-making act will be hazardous to your authority. It needn't be. First of all, make it clear that you'll always retain a veto power over group decisions (but don't exercise it unless absolutely necessary). Second, establish ground rules for the group's participation beforehand. Explain what's negotiable and what's not. Make these limitations clear. Finally, provide enough information for the group so that its members can see situations as you do. It's when people don't have enough facts that they rebel against authority.

In dealing with work groups, try to make your role that of a coach. Help employees to see why cost cutting, for instance, is desirable and necessary to prevent layoffs. Encourage them to discuss ways of cutting costs. Welcome their suggestions. Try to find ways of putting even relatively insignificant ideas to work. And report the team's achievements frequently. Emphasize that good records are the result of the team's united effort, not your own bright ideas.

Of course, it goes without saying that certain decisions—such as those concerning work standards or quality specifications—may be beyond the group's control or even yours. (See Figure 8-3.) Consequently, you should make it clear at the start what work conditions are off limits as far as group participation is concerned.

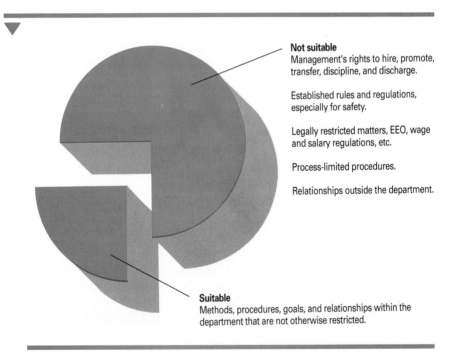

Not suitable
Management's rights to hire, promote, transfer, discipline, and discharge.

Established rules and regulations, especially for safety.

Legally restricted matters, EEO, wage and salary regulations, etc.

Process-limited procedures.

Relationships outside the department.

Suitable
Methods, procedures, goals, and relationships within the department that are not otherwise restricted.

FIGURE 8-3 **Areas suitable for and areas usually not suitable for participatory management methods**

WHAT MAKES GROUP
PARTICIPATION SO EFFECTIVE?

You'll hear a lot about the wonders of participation in one form or another, such as "consensus management" or "Quality Circles." Most of what you'll hear is true. In today's employer-employee relations, few techniques have been as successful in developing harmony and attaining common goals as has the development of participative methods by management and supervision.

Participation is an amazingly simple way to inspire people. And its simplicity lies in the definition of the word: "to share in common with others."

Sharing, then, is the secret. You must share knowledge and information with others in order to gain their cooperation. You must share your own experience so that employees will benefit from it. You must share the decision-making process itself so that employees can do some things the way they'd like to. And you must share credit for achievement.

REVIEW ▼8▼ QUESTIONS

1. What sorts of things affect the development of an individual's personality?
2. If an employee's survival, social, and esteem needs have been satisfied, which of Maslow's five needs should a supervisor appeal to next? Why?
3. How might the order of priorities for Maslow's five basic needs change as a person matures?
4. Comment on the relationship between an individual's needs for esteem and to do meaningful work.
5. How does Herzberg distinguish between satisfaction and dissatisfaction?
6. After changes were made in her job, an employee complained to the supervisor, "This may be job enlargement, but it sure isn't job enrichment." What did the employee mean?
7. Should a supervisor force an employee to choose between loyalty to the group and loyalty to the supervisor? Why or why not?
8. Why would a supervisor encourage group participation in solving work problems?

A CASE IN POINT

The Unhappy Lab Technician

The following episode takes place in the research laboratory of a major pharmaceutical firm. All the employees involved hold some sort of professional status, ranging from technician to senior research scientist. The organization is structured so that a project leader supervises a team of from five to eight of these employees. There are several teams in the laboratory. The project (or team) leader is, essentially, a supervisor. Team leaders report to the laboratory director.

Golda, leader of Team B, manages to get satisfactory performance from all but one member of her team. The problem member is Karen, a laboratory technician. Karen is a high school graduate who became a state certified technician by taking a series of specialized courses at a local technical institute and passing a certification examination. Compensation for lab technicians is relatively high, as is their status in the community. Compared with other members of Team B, however, Karen's status is at the bottom of the totem pole. The other members are all graduates of prestigious colleges—two with advanced degrees.

Golda reasons, "Karen is well paid. Lab work is relatively simple and undemanding, and the hours are good. Karen has a quick mind, and she has shown that she is capable of satisfactory performance."

Karen was friendly with other team members when she first joined the staff. Now she takes her coffee breaks by herself. At staff meetings, she has little to say. Increasingly, other members of the team complain about Karen's work. They say she lets the samples they send her for testing pile up, and when she does get to them, her tests are often unreliable.

Golda has approached Karen about the problem a couple of times with no success. Karen's reactions have been unclear except to indicate that she is unhappy that she gets so little satisfaction from her work, which she considers routine. She says, "Perhaps it's me they don't like."

The matter comes to a head when two junior scientists meet with Golda and ask that Karen be transferred off their team. "Karen doesn't fit in with us. She's not a genuine professional, nor is her work professional. Besides, lab technicians aren't so important that they can't be replaced."

What should Golda do now? Five alternative courses of action are listed below. Rank them in the order in which they appeal to you (1 most effective, 5 least effective). You may add another approach in the space provided, if you wish. In any event, be prepared to justify your ranking.

_____ **A.** See what can be done to reduce Karen's work load so that she can get on top of her job again.

_____ **B.** Examine Karen's job to see how it can be made more interesting and more challenging for her.

_____ **C.** Comply with the junior scientists' request and speak to the lab director about transferring Karen to another team.

_____ **D.** Speak to Karen about her performance and promise her you'll try to get her a pay raise if her work improves.

_____ **E.** Look for ways to make Karen and her work a more integral part of the team's activities, social as well as professional.

If you have another approach, write it here.

▶ _____

_____

_____

Complete the ACTION PLANNING CHECKLIST
for this chapter, which can be found on page 318.

CHAPTER

9

COMMUNICATING CLEARLY WITH EMPLOYEES

LEARNING OBJECTIVES

After studying this chapter, you should be able to:

1. Explain the steps in the communication process, including the factors that contribute to, or detract from, its effectiveness.

2. Know what to communicate to employees and your boss.

3. Be aware of the effects of nonverbal communications and improve your listening skills.

4. Choose appropriate spoken and written methods for communicating with individuals and groups.

5. Issue orders and instructions in a trouble-free manner so as to make them more acceptable to employees.

OVERVIEW OF KEY CONCEPTS IN THIS CHAPTER

▶ The effectiveness of employee communication depends on the extent to which supervision and management strive to maintain an open, honest, and three-dimensional system. The resultant effectiveness of this effort will become a major factor in strengthening or weakening of organizational unity and morale.

▶ Information can be exchanged only when reception as well as sending takes place and if distractions (or "noise") are held to a minimum. Although this exchange is greatly influenced by nonverbal factors such as anxieties, personalities, facial expressions, and tones of voice, a great deal of organizational information must inevitably be transmitted by words.

▶ Communication techniques are most effective (1) when used in combination, one with another, rather than singly; and (2) when appropriately tuned to the situations and the individuals involved.

▶ The issuance of orders and the giving of instructions are acts of communication. As such, they are susceptible to the shortcomings and misfires that obscure, distort, or otherwise interfere with the exchange of information. Therefore, clarity, consistency, restatement, specificity, and rapport are essential to the order-giving, instructional process.

▶ Manner and tone, as well as sensitivity and empathy, provide a basis for employees' understanding and acceptance of orders and instructions—and even the most arbitrary commands. When employees can be helped to grasp the reasons for, and the rationality of, the directions they are expected to follow, they are likely to accept these directions more readily and to carry them out with alacrity and enthusiasm.

161

WHAT ARE THE MEANING AND SIGNIFICANCE OF THE TERM *COMMUNICATION* IN SUPERVISION?

The term **communication** is defined as the process of passing information and understanding from one person to another. As a supervisory responsibility, the process is frequently called employee communication, although the communicating process is equally important between supervisors and between supervisor and manager.

The term *communications* is more narrowly used to describe the mechanical and electronic means of transmitting and receiving information, such as newspapers, bulletin-board announcements, computer printouts, radios, telephones, and video screens. Employee communication has many of the qualities—and limitations—of these means, but it is infinitely more subtle and complex. So employee communication needs to be managed carefully.

HOW DOES COMMUNICATION ACTIVATE THE ORGANIZATION?

By providing the linking pin between plans and action. You may have a great set of plans and a fine staff, but until something begins to happen, you will have accomplished nothing. Neither motivation nor leadership can bring about action without communication. This is what starts and keeps the whole plan in motion.

WHAT IS MEANT BY THE COMMUNICATION PROCESS?

In a broad sense, it is the series of steps that enables an idea in one person's mind to be transmitted to, understood by, and acted on by another person. This process is illustrated in greater detail in Figure 9-1. Clearly, it is an essential ingredient in all human relationships. To be effective, it requires that supervisors establish rapport with employees, be sensitive to how others perceive ideas and information, and minimize the noise that can detract from the process. It also requires that supervisors have better-than-average skill in using the spoken word, the written word, and the nonverbal signals that the face and body send out to others. Last, but far from least, it demands of supervisors that they be good at receiving communications from others. That is, they must be good listeners who are receptive to feedback and questions.

▼ FIGURE 9–1
The com-
munication
process

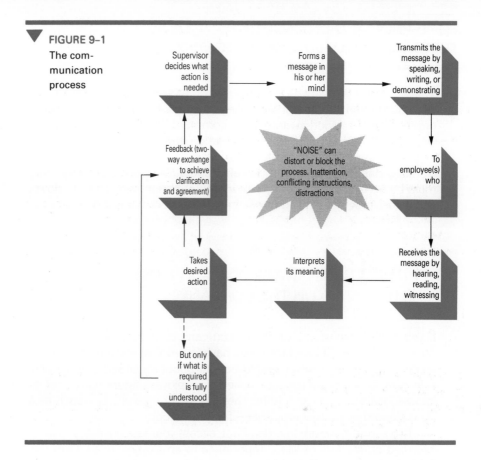

| Supervisor decides what action is needed | Forms a message in his or her mind | Transmits the message by speaking, writing, or demonstrating |

"NOISE" can distort or block the process. Inattention, conflicting instructions, distractions

Feedback (two-way exchange to achieve clarification and agreement)

To employee(s) who

Takes desired action

Interprets its meaning

Receives the message by hearing, reading, witnessing

But only if what is required is fully understood

NOISE AND FEEDBACK—WHAT ARE THEY?

These are two very important terms in the language of communication. *Noise* is any kind of distraction, physical or emotional, within an individual or in the environment that distorts or obstructs the transmission of a message—such as an order or instruction—from one individual to another. Noise is ever present and must be anticipated and coped with. This can be done by seeking a quieter place to have a conversation, for example, or by postponing a disciplinary session until either the supervisor or the employee has had time to calm down. *Feedback* is information provided by either party that serves to clarify and/or verify understanding and to indicate either agreement or dissent. Without feedback, communication is doomed to fail.

SOME PEOPLE TALK ABOUT THREE-DIMENSIONAL COMMUNICATION. WHAT ARE THEY REFERRING TO?

Communication should not be a one-way street. For a complex, modern organization to function smoothly, communication must move three ways. Not only must you furnish information downward to employees, but employees must communicate their ideas and feelings upward to you. Because staff and interdepartmental cooperation is so important, there must be horizontal, or sideways, flow of information, too. This up, down, and across process is called three-dimensional communication.

BUT WHAT SHOULD YOU DO WHEN YOU DON'T HAVE THE ANSWERS TO EVERYTHING THAT IS HAPPENING IN THE COMPANY?

If you don't know what's going on, you can't tell others or answer their questions. But you'll lose face if you have to say that you'll find out from someone else every time an employee asks about social security, the pension plan, or a leave-of-absence policy. If employees figure you're not as knowledgeable as you should be, they'll go to someone else—such as a shop steward or another employee—for information.

Two suggestions are in order. First, accept your responsibility to keep informed on matters of likely importance to employees. Read. Observe. Ask questions yourself. Anticipate what employees are interested in. Second, never bluff or pass the buck when you are caught unprepared. You may need to admit, "I don't know the answer to that one, but I'll certainly find out and let you know by tomorrow morning."

WHERE ARE THE GREATEST DANGERS IN COMMUNICATING WITH EMPLOYEES?

There are many common hazards for supervisors. Some supervisors try too hard and wind up overcommunicating. They talk too much and listen too little, or they may be indiscreet and violate confidences. You must decide what employees are interested in hearing and what level of detail they need to know.

Other supervisors get into difficulty by expressing their views on intensely personal matters such as politics, religion, and social values. And whatever you say, never make comments that have sexual overtones or use language that could create an offensive work environment. These can easily be interpreted by employees as a form of sexual harassment.

Another problem involves stepping on someone's ego. Many employees are quite sensitive and may feel threatened or hurt if you are tactless. Even a sharp tone of voice, being brusque, or using a poor choice of words may offend someone. Avoid putting people on the defensive, for it will defeat your purpose.

WHAT KINDS OF THINGS SHOULD I TELL MY BOSS?

Your success as a leader depends on how freely employees will talk to you and tell you what's bothering them. Your superior, too, needs similar information from you. Make a point of voluntarily keeping your boss informed on the following:

> *Progress toward performance goals and standards.* This covers items such as deliveries, output, and quality. If possible, warn your boss in advance about foreseeable problems, while there is still time to obtain help.

> *Matters that may cause controversy.* Arguments with other supervisors, a controversial interpretation of company policy, a discipline problem within your department—all are issues that should be brought to the attention of your superior. It's better to explain your side first and support it with the facts.

> *Attitudes and morale.* Middle and top managers are relatively isolated from direct contact with the work group. This can not only frustrate them but deprive them of needed information about how employees feel. So make a point of telling your boss regularly about both the general level of morale and employee reactions to specific issues.

WHAT KINDS OF COMMUNICATIONS ARE LIKELY TO SPEAK LOUDER THAN WORDS?

The messages transmitted by your actions. Talking and writing are the communication methods most frequently used, of course. But regardless of what you say, employees will be most affected by what you communicate to them by your actions. What you do—how you treat them—is the proof of your real intentions. Going to bat for an employee who needs help provides concrete evidence of how highly you value that person's contributions on your team.

Even on simple matters, such as training an employee to do a new job, the act of showing how to do it (demonstration) is eloquent even when no words are spoken. Similarly, going to an employee's work site to chat rather than always requesting that the employee come to your office helps project a supportive image. The best communications are generally those that combine spoken or written words with compatible actions.

BODY LANGUAGE—WHAT'S THAT?

Nonverbal body movements or facial expressions that may convey to others what is really on your mind are referred to as *body language.* These signals may be no more than a frown, a shrug of the shoulders, or a gesture with your hands. Unfortunately, they can be misinterpreted. For example:

▶ Nodding the head up and down can imply agreement with the speaker; shaking the head from side to side can be perceived as disagreement.

▶ Drumming the fingers or tapping the foot may mean "Hurry up. I'm impatient for you to get to the point."

▶ Raising the eyebrows may signal doubt, surprise, or skepticism.

▶ Rolling the eyes often expresses disbelief.

▶ Tight-lipped frowning may indicate displeasure or even disgust.

Many body movements such as these are unconscious and deeply ingrained, and they would be difficult for you to change. But try to assess whether people are reacting primarily to your words or to your body language. Observe the nonverbal signals from others; these can often provide you with solid clues to what is on another person's mind.

HOW CAN YOU BE SURE THAT AN EMPLOYEE UNDERSTANDS WHAT YOU MEAN?

A very simple device is to ask the employee to repeat back to you what you have said. That, of course, is feedback. If the person can't accurately repeat what you have said, it's a signal for you to tell your story over again.

Another way is to get the employee to ask questions. This, too, is a form of feedback. What is queried will tip you off to areas of weak understanding. Once a conversation is established on a give-and-take basis, communication is always improved.

Many words and phrases have double, or at least unclear, meanings. Avoid such words or terms when handing out assignments. Instead, add clarifying details to make your message more specific. For example:

Quality factors. Avoid words such as *good, smooth, well-done,* and *clean.* Try instead: *fewer than three rejects a day; so smooth that a dust cloth won't catch on the surface; a "well-done" steak cooked without a trace of red in it; completely free of the grease that pro-tected the part when it was shipped.*

Time factors. Avoid terms such as *quickly, as soon as possible, in a few days.* Try instead: *25 per minute; within 24 hours; by Thursday at 2 p.m.*

WHAT WILL ENCOURAGE EMPLOYEES TO COMMUNICATE WITH YOU?

Good faith, mutual confidence, appreciation for their ideas, and a friendly attitude are the foundations on which employees will build their trust and learn to talk to you. A more specific method is the development of the fine art of listening.

Real communication is a two-way process. In the long run, people won't listen to you if you won't listen to them. But listening must be more than just a mechanical process. Many employees (in fact, most people) are poor communicators. This means that you have to be an extraordinary receiver to find out what workers may be trying to say. Here are a few suggestions that may improve your listening power.

Don't Assume Anything. Don't anticipate. Don't let an employee think that you know what is going to be said.

Don't Interrupt. Let the individual have a full say. The employee who is stopped may feel that there will never be an opportunity to unload the problem. If you don't have the time to hear the employee out just then, ask that the discussion stay within a time limit. Better still, make an appoint-ment (for the same day, if at all possible) for a time when you can get the whole story.

Don't React Too Quickly. We all tend to jump to conclusions. The em-ployee may use a word that makes you see red, or may express the situa-tion badly. Be patient in trying to make sure that you are both talking about the same thing. Above all, try to understand—although not neces-sarily agree with—the other's viewpoint.

HOW CAN ACTIVE LISTENING IMPROVE YOUR COMMUNICATIONS?

A supervisor who actively listens to an employee's negative reaction to an order, for example, may hear the reason for that resistance. Usually, however, we tend to put our minds into neutral when others resist us. We engage in passive listening, hardly hearing what the other person says, and we are ready to attack again. Compare these two examples:

Passive Listening

Employee: What does the scheduling office think I am, Rose—a miracle worker? There is no way this job can be finished today.

Supervisor: That's the order, whether you like it or not. Just make sure you've finished it by 5 p.m.

Employee: I'm already behind schedule because of the press breakdown this week. Doesn't anybody understand what kind of pressure that puts on me?

Supervisor: Look, I don't make up the schedules here. It's my job to see that they get carried out. We're all under pressure this week. So, like it or not, you've got to get hopping right away so that we meet the deadline.

Employee: I'll do it, but this is the last time you're going to treat me like dirt.

Active Listening

Employee: What does the scheduling office think I am, Rose—a miracle worker? There is no way this job can be finished today.

Supervisor: Sounds like you're really angry about it, Joe.

Employee: You're darned right I am. I've been working all week to catch up after that press broke down. Now that I'm about on schedule, this lousy order comes in.

Supervisor: As if you didn't have enough to do already. Seems as if you're shoveling sand against the tide.

Employee: Yeah. It's all uphill around here. I can hardly catch a breath.

Supervisor: You feel like it's unfair to unload a rush job on you when you've been trying so hard to get back on schedule?

Employee: That's right. I'm willing to pull my share of the load, Rose, but it's discouraging to feel that you're being dumped on all the time.

Supervisor: You feel that we have been asking more than you can handle?

Employee: Not more than I can handle. I can get this job out today. But it sure puts me near my breaking point.

Supervisor: I understand how you feel. Actually, Joe, we haven't been picking on you. The whole department is in a bind this week. But I appreciate your taking on what seems like an unjustified overload.

The difference between these two examples is that the supervisor is actively listening in the second one. Joe is, in effect, saying that he is being misused. Rose is listening and responding to make it clear to Joe that she appreciates the feeling he is expressing. Active listening won't solve all communication problems, but it does provide a good base for improving clarity and understanding.

CAN LISTENING BE OVERDONE?

Listening should make up at least a third of your communication time, but it shouldn't take the place of definite actions and answers on your part.

When an employee begins to ramble too far afield in a discussion, return to the point with astute questioning. If an employee is clearly wrong on a point of fact, make this clear even if it means contradicting the individual. But watch your tone!

When conferences or group discussions turn into purposeless rap sessions, it's time for you to set talk aside and take action.

Finally, when an employee comes to you with a problem, and its solution is clear to you, give a straightforward reply. It does help, if you have the time, to permit the employee to develop a solution. But when you have been approached because of your knowledge and experience, chances are a direct answer is wanted, not a session of hand holding.

IS ANY ONE METHOD OF COMMUNICATION BETTER THAN ANOTHER?

Each situation has its own best method or combination of methods. Some problems are urgent and demand an immediate response (an informal talk, telephone call, or handwritten memo). Some employees believe only what you put down on paper, so time spent communicating face to face with them is virtually wasted. If the same message must be conveyed to a large number of people, a memo or a mass meeting is best. So it seems that the most successful communicating is done by supervisors who (1) quickly analyze the situation they are encountering and (2) know and use many ways of getting their ideas, instructions, and feelings across to others.

SHOULD A SUPERVISOR USE THE COMPANY GRAPEVINE AS A MEANS OF COMMUNICATION?

Listen to it, for it's one way of getting clues about what's going on. But don't depend on it to provide totally accurate information. And don't make a deliberate practice of leaking information to the work group through the grapevine, for employees will then rely even less on your formal communication methods.

The grapevine gets its most active usage in the absence of good communication about company rules, employee benefits, opportunities for advancement, and performance feedback. If you don't tell employees—promptly—about the things that interest or affect them, the grapevine will quickly emerge. However, much of the grapevine information will be based on incomplete data, partial truths, and outright lies. And surveys show that even though employees receive a lot of information from the rumor mill and enjoy participating in it, they'd much rather get the real story from a responsible party—their supervisor. You can prevent a lot of emotional upsets among your employees, and build a lot of goodwill, by spiking rumors as soon as they appear. So show employees you welcome the chance to tell the truth.

HOW CAN PERSON-TO-PERSON COMMUNICATIONS BE CONDUCTED EFFECTIVELY?

The maximum of "custom tailoring" for the individual is not only feasible but definitely in order. It becomes increasingly so as the relationship accumulates a common background. This is because an individual who is addressed singly, but like anyone else, is usually resentful in proportion to the degree of previously assumed familiarity.

Spoken. In spoken communication the immediate situation is shared, and the person addressed is aware of the conditions under which the communication takes place. Therefore, haste, tone, mood, gestures, or facial expressions may seriously affect the way the person reacts.

1. *Informal talks.* Still the most fundamental form of communication. They are suitable for day-to-day liaisons, directions, exchanges of information, conferences, reviews, discipline, checking up, and maintenance of effective personal relations.

2. *Planned appointments.* Appropriate for regular reviews or liaisons, recurring joint work sessions, and so forth. The parties should be adequately prepared to make such meetings complete and effective by

being up to date, by providing adequate data and information, and by limiting interruptions to the fewest possible.

3. *Telephone calls.* For quick checkups or for imparting or receiving information, instructions, or data.

Written. All messages intended to be formal, official, or long-term, or that affect several persons in a related way, should be written. Be sure that you use only a written communication to amend any previous written communication. Oral changes will be forgotten or recalled indifferently.

4. *Interoffice memos.* For recording informal inquiries or replies. They can be of value, too, if several people are to receive a message that is extensive, or when data are numerous or complex. The use of memos should not be overdone, or they will be ignored.

5. *Letters.* More individualized in effect than a memo and usually more formal. They are useful for official notices, formally recorded statements, or lengthy communications, even when the addressee is physically accessible.

6. *Reports.* More impersonal than a letter and usually more formal. Reports are used to convey information associated with evaluation, analysis, or recommendations to superiors or colleagues.

HOW CAN YOU COMMUNICATE MOST EFFECTIVELY WITH GROUPS OF EMPLOYEES?

Groups that are uniform in status, age, sex, compensation level, occupation, and length of service provide a valid basis for highly pointed messages. This approach helps avoid the gradually numbing stream of form letters, memos, and announcements that really have meaning for only a few of the recipients.

Spoken. Effective spoken communication with groups calls for special skills. For instance, those who are effective in a committee of equals may be inadequate in a mass meeting. Having the ability to conduct a conference of your own staff doesn't mean you will have equal ability to participate effectively as a staff member in a conference called by your superior.

1. *Informal staff meetings.* These provide an opportunity for development of strong group cohesiveness and response. Properly supplemented with individual face-to-face contacts, such meetings offer outstanding means of coordinating activities and building mutual understanding.

2. ***Planned conferences.*** Relatively formal affairs. The commonest error is for the person calling the conference to set up the agenda without previous consultation with those who will attend. It is usually desirable to check with most of the prospective participants in advance; provide time for preparing and assembling needed data, information, reports, and recommendations; and allow opportunity for suggestions as to agenda and conduct of the meeting.

3. ***Mass meetings.*** Of large numbers of employees or management. These meetings can be a valuable means of celebrating occasions, building morale, changing attitudes, meeting emergencies, introducing new policies or key personnel, or making special announcements.

Written. The effect of a single, isolated written communication to a group of employees is generally unpredictable. But a carefully planned program of written communications can develop a desirable cumulative effect.

4. ***Bulletin board notices.*** For lengthy or formal announcements. These notices can be used for a series of illustrated messages and are most effective when readership is constantly attracted by changes and by careful control of content, including prompt removal of out-of-date material. Most bulletin board announcements should be supplemented by other forms.

5. ***Posters.*** Small or large, at suitable locations, used in series, and changed frequently, posters can do much to supplement your other communications media.

6. ***Exhibits and displays.*** Can serve a useful purpose when appropriate space is available and when they can be properly prepared.

7. ***Visual aids.*** Films, videos, easel presentations, audio cassettes, and other special visual materials have great potential value but are only as good as the way they are used. Few are self-administering. A good video will be far more effective, for instance, if presented with a soundly planned introduction and follow-up.

HOW ARE ORDERS AND INSTRUCTIONS LINKED TO THE COMMUNICATION PROCESS?

Orders and instructions are the most direct, authority-based kinds of communications. Although it is desirable for employees to agree with your rationale for an order, it is absolutely imperative that employees *understand* what must be done and do it. So, as their supervisor, you have a double responsibility: (1) to make sure that employees know what to do and (2) to make sure that they do it properly. A sound understanding and application of the communication process will help you meet both these responsibilities.

HOW CAN YOU GET BETTER RESULTS FROM THE INSTRUCTIONS AND ORDERS YOU ISSUE?

By being sure your order is the right one for the particular situation at hand and by being specific about what the employee is to do and what kind of results you expect.

Your orders are even more effective when you use care in selecting the person most likely to carry them out well. You add power to your orders by being confident (not arrogant) and calm as you deliver them. Finally, your orders will stand the best chance of accomplishing what you intend if you make a practice of checking to be sure they are carried out at the time and in the manner you prescribe.

SHOULD YOU REPEAT AN ORDER?

Yes, by all means. Repeat your instructions to be certain the employee understands them clearly. All of us are experts at misunderstanding. So give a worker an opportunity to ask questions if there seems to be doubt about what you want. In fact, it's a good practice to ask the employee to repeat your instructions back to you. In this way you can readily find out where the stumbling blocks might be.

WHEN SHOULD YOU ASK—RATHER THAN ORDER—AN EMPLOYEE TO DO SOMETHING?

As often as possible. Many of today's employees resent being in positions where they must take orders. They want and deserve more consideration. Psychologists who study employee behavior report that most workers will rate a boss highly and will cooperate more willingly as a result if the boss phrases orders as requests. We know, too, that employees like to feel they have some say in decisions that affect them. Often they will work harder and be more committed when they have had a chance to participate in decision making.

So there's nothing wrong (and there's much good) in saying, "Will you try to get that machine cleaned up before quitting time?" or "Won't you please hold your coffee break time down to fifteen minutes?" Such requests give workers the feeling that they have some freedom of action, and this autonomy is a source of job satisfaction for them. In addition, the use of requests instead of orders will make you seem less like a dictator.

WHEN SHOULD YOU "COMMAND" AN EMPLOYEE TO DO SOMETHING?

Although commands are dangerous, they may be necessary in emergencies. In case of accident or fire, for instance, your instructions should be direct, clear, and unequivocal to avoid conflicting actions.

Orders should be specific and firm, too, in operating situations that demand active leadership. It's desirable to be especially decisive, for instance, in directing a crew that requires rapid coordination on an unfamiliar job—such as supervising workers who are lowering a 100-ton machine onto its foundations, or starting up a new and complex machine.

But, in general, commands cause resentment. It's best to avoid them until you need them. If you use commands only occasionally, your employees will know that you're not being bossy for the sake of showing your authority. They will recognize that your change in approach is necessary and will snap to accordingly.

WHAT SHOULD YOU DO WHEN AN EMPLOYEE WILLFULLY REFUSES TO DO WHAT YOU ASK?

The first piece of advice and the toughest to follow is don't fly off the handle. Review the order's fairness, the selection of the person to carry it out, and the probability that you were understood. If you think you've done your part, find out what the employee objects to. Ask for specifics: "What is it you object to? Why do you think it's unreasonable?" Chances are, a nonthreatening exploration of the situation will let both of you cool down and help you clarify the real problem. Perhaps you can even modify the order so that it will be accepted.

But if the employee continues to resist a reasonable request, you're faced with a disciplinary problem. Find a private place where you can talk calmly but firmly. Let it be known that you will take disciplinary steps if the problem isn't resolved. But try to avoid a showdown situation in which one (or both) of you will wind up losing.

WHEN SHOULD YOU PUT AN ORDER IN WRITING?

Whenever you change an order that was previously in writing, put the new order in writing, too. Or if you give an order that must be carried over into another shift, it's wise to jot it down in writing—on the bulletin board, in the department logbook, or as a note to be passed on to the employees concerned. This is much more reliable than word of mouth.

When instructions are complex and contain variations from normal in amounts and sequence, it's wise to write them down, too. On the other hand, don't depend too much on written orders. Not everyone follows written instructions easily. In fact, if you do write down instructions, look for an opportunity to review them orally with employees to see if they understand them. The written orders thus serve as a reference.

HOW IS YOUR TONE OF VOICE IMPORTANT?

Remember the story of the cowboy who said, "When you call me that, smile"? Employees feel the same way. They can read your voice like a book and can tell if you're trying to throw your weight around, if you mean what you say, or if you're just talking through your hat. When you give an order, for example, that you know is going to be hard to carry out, smile to indicate that you know that what you ask isn't easy; but let the tone of your voice show that you expect it to be done, regardless.

WHAT GUIDELINES ARE THERE FOR AVOIDING PROBLEMS WHEN ISSUING ORDERS, MAKING ASSIGNMENTS, OR GIVING INSTRUCTIONS?

There can be no guarantees that employees won't balk about a particular assignment or set of instructions. Nevertheless, there are ten solid guidelines that will help you minimize problems:

1. *Don't make it a struggle for power.* If you typically project an I'll-show-you-who's-boss image, you'll soon be fighting the whole department. Try to focus your attention—and the worker's—on the goal that must be met. The idea to project is that it is the *situation* that demands the order, not a personal whim of the supervisor.

2. *Avoid an offhand manner.* If you want employees to take instructions seriously, then deliver them that way. It's all right to have fun occasionally, but be clear and firm about those matters that are important.

3. *Watch out for your words.* Most employees accept the fact that the supervisor's job is to hand out orders and instructions. Their quarrel is more likely to be with the way these are given. Therefore, select words that will clearly convey your thoughts, and watch your tone of voice.

4. ***Don't assume that the worker understands.*** Encourage the employee to ask questions and to identify problems. Have the employee confirm understanding by repeating or demonstrating what you've said.

5. ***Seek feedback right away.*** Give the employee who wishes to complain about the assignment a chance to do so at the time. It's better to discover resistance and misunderstandings while there is still time to iron them out.

6. ***Don't give too many orders.*** Communication overload will be self-defeating, so be selective in issuing instructions. Keep them brief and to the point. If you can, wait until an employee has finished one job before assigning another one.

7. ***Provide just enough detail.***   Jobs differ in the complexity of information required to do them well, and workers differ in their needs for detail, too. Old hands get bored listening to unneeded information; new employees may be hungry for supporting details.

8. ***Watch out for conflicting instructions.*** Check to make sure you're not telling your employees one thing while supervisors in adjoining departments are telling their people another. Also, be consistent from day to day and from employee to employee in the directions you provide.

9. ***Don't choose only the willing worker.*** Some people are naturally cooperative. Others make it difficult every time you ask them to do anything. Be sure you don't overwork the willing person and neglect the hard-to-handle people just to avoid confrontations.

10. ***Try not to pick on anyone.*** It is tempting to punish problem employees by handing them the unpleasant assignments. Resist this if you can. Employees have the right to expect the work to be distributed fairly, even if you have a grudge against one of them.

REVIEW ▼9 QUESTIONS

1. What is meant by "noise" and why is its presence in the communication process so undesirable?
2. Discuss the shortcomings of the grapevine.
3. How can the credibility gap be narrowed between a supervisor and his or her employees?
4. Is it possible for a supervisor to overcommunicate? If so, what's the harm?
5. Why shouldn't a supervisor who is quick to grasp the gist of an employee's query or complaint cut off the conversation right away to give an answer or a decision?
6. Why is the ability to listen actively so valuable to a supervisor?
7. Contrast a direct order and a request.
8. Under what circumstances might a supervisor be advised to command an employee to carry out an order?

A CASE IN POINT

Delay at the Airport

When it rains or snows, duty at the SkyWay Airlines passenger registration counter can be just as unpleasant as the weather. Claire, a passenger agent, had come on duty at 6 a.m. on just such a day. Now, after having dealt with long lines of delayed, irritated, and sometimes abusive passengers, Claire sighed with relief when she was about to come off her shift. As she was preparing to sign over her terminal position to her replacement, however, Claire was confronted by a visibly agitated passenger. The passenger's noontime flight had been canceled and rescheduled for later that evening. Upon receiving this information, the passenger's complaints were loud and strong. A later flight would not be satisfactory, because it would bring him to his destination too late to be of use that day. Furthermore, the passenger declared, if he could not get an earlier flight, he expected the airline to provide him with vouchers for overnight hotel accommodations.

Claire could find no way to book the passenger on an earlier flight. She reported this to the passenger. She also explained that because the cancellation was due to weather, the airline would not provide the vouchers the passenger requested. This, too, was unsatisfactory, and the passenger demanded to see Claire's supervisor. Claire told the passenger that this was impossible, but she would check with her supervisor by telephone.

When Claire telephoned Ms. Jackson, her supervisor, Ms. Jackson asked, "How insistent is this passenger?"

Claire replied, "No more than anyone else has been today."

Ms. Jackson then gave Claire this advice: "Try to cool him off. If he persists, however, check page 27 of the SkyWay Passenger Agent Manual to see what exception might be made under the circumstances. If there's any problem, I suggest that you get back in touch with me."

Claire looked up page 27 in the manual. In her opinion, the relevant sentence read: "If a flight has been delayed or canceled by weather and a passenger can be scheduled to the same destination later on the same date, no accommodations or meal vouchers will ordinarily be provided." Except for the word "ordinarily," the statement seemed clear and unequivocal to Claire. Accordingly, Claire advised the passenger that he could accept booking on the later flight or wait until the next morning, but in neither case would vouchers for accommodations or meals be forthcoming.

The matter did not end there. The passenger fumed at this reply and ultimately wrote a letter of complaint to the president of the airline. When the complaint came down through channels and finally reached Ms. Jackson, she called Claire into her office. After Claire explained her decision, Ms. Jackson said, "If there was any question in your mind, why didn't you check back with me as I suggested? Also, you should have recalled that at a recent meeting of passenger agents, I mentioned that the instructions on page 27 of the manual— and especially the term "ordinarily"—had been interpreted to mean that in cases judged to be extreme by the passenger agent, she could exercise discretion in deciding whether or not to issue vouchers. I think the situation *was* extreme. If you had listened to my advice in the first place, or followed the instructions in the manual, we could have avoided this problem."

Claire retorted, "*I* think the problem could have been avoided if *you* had made yourself clear to me in the first place!"

How could Ms. Jackson have made herself more clear? Five alternative courses of action are listed below. Rank them in the order in which they appeal to you (1 most effective, 5 least effective). You may add another approach in the space provided, if you wish. In any event, be prepared to justify your ranking.

_____ **A.** Come to Claire's terminal position immediately and shown her in person how to handle a difficult situation.

_____ **B.** When speaking to Claire on the telephone, requested— rather than suggested—that she call back before giving the passenger her decision.

_____ **C.** Provided beforehand, orally and in writing, several examples of when the instructions on page 27 of the manual might allow for discretion on the part of the agent.

_____ **D.** Made a written notation on page 27 of the manual as to the interpretation of the word "ordinarily."

_____ **E.** Placed a notice on the agents' bulletin board regarding care in interpreting the word "ordinarily" on page 27 of the manual.

If you have another approach, write it here.

▶ _____

_____

_____

Complete the ACTION PLANNING CHECKLIST
for this chapter, which can be found on page 319.

10

PROVIDING LEADERSHIP TO BUILD EFFECTIVE TEAMS

LEARNING OBJECTIVES

After studying this chapter, you should be able to:

1. Describe and evaluate the essential skills of leadership.

2. Explain the relationships between leadership and motivation and differentiate between the assumptions of Theory X and Theory Y.

3. Recognize various leadership styles, explain the contingency model of leadership, and identify the two concerns of the Managerial Grid©.

4. Discuss the factors a leader should consider when choosing a leadership style and explain the continuum of leadership styles.

5. Discuss the influences of employee expectations and a supervisor's personality on a leader's effectiveness and popularity.

▶ Leadership requires the ability to develop rapport with others and to apply appropriate persuasion and influence so as to obtain the willing cooperation of others in pursuing legitimate organizational goals. Given sound character in the supervisor, the skills of leadership can be acquired and developed.

▶ Leadership relies on gaining a firm understanding of another person's motives and providing conditions in the workplace that enable that person to satisfy his or her needs while also helping the organization to attain its goals. Assumptions about the needs of others are simplified by applying Theory X and Theory Y analysis.

▶ Styles of leadership range from autocratic approaches (which are forceful and demanding), through democratic and consultative approaches, to free-rein or participative approaches (which encourage employee responsibility and initiative.) Further refinements include the results-centered approach, the contingency approach, and the Managerial Grid©, which classifies leadership by rating it on two scales: a concern for people and a concern for production.

▶ A leadership approach can be selected from a continuum of styles that range from strictly autocratic to purely participative. The best choice of style is one that most nearly matches the personality of the individuals involved and the circumstances of the situation.

▶ The success of leadership depends less on technique than on the creation of an enthusiastic attachment and deep-seated trust between supervisor and subordinate.

181

IS LEADERSHIP THE SAME AS MANAGEMENT?

Not exactly. Leadership is only one of the many functions a manager must perform for the work force. In addition, a manager must plan, organize, communicate, and exercise control. Nevertheless, leadership is a basic requirement of all managers. It is especially important at the supervisory level, where the majority of personal contacts are made between managers and employees.

HOW IS LEADERSHIP DEFINED?

Everyone will give you a different answer to this one. Our definition is this: **Leadership** is the knack of getting other people to follow you and to do willingly the things that you want them to do. It should go without saying that these things should be legitimate. They should represent actions that will advance your department toward its goals of higher productivity, improved quality of product or service, and conservation of resources.

WHAT PERSONAL SKILLS DOES LEADERSHIP REQUIRE?

Here again, answers will differ. Most people will agree, however, that good leaders have mastered the following skills:

Persuasion. Some would call this sales ability. It is the ability to assemble and present to others a good case for what you think should be done. Persuasive talent alone will not make you a leader.

Influence. This is the ability to exert power over others. Many people possess or are given power, but few learn how to use it. Supervisors, for example, have the power and authority of their positions. They have the power of greater knowledge of departmental and company operations than is possessed by their employees. They also have the power that comes from the prestige that is commonly associated with their work. None of this, however, will make you a leader until you learn to use this power to move others.

Rapport. In this sense, rapport is the art of creating among others a willingness to cooperate. It has a great deal to do with what behavioral scientists call "interpersonal skills." It requires a deep understanding of motivation and the ability to perceive the needs of others. Leaders first establish rapport; then they use their powers of influence and persuasion to activate individuals and groups in the pursuit of worth-while goals.

ARE GOOD LEADERS BORN OR MADE?

Very few are born leaders. Most leaders learn their skills. They do so mainly through hard work and careful study of their employees and the situations in which they do their jobs.

HOW ARE MOTIVATION AND LEADERSHIP RELATED?

Motivation is a power that arises within an individual to satisfy a need. As you've seen earlier in discussions about Maslow's and Herzberg's views of motivation, needs cover a broad span, from the needs for survival and safety to the needs for self-esteem and fulfillment, and from the need for achievement to the needs for affiliation and power. Leaders, as shown in Figure 10-1, act to provide satisfaction—or to offer a means of satisfaction—for the needs of others. Leaders don't really motivate. A leader succeeds by first understanding the needs of others and then applying persuasion and influence to show others that they will get the most satisfaction from following the leader's views.

A person can have motivation without another person's leadership. Leadership, however, cannot succeed without motivation on the follower's part. Take Mary, for example. She has a powerful need to show that she can perform a higher-level job. This may be a strong-enough motivation for her to attend night courses to acquire the necessary knowledge and skills. She will do this with or without the encouragement of her supervisor. On the other hand, there is Peter. He has the same aptitudes as Mary. With additional training, he, too, could perform a higher-level job. Peter's supervisor sees this aptitude and offers Peter all sorts of encouragement and assistance in acquiring the necessary skills. Peter, however, is content to stay where he is. His social needs are very strong. He wants to enjoy working with the people he's become friendly with. Enrolled in a night course at the supervisor's suggestion, he soon drops out. The leadership failed, despite the supervisor's influence and persuasion, because the supervisor was not properly tuned to Peter's motivational needs.

Turn Peter's situation around a little bit and look at it again. Suppose Peter is such a fun-lover that his work suffers. His boss tells him that if his performance doesn't improve, he'll lose his job. Peter's reaction is: "So what! I can get another job." At this point the supervisor uses the knowl-

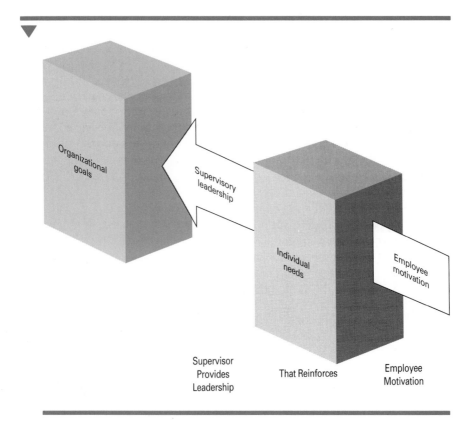

FIGURE 10-1 **How leadership and motivation are related**

edge of Peter's social needs to persuade him that he'll enjoy working with his friends at his current job more than he might enjoy working with strangers at some other job. Peter accepts this advice and gets his act together so that he can hold his present job. The leadership provided by Peter's supervisor has succeeded. The supervisor established rapport and was tuned to Peter's motivational needs. She used the power of her position to influence Peter's judgment about the consequences of his performance. And then she persuaded Peter that it was in his best interests to improve the quality of his work.

THEORY X, THEORY Y. WHAT'S THIS ALL ABOUT?

To get along with people effectively, you must make a couple of fundamental decisions. First you must recognize your responsibility for managing human affairs at work. But you must always weigh this concern of yours against the practical urgencies of technical and administrative matters.

Douglas McGregor, late professor of industrial management at the Massachusetts Institute of Technology, had much to offer supervisors in his thoughtful work *The Human Side of Enterprise.* Most of today's management thinking was forged to meet the needs of a feudal society, reasoned McGregor. The world has changed, and new thinking is needed for top efficiency today. That's the core of this unique philosophy of pitting Theory X against Theory Y.

Theory X, the traditional framework for management thinking, is based on the following set of assumptions about human nature and human behavior:

1. The average human being has an inherent dislike of work and will avoid it if possible.

2. Because of this human characteristic of dislike of work, most people must be coerced, controlled, directed, or threatened with punishment to get them to put forth adequate effort toward the achievement of organizational objectives.

3. The average human being prefers to be directed, wishes to avoid responsibility, has relatively little ambition, and wants security above all.

Do these assumptions make up a straw person for purposes of scientific demolition? Unfortunately, they do not. Although they are rarely stated so directly, the principles that constitute the bulk of traditional management action could have been derived only from assumptions such as those of Theory X.

Theory Y finds its roots in recently accumulated knowledge about human behavior. It is based on the following set of assumptions:

1. The expenditure of physical and mental effort in work is as natural as play or rest.

2. External control and the threat of punishment are not the only means for bringing about effort toward organizational objectives. Individuals will exercise self-control in the service of objectives to which they are committed.

3. Commitment to objectives depends on the rewards associated with their achievement. The most important rewards are those that satisfy needs for self-respect and personal improvement.

4. The average human being learns, under proper conditions, not only to accept but also to seek responsibility.

5. The capacity to exercise a relatively high degree of imagination, ingenuity, and creativity in the solution of organizational problems is

widely, not narrowly, distributed in the population among both men and women.

6.   Under the conditions of modern industrial life, the intellectual potentialities of the average human being are only partially realized.

WHAT MAKES THEORY Y SO APPLICABLE TODAY?

Under the assumptions of Theory Y, the work of the supervisor is to integrate the needs of employees with the needs of the department. Hard-nosed control rarely works out today. Here are McGregor's words:

[Supervisors] are dealing with adults who are only partially dependent. They can—and will—exercise remarkable ingenuity in defeating the purpose of external controls that they resent. However, they can—and do—learn to exercise self-direction and self-control under appropriate conditions. . . . [The supervisor's] task is to help them discover objectives consistent both with organizational requirements and with their own personal goals.

In McGregor's mind, the ability to help employees discover goals consistent with those of the organization is the essence of leadership. When a genuine commitment to these objectives is secured, said McGregor, "supervision consists of helping employees achieve these objectives: to act as teacher, consultant, colleague, and only rarely as authoritative boss."

You can see that Theory Y and the style of leadership it implies are far more in tune with today's employees than are Theory X and its autocratic style of leadership. For you, the important variable will be your own assumptions about the motivation of the people you will supervise. If your assumptions are along the lines of Theory X, you will lean toward styles of leadership that differ from those you would use if your beliefs followed Theory Y. If your assumptions are correct about the motivations of others, then your leadership problems should be minor. But if your assumptions are wrong, your leadership is likely to be weak and ineffective.

WHAT IS MEANT BY "STYLES" OF LEADERSHIP, AND WHICH ARE THE MOST BASIC?

A *style of leadership* refers to the kind of approach a supervisor uses in trying to direct, activate, stimulate, or otherwise provide a motivational atmosphere for employees. The most traditional styles of leadership are these:

Autocratic, or directive, leadership. Many people think that this style is old-fashioned, but it often works. The leader makes the decisions and demands obedience from the people supervised. The trouble with this "tell-and-sell" approach is that the supervisor better be right in what is demanded. This style reflects, of course, the assumptions of Theory X.

Democratic, or consultative, leadership. This style continues to be a popular approach. The leader discusses options with, consults with, and draws ideas from the people supervised before making decisions. This promotes involvement and strong teamwork. Some critics, however, say that it leads to less than optimum compromises. In many ways, the consultative style is similar to what the Japanese call "consensus" management.

Free-rein, or participative, leadership. This style is the most difficult approach for a supervisor. The leader acts as information center and exercises minimum control, depending on the employee's sense of responsibility and good judgment to get things done. Advocates of this approach describe it as "integrative" leadership. Obviously, this style is in harmony with the assumptions of Theory Y. There are serious dangers, however, in using participative leadership: only mature individuals respond to it well, and there is always the risk that you will lose control of your operations. For another perspective, see the discussion of participation and its risk to authority on pages 155 to 156 and in Figure 8-3.

ARE THE TRADITIONAL STYLES
THE ONLY WAYS TO LEAD?

Not at all. Two somewhat related approaches have become popular in recent years.

Results-centered leadership is akin to the "work itself" approach to motivation described on pages 150 and 151 in Chapter 8 or to what you have read about management by objectives on page 75 in Chapter 4. Using this technique, the supervisor tries to focus on the job to be done and to minimize the personalities involved. In effect, the supervisor says to the employee: "This is the goal the organization expects you to reach each day. Now let's work together to see how your job can be set up so that you can make your quota."

Contingency, or *situational, leadership* maintains that leaders will be successful in a particular situation only if three factors are in balance. This approach, advanced by Professor Fred Fiedler and documented in many studies, asks the leader to examine (1) the extent of rapport or good feelings between the supervisor and those supervised, (2) the nature of the job to be done, in terms of how carefully procedures and specifications must be followed, and (3) the amount of real power invested in the supervisor by his or her superiors.

WHAT IS THE PARTICULAR SIGNIFICANCE OF THE CONTINGENCY APPROACH?

It adds an important consideration when a supervisor is choosing a leadership style. As the term *contingency* implies, the style chosen depends on the conditions of Fiedler's three factors in any given situation. Surprisingly, the autocratic, or authoritative, approach, which uses forceful directing and controlling, is most effective in either very favorable or very unfavorable circumstances. That is, it works best when relationships are either very good or very poor, job methods are either precisely defined or not defined at all, and the leader's true authority is either very strong or very weak. In the less clearly defined, or middle, situations, the participative approach is more likely to be successful.

In other words, an *authoritative style* works out best (1) in situations where the supervisor has lots of real power, the process requires strong control, and rapport with employees is good and (2) in situations where exactly the opposite conditions prevail.

A *participative style* is best where the supervisor's authority hasn't been clearly spelled out by top management or acknowledged by the employees, where the process and procedures are somewhat flexible, and where the rapport between supervisor and employees is only middling good.

The contingency approach tends to explain why dictatorial supervisors can be effective in some situations and not in others. Similarly, it helps to show where participative leadership may work best and to suggest where it might fail. An authoritative approach looks good for assembly-line workers or for labor crews cleaning up the area. A participative approach seems favorable on jobs for which exact procedures are hard to set or for jobs that require creativity or initiative. These conclusions are contingent on the authoritative leader's having either high or low position power and high or low rapport and on the participative leader's having moderate rapport and only so-so authority.

WHERE DOES THE MANAGERIAL GRID© FIT IN?

The *Managerial Grid©* helps supervisors assess their leadership approaches. The Grid, devised by industrial psychologists Robert R. Blake and Jane S. Mouton, makes two measurements of a leader's approach: concern for production and concern for people. As shown in Figure 10-2 (which is a special revision for supervisory management), these two factors are typically plotted on a grid chart. The least concern for each factor is rated 1, the highest 9. To judge your own approach, first rate yourself according to your concern for people; say you think it is fairly high—a 6 score. Next rate your emphasis on production or job results; say you rate that as medium—a score of 5. You then find your place on the Managerial

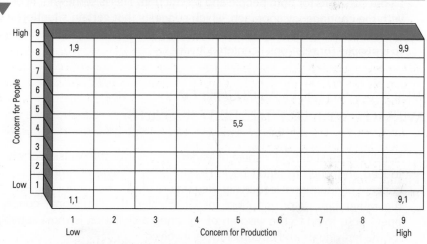

1,9   **Comfortable and Pleasant.** Attempts are made to promote harmony and goodwill. Issues which may cause disruption are smoothed over with the hope that things will continue to go well in the work situation.

9,9   **Quality Achievement.** People work together to get high-quality results and are willing to measure their accomplishments against the highest possible standard. All involved support and hold one another accountable for actions influencing the result.

5,5   **Accommodation and Compromise.** With this go-along-to-get-along, "don't-rock-the-boat" approach, progress may be made, but only within the company's rules and regulations.

1,1   **Do-Nothing Neutrality.** An approach associated with low concern, "passing the buck," and skillfully camouflaged "doing little or nothing."

9,1   **Produce or Perish.** Results may be achieved for a short time. Used over the long term, it motivates people to "beat the system" or, at the very least, decreases their willingness to contribute.

FIGURE 10-2 **The supervisory grid**

(From Robert R. Blake and Jane S. Mouton, *The Grid for Supervisory Effectiveness*, Scientific Methods, Inc., Austin, TX, 1975, p. 5. With permission of the copyright holders.)

Grid© by putting a mark on the chart six squares up and five squares across.

Blake, Mouton, and others have given nicknames to various places on the grid. The lower left-hand corner (1,1) could be called the cream puff, a supervisor who doesn't push for anything. The upper left-hand corner (1 for production, 9 for people) can be called the do-gooder, a person who watches out for people at the cost of overlooking production needs entirely. The lower right-hand corner (9 for production, 1 for people) is the hard-nose, a supervisor for whom production is all that counts. The supervisor near the middle of the chart (5 for both production and people) is the middle-of-the-roader, a person who makes a reasonable push for both concerns. In the eyes of many, all supervisors should strive to make their leadership performance score 9, 9 (highest for both production and people) so that they might be called professionals.

The Grid implies the need for leadership that is fully balanced between all-out concerns for both people and production. This is somewhat at odds with the contingency approach, which suggests that certain situations respond best to a task- (or production-) centered leader and other situations to a people- (or relations-) centered leader.

WHICH STYLE OF LEADERSHIP, ON AVERAGE, WILL GET THE BEST RESULTS?

Surely the most difficult aspect of leadership involves the decision of when to lead and when to stand back. Herein lies the value of employing the concept of situational leadership. Regardless of whether or not you accept the rather narrow prescriptions of Dr. Fiedler, the situational concept opens your mind to the wisdom of selecting a style that is most suitable for the individuals and circumstances involved.

Many successful managers will tell you that democratic leadership is the best method to use. The fact is, however, that whereas the democratic way may involve the least risk, you'll hamper your leadership role if you stick only to this method. You can play a round of golf with a driver, but you'll get a much better score if you use a wedge in a sand trap and a putter on the greens.

Suppose you have a need to cut down scrap in your department. You may find it wise to consult with all your workers in a group meeting to let them decide how they'll approach the problem (democratic leadership). Then let the inspector, when informed of the plan, adjust inspection techniques accordingly (free-rein). Then tell the scrap collector how you want the waste sorted (autocratic). You see, this way you'll be using all three styles of leadership to deal with the same problem.

A good way to consider such choices is to think of leadership as ranging along a *continuum* of styles, as shown in Figure 10-3. At one extreme,

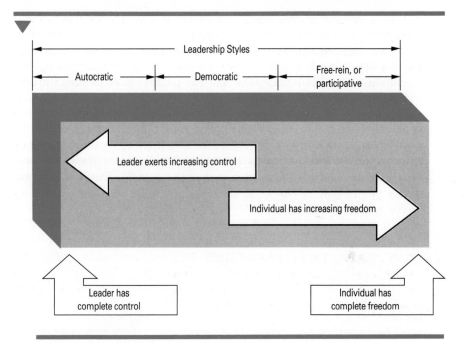

FIGURE 10-3 **Continuum of leadership styles**

(Adapted from Robert Tannebaum and Warren H. Schmidt, "How to Choose a Leadership Pattern," *Harvard Business Review,* March-April 1958, pp. 95-101.)

a supervisor relies on complete authority; at the other, subordinates are allowed a great deal of freedom. Between the extremes are an infinite number of shadings of leadership styles to choose from.

WHAT KIND OF LEADERSHIP WORKS BEST IN AN EMERGENCY?

Autocratic leadership is fast. When an emergency arises—say a live-steam hose breaks loose and whips about, endangering lives—you wouldn't want to pussyfoot around consulting employees as to what to do. You'll probably shout, "Hey, Smitty, cut the steam valve! Carl, watch the safety!"

MUST A PEOPLE-CENTERED LEADER ALWAYS GET PARTICIPATION?

No. If you plan your big targets by first asking for and considering the opinions of your employees, they'll understand that there isn't time to handle every decision in this way. Participation is a long-range affair. If you show that you want and respect employees' opinions—and that your decisions are affected by these opinions—you'll have achieved the goal of making employees feel they are part of a team. An occasional oversight or an infrequent decision made without their counsel won't destroy the feeling that generates cooperation.

By sowing the seeds of participation generously, you'll also find that you won't have to take over many of the minor decisions that otherwise would occupy your attention. Employees who know from experience that their opinions are desired know in advance how the team (their team and yours) would act if it had a chance to go into a huddle. They'll act accordingly.

HOW MUCH DOES A SUPERVISOR'S PERSONALITY HAVE TO DO WITH LEADERSHIP?

A good personality helps. Employees may react more easily to a supervisor who has a ready smile and who is warm and outgoing. But personality must be more than skin-deep to be effective. Much more important is your real desire to understand and sympathize with the people who work for you. Fair play, interest in others, good decisions, and character will help make you a stronger leader than you would be if you relied solely on personality.

Likewise, one kind of leadership may fit your personality better than the other two do. And you may rely more on this kind of leadership than on the others. But work hard to keep from depending on just one approach.

WHAT DO EMPLOYEE PERSONALITIES HAVE TO DO WITH THE KIND OF LEADERSHIP YOU EXERCISE?

Noted author Auren Uris advises that you'll find the following connections between leadership methods and types of personality:

Aggressive, hostile persons do better under autocratic leaders. Their latent hostility must be firmly channeled to confine their work to constructive ends.

Aggressive, cooperative persons work better under democratic or free-rein leadership. Their self-assertiveness takes constructive paths, and they will head in the right direction when on their own.

Insecure persons, who tend to depend on their superiors, do better under the firmer hand of the autocratic leader.

Individualists, or solo players, are usually most productive under free-rein leadership—if they know the job well.

Uris calls this point of view "followership." It is based on the well-established fact that certain kinds of persons naturally follow certain kinds of leaders better than others. The trick is to match them when you can.

HOW DO LEADERS WIN LOYALTY FROM THEIR FOLLOWERS?

You win loyalty be being loyal to your employees—by supporting their best interests and defending their actions to others who would discredit them. "We may not have made a good showing this month," a supervisor who is loyal to the group will say, "but no one can say the staff wasn't in there trying."

Loyalty is also inspired when you show employees your own loyalty to your superiors. For instance, if you have to pass along an order from your superior, you will breed only contempt among your subordinates if you say, "Here's the new operating instruction from the central office. I don't think any more of it than you do. But it was sent down from the top, so we'll have to try to make sense out of it, even if they don't know what they're doing."

WHAT ARE SOME OF THE PERSONAL QUALITIES EMPLOYEES LIKE TO SEE IN THEIR LEADERS?

Although our leaders don't always measure up to our expectations, there are a number of characteristics that most of us respond to. The following qualities not only are desirable but also tend to provide the foundation for leadership effectiveness:

Sense of mission. This is a belief in your own ability to lead, a love for the work of leadership itself, and a devotion to the people and the organization you serve.

Self-denial. This essential of leadership is too often played down. It means a willingness to forgo self-indulgences (such as losing your temper) and the ability to bear the headaches the job entails.

High character. Few persons become successful leaders who aren't honest with themselves and with others, who can't face hard facts and unpleasant situations with courage, who fear criticism or their own mistakes, or who are insincere or undependable.

Job competence. There's been too much talk about the insignificance of technical job skill for the supervisor. A person who knows the job that is being supervised has one of the best foundations for building good leadership.

Good judgment. Common sense, the ability to separate the important from the unimportant, tact, and the wisdom to look into the future and plan for it are all ingredients that tend to make the best leaders.

Energy. Leadership at any level means rising early and working late. It leaves little time for relaxation or escape from problems. Good health, good nerves, and boundless energy make this tough job easier.

CAN LEADERS ALWAYS BE POPULAR WITH THE PEOPLE THEY SUPERVISE?

Probably not. The very best leaders seem to combine the knack of leading with the knack of winning friends. But most supervisors are not that successful. Instead, they must be satisfied with respect and with followers. Why? Because many of the decisions that you must make as a supervisor will not favor everybody. Sometimes you will please nobody. The result is that you must often be satisfied with the knowledge that your leadership has been responsible, considerate, and equitable—regardless of how unfairly others may judge you.

REVIEW ▼ 10 ▼ QUESTIONS

1. Which are the three skills most likely to be required of leaders? Can they be learned, or must a leader be born with them?
2. Give an example of how an individual's motivational needs offer an opportunity for effective action on the part of a supervisor.
3. As supervisor of the catalog section of a direct mail house, Mary has come to believe that without her close supervision, employees in her department would never get their work done. Which of McGregor's assumptions about employees at work does Mary's view represent?
4. Compare democratic leadership with participative leadership.
5. According to Fiedler's contingency model of leadership, what is likely to be the best approach in a situation where the supervisor has been newly appointed, relationships with the new group are standoffish, and the task to be performed requires great accuracy? Why?
6. In what ways is the Managerial Grid© related to Theory X and Theory Y?
7. Provide examples of the use of a leadership style at three different points along the continuum of leadership styles.
8. Which kind of leadership style best fits an insecure employee? An aggressive, hostile person? A highly creative individualist? Why?

A CASE IN POINT

The Flexitime Option

You supervise a clerical section for a government agency in a congested downtown area. In a widely distributed memo, the agency has suggested that because of heavy traffic at opening and closing times, each department may stagger its hours according to a flexitime schedule, *if it wishes* and *only if this does not have an adverse effect on the department's operations.* A flexitime schedule would allow employees to stagger their hours so that—as long as each person works a total of eight hours daily—some could come in early (say at 7 a.m.) and leave early, whereas others could come in later (say at 10 a.m.) and leave later. Flexitime does not appear to be suitable for the section that you supervise, because the work there requires considerable interchange among employees. Many of your employees, however, favor the flexitime schedule. Flexitime appeals to them especially because they have obligations such as home care for aging parents and day-care drop-off and pickup for children.

You are sympathetic with your employees' interests. Nevertheless, you feel certain that any changes in work schedules that interfere with the prompt exchange of information, advice, and services among the various operations will greatly lower the department's productivity as well as the quality of the services it renders. Several of your employees are pressing you now to switch to a flexitime schedule, and they cite the fact that a couple of other sections in the agency have adopted it already.

You check back with your boss for clarification regarding the memo. She tells you that it means just what it says. You can adopt a flexitime schedule *if* you wish and *only if* it does not affect your department's operations in a negative way.

How would you provide the leadership needed to find the best solution to this problem? Five alternative courses of action are listed below. Rank them in the order in which they appeal to you (1 most effective, 5 least effective). You may add another approach in the space provided, if you wish. In any event, be prepared to justify your ranking.

_____ **A.**   Meet separately with each of your employees to gather information about their feelings toward a flexitime schedule.

_____ **B.**   Issue a memo to your section saying that the flexitime option is not appropriate for their work and that no changes in work schedules will be made.

_____ **C.**   Get your employees together and explain to them why no changes can be made in their work schedules.

_____ **D.**   Advise employees that you will work with them to see whether or not a flexitime plan can be developed that meets the productivity and quality goals established for your section.

_____ **E.**   Turn the problem over to your subordinates and tell them you'll abide by their decision.

If you have another approach, write it here.

▶ _____

_____

_____

Complete the ACTION PLANNING CHECKLIST
for this chapter, which can be found on page 320.

Test your comprehension of the material in Chapters 6, 7, 8, 9, and 10. Correct answers are in the Appendix.

True-False

By writing T or F in the space provided, indicate whether each statement is true or false.

1. Staffing includes these five steps: specifying the kinds of jobs to be filled, estimating the number of employees needed, recruiting applicants, interviewing candidates, and selecting the most appropriate.

   1. _____

2. A job specification differs from a job description in that the job specification puts its emphasis on the qualifications needed by the *person* who will fill the job.

   2. _____

3. Given a choice, supervisors are better off if they understaff than if they overstaff.

   3. _____

4. When interviewing job candidates, answers to yes-or-no questions provide better information than those to open-ended questions.

   4. _____

5. A test that asks a carpenter to show how well he or she can drive a nail or saw a piece of wood is an aptitude test.

   5. _____

6. The time when an employee is most receptive to instruction is called the key point.

   6. _____

7. The four-step method of training puts great emphasis on preparing an employee to learn or to receive instruction.

   7. _____

8. A supervisor is freed from the responsibility of training employees if the organization has a human resources development (or training) staff.

   8. _____

9. A job should be taught to an employee in the exact sequence in which it is performed.

9. _____

10. Reading programs, correspondence courses, and manufacturers' instruction manuals are not particularly good methods of job training for employees.

10. _____

11. An employee's behavior may occasionally appear to be irrational, but, underneath, there is probably a logical reason for it.

11. _____

12. Bonita continues to work even though she no longer needs the money; she works for the fun of being around people. She is probably largely motivated by social needs.

12. _____

13. According to Herzberg, adequate pay and good working conditions help to create job satisfaction.

13. _____

14. The people-centered approach focuses on the work itself and emphasizes the supervisor's role as a facilitator.

14. _____

15. Although informal groups are sure to emerge at work, they are largely powerless because they have no recognizable authority.

15. _____

16. "Static" is the term applied to any extraneous distraction that interferes with the communication process.

16. _____

17. A supervisor should let the boss know about a situation if it is something the boss will be held accountable for, even if the supervisor handled it well.

17. _____

18. Listening passively encourages communication because it doesn't interfere with what the speaker is saying.

18. _____

19. A written communication is essential to amend a previous written communication.

19. _____

20. When it has been properly given, it should not be necessary for a supervisor to repeat an order.

20. _____

21. Daphne can persuade her employees to follow her instructions willingly. Daphne has become a leader.

21. _____

22. When a supervisor asks for, receives, and considers an employee's opinion before setting policy, not only does this illustrate participation, it is also an example of rapport.   22. _____

23. The ratio between a supervisor's concern for people and concern for production can be shown on the continuum of management styles.   23. _____

24. The most effective leaders stick to one style of leadership, regardless of the situation or the people involved.   24. _____

25. Success of leaders does not necessarily depend on how pleased their subordinates are with their leadership.   25. _____

Multiple Choice

For each of the following items, choose the response that best completes the statement or answers the question. Write the letter of the response in the space provided.

1. The number of employees a supervisor needs to run a department depends mainly on two factors—the scheduled output required of the department and:

   a. the productivity expected from each employee.
   b. the total machine capacity of the department.
   c. the department's record of employee absences and turnover.
   d. the company's policy toward understaffing and overstaffing.   1. _____

2. When interviewing job applicants, it is permissible to ask questions about which of the following?

   a. Race or color.
   b. Marital status.
   c. Religion or national origin.
   d. Experience and education.   2. _____

3. When persons who take an employment test tend to get a different score each time they take the test, the test is said to be lacking in:

a. test validity.
b. test reliability.
c. performance.
d. aptitude.   3. _____

4. The average employee turnover rate in the United States is about:

a. 10 percent per year.
b. 15 percent per year.
c. 80 percent per year.
d. 3 percent per year.   4. _____

5. The biggest problem that supervisors face in planning work-force size from day to day is:

a. employee turnover.
b. holidays and vacations.
c. employee morale.
d. employee absences.   5. _____

6. The teachable moment is most evident during:

a. orientation training.
b. refresher training.
c. apprenticeship programs.
d. programmed instruction.   6._____

7. The last step in the four-step JIT process is:

a. teaching the most difficult step.
b. outlining the key points.
c. putting the trainees on their own.
d. breaking the job down.   7._____

8. Nora wants to prepare a skills inventory of each worker's training needs. Which of the following would be an important part of that inventory?

   a. What each worker knows or can already do.
   b. What each worker doesn't know and needs to be able to do.
   c. A plan for providing the training each worker needs.
   d. All of the above.   8. _____

9. Mel is disappointed that Marsha hasn't transferred the training she has received from the training department back to her job. Mel should:

   a. let Martha know he is disappointed that she has wasted the time and money spent on her training.
   b. monitor Marsha's performance, correcting her when it is not on target and praising her when it is.
   c. discipline Marsha for not applying herself.
   d. send Marsha back for further training.   9. _____

10. Computer-assisted instruction (CAI) is most commonly offered in connection with:

    a. vestibule training.
    b. apprenticeship programs.
    c. programmed learning.
    d. key-point training.   10. _____

11. The human need that serves as the strongest motivator is:

    a. the one that stands highest in the hierarchy—the desire to do worthwhile work.
    b. the one that comes first in the hierarchy—the survival need.
    c. the need that has not yet been satisfied.
    d. the need that is easiest to satisfy.   11. _____

12. Alva tells an employee, "This may be a grim assignment, but you'll really be a hero if you can pull this report together by next Monday." Alva is probably trying
to motivate by:

    a. providing satisfaction.
    b. preventing dissatisfaction.
    c. appealing to security needs.
    d. appealing to social needs.   12. _____

13. As compared with process-centered job design, people-
centered job design emphasizes:

    a. tool and machine requirements.
    b. process flow sequences.
    c. personalities.
    d. the work itself.   13. _____

14. Zack, the congresswoman's secretary, has recently
been asked to pick up and deliver his boss's mail. From
a people-centered point of view, this is an example of:

    a. job enlargement.
    b. job enrichment.
    c. work simplification.
    d. goal orientation.   14. _____

15. Worker participation is most likely to be useful in:

    a. disciplinary actions.
    d. establishing quality specifications.
    c. solving work problems.
    d. revising compensation policies.   15. _____

16. Which of the following is not characteristic of good
communication?

    a. Involves listening.
    b. Discourages feedback.
    c. Is three-dimensional.
    d. Encourages understanding.   16. _____

17. An employee asks a supervisor, Ms. Smith, about an incentive plan. Ms. Smith does not know the answer. Her reply to the employee should be:

    a. "You'd best check that out with the Human Resources Department."
    b. "Try asking Pete about it. He keeps up on things like that better than I can."
    c. "I'm not sure of the answer, but I'll find out and let you know as soon as possible."
    d. "See if you can find an answer in your Employee Handbook."   17. _____

18. Nonverbal communication signals are called:

    a. interpersonal communications.
    b. active listening.
    c. two-way communications.
    d. body language.   18. _____

19. Written communications are generally better than oral communications for which of the following purposes?

    a. Speed.
    b. Lengthy messages.
    c. Informality.
    d. Personal impact.   19. _____

20. Which of the following instructions is least likely to be misunderstood?

    a. Speed up the machine a little bit.
    b. I want you to do a good job on this.
    c. Type this as soon as possible.
    d. Finish this within the next two hours.   20. _____

21. Ruth wants to become a good leader. Which of the following statements will most help her to develop her leadership skills?

    a. Forget it—leaders are born, not made.
    b. Master the skills of persuasion, influence, and rapport.
    c. Develop one leadership skill and stick with it.
    d. Concentrate on the best aspects of your personality; all else will follow.   21. _____

22. The situational (or contingency) approach to leadership is based on the idea that:

   a. the task to be done determines the leadership style
      needed.
   b. times have changed, and autocratic leadership is no
      longer acceptable.
   c. the leadership style needed is based on the relation-
      ship of three factors.
   d. a situation can be manipulated to accommodate
      your leadership style.   22. _____

23. The belief that assumptions about human nature
should determine the leadership style of a supervisor is
part of:

   a. Theory X only.
   b. Theory Y only.
   c. both Theory X and Theory Y.
   d. neither Theory X nor Theory Y.   23. _____

24. One of your employees, Manny, has an aggressive, hostile personality. The style of leadership that is most
likely to be effective with Manny is:

   a. autocratic.
   b. democratic.
   c. participative.
   d. none of the above.   24. _____

25. Most employees respond favorably to each of the following personality traits in a leader except:

   a. self-denial.
   b. self-indulgence.
   c. sense of mission.
   d. boundless energy.   25. _____

PART THREE

Handling Vital
Personnel Problems

Not all runs smoothly and serenely for supervisory managers. There are times when their skills—especially their interpersonal skills—are sharply tested. These times occur mostly when employees feel mistreated, when they are deeply troubled by personal problems, when their performance must be criticized, or when they misbehave and must be disciplined. To make it even more trying for supervisors, these situations must be handled not only deftly and sensitively, but also within the framework of legal guidelines and restrictions.

▶ Chapter 11 alerts supervisors to the importance of employee complaints and grievances and outlines several proven policies and approaches for handling them.

▶ Chapter 12 encourages supervisors to develop a sensitivity to employees' emotional problems when they affect job performance and to counsel employees effectively regarding absenteeism and drug and alcohol abuse.

▶ Chapter 13 explains how to evaluate employee performance fairly and objectively and to conduct appraisal interviews in a positive way.

▶ Chapter 14 deals with the need to think of discipline in a constructive way and suggests methods for administering it firmly and equitably.

▶ Chapter 15 outlines the aspects of equal employment opportunity, labor relations, and safety and health legislation that most greatly restrict supervisory management.

HANDLING COMPLAINTS AND MINIMIZING GRIEVANCES

LEARNING OBJECTIVES

After studying this chapter, you should be able to:

1. Understand the need for handling grievances promptly.

2. Describe appropriate methods for recognizing, responding to, and preventing grievances.

3. Recognize a formal procedure for handling grievances and the supervisor's role in it.

4. Identify the common sources of conflict in an organization.

5. Discuss some effective ways of reducing and minimizing conflict.

▶ A grievance, even when trivial, unjustified, or fancied, can be very real to the employee who raises it; consequently, it deserves serious and emphatic consideration by the supervisor.

▶ Unless objectivity, consistency, and absolute fairness characterize a supervisor's handling of grievances, the supervisor's rulings are unlikely to gain the acceptance by employees that is needed to maintain harmony and discipline.

▶ A careful and thorough examination of all the specific facts, events, and attitudes that make up the circumstances of a grievance is a fundamental step that must be taken for the eventual resolution of the grievance.

▶ Grievance discussions should be conducted by the supervisor in a businesslike manner, the settlement concluded without undue delay, and corrective action discharged promptly without future prejudice toward the complainant.

▶ Conflicts, like grievances, occur in all organizations. Each conflict requires an understanding of its causes and a resolution that is consistent with the objectives of both the work group and the organization.

HOW MUCH ATTENTION SHOULD SUPERVISORS PAY TO EMPLOYEES' COMPLAINTS?

Just as much as is necessary to remove the employees' complaints as obstacles to their doing willing, productive jobs. This is the main reason supervisors should act as soon as they even sense a complaint, gripe, or grievance. A gripe, imagined or real, spoken or held within, blocks an employee's will to cooperate. Until you've examined the grievance and its underlying causes, the employee isn't likely to work very hard for you. If the complaint has merit, the only way for you to get the employee back on your team 100 percent is to correct the situation.

CAN YOU SETTLE EVERY GRIEVANCE TO THE EMPLOYEE'S SATISFACTION?

No. It's natural for people sometimes to want more than they deserve. When an employee complains about a condition that the facts don't support, the best you can do is to demonstrate that the settlement is a just one—even if it isn't exactly what the employee would like.

IS THERE DANGER IN TRYING TO TALK AN EMPLOYEE OUT OF A COMPLAINT?

Yes. Talk if you will. But don't try to outsmart an employee—even if this is what the employee is trying to do to you. Grievances are caused by facts—or what employees believe to be facts. Clever use of words and sharp debating tactics won't change these facts or dissolve the grievances.

Patience and sincerity are the two biggest keys to settling a grievance. In many cases, just listening patiently to an explanation will result in the employee's dropping the grievance.

WHAT IS AN IMAGINED GRIEVANCE? IF IT IS A FIGMENT OF A WORKER'S IMAGINATION, WHY GIVE IT SERIOUS ATTENTION?

Facts and situations appear differently to different people. What may appear imaginary to a supervisor who has a broad knowledge of the facts may seem to be a very real injustice from an employee's point of view. This does not in any way make it a grievance that can be ignored or, worse still, ridiculed. Suppose Marie, for example, feels that she has been given an unpleasant assignment because the supervisor is picking on her. The supervisor, however, knows that an unexpected schedule change has made the assignment unavoidable. Furthermore, other employees also have had to accept undesirable assignments as a result of the change. Until Marie has had a chance to voice her complaint fully, however, she will not be ready to listen to an explanation. And without being given all the facts, she is likely to consider the explanation just an excuse.

Most grievances are advanced because the employee believes that she or he is the victim of an injustice. To the employee, the grievance is real, not imaginary. Accordingly, good supervisors will give fair hearings to all grievances, whether real or imaginary, justified or contrived.

WHAT'S THE MOST IMPORTANT THING YOU CAN DO WHEN HANDLING GRIEVANCES?

It can't be said too often: Above all, be fair. Get the employee's point of view clear in your mind. If the employee has an opportunity to be understood, the grievance may turn out to be something different from what it first appears to be.

To be really fair, you must be prepared to accept the logical conclusion that flows from the facts you uncover in the process. (See Figure 11-1.) This may mean making concessions. But if the facts warrant it, you often have to change your mind or your way of doing things if you are to gain a reputation for fair dealing.

If you find you've made a mistake, admit it. A supervisor isn't expected to be right all the time. But your employees expect you to be honest in every instance—even if it means "eating crow" on occasion.

SHOULD A SUPERVISOR BARGAIN ON GRIEVANCES?

No. Be like a good baseball umpire: Call each one as you see it. An umpire who blows a decision is really in for trouble if he or she tries to make up for it on the next call. It should be the same with grievances. An employee either has a case or hasn't a case. Consider each case on its merits, and don't let grievances become political issues.

▼ FIGURE 11-1

The grievance handling process

1. LISTEN to the complaint attentively. *don't judge*

2. INVESTIGATE the facts to verify them.

3. OBTAIN INFORMATION relevant to the case: absence, lateness, accident records, etc.

4. SEEK EXPERT ADVICE if necessary.

5. MAKE A DECISION based on the facts.

6. GIVE YOUR ANSWER promptly.

7. KEEP A RECORD of the statement.

SHOULD SUPERVISORS CHANGE THEIR STORIES IF THEY FIND THE FACTS WON'T SUPPORT THEIR ORIGINAL CONCLUSIONS?

Supervisors have no other choice if on investigation they find their actions or decisions have been wrong. But they should avoid this embarrassing situation in the first place. Just be sure to get the facts—all the facts. Get them straight to begin with—before you give the employee or a union steward your decision. It costs you nothing to say, "Give me a couple of hours (or a couple of days) to look into this matter thoroughly. Just as soon as I know all the facts, I'll be able to discuss this grievance so that we can come up with the fairest solution."

In trying to round up the facts of a case, explore further than just the obvious places. For example, if the grievance involves a dispute over pay, look beyond just the time-card and payroll data. Ask yourself: Has the worker been upset about the jobs assigned? Has the worker had a fair share of easier jobs? Have we had occasion to turn the worker down on a bid for a better job? Does the worker know how to fill in a time card properly? Does the worker know the procedure for getting credit for machine breakdown time? Have the worker's materials and tools been up to standard?

All these factors could affect a person's pay and should be examined before you commit yourself.

Records are especially useful in assembling the facts and backing you when you present your decision to the employee or the union. If your complaint is that someone's output has been below par, you'll need the worker's records and the records of others to prove it.

WHEN YOU GIVE YOUR DECISION ON A GRIEVANCE, HOW SPECIFIC SHOULD YOU BE? SHOULD YOU LEAVE YOURSELF A LOOPHOLE?

A supervisor is paid to make decisions. When the grievance has been fully investigated and you've talked it over with the parties involved, make your decision as promptly as possible. Be definite in your answer. State your decision so that there's no mistake about what you mean. If it involves a warning rather than a more serious penalty, don't give this kind of reply: "I'll withhold the warning this time, but next time it happens it won't be so easy for you."

Instead, use this clear-cut approach: "There appears to be good reason to believe that you misunderstood what I expected of you. So I'll tear up the warning and throw it away. Next time you'll get a written warning. And if it happens a second time, it will cost you a week off without pay."

MUST YOU GIVE YOUR DECISION RIGHT AWAY?

No, but don't sit on it forever. Nothing breaks down the grievance procedure like procrastination. If you can't make up your mind on the spot, or need to check even further than you did originally, tell the employee and the steward that you'll give them a definite answer "this afternoon" or "tomorrow." Stick to this promise. If you run into an unexpected delay, let them know about it. "Sorry I can't let you know this afternoon as I'd hoped, because the paymaster has been tied up all morning. I won't be able to check the time sheets until late this afternoon. But I will let you know first thing in the morning."

SUPPOSE YOUR BOSS OR YOUR BOSS'S SUPERIOR ASKS YOU TO HAND DOWN A GRIEVANCE DECISION THAT YOU DON'T AGREE WITH. SHOULD YOU ACCEPT RESPONSIBILITY FOR IT?

This is the old "supervisor-in-the-middle" situation. It's bound to come up from time to time. Sometimes you'll find that company practice is easier on the employee than you think it should be. Sometimes you'll find just the reverse—that it's tougher than what you'd do if you had no one to answer to but yourself. In either case, don't pass the buck. If you as a supervisor say that you agree with the employee but that the company manager can't see it your way, you destroy the whole process of management teamwork. If you don't agree with company policy, try to adjust your own thinking. In any event, and as hard as it may be to swallow, you should pass the decision along as your own.

SHOULD A SUPERVISOR HELP EMPLOYEES SAVE FACE WHEN GRIEVANCES GO AGAINST THEM?

It seems as if it's asking too much for a supervisor to be noble about winning a grievance—especially when the employee or the union has been nasty or aggressive in pursuing it. But here again, it's a bad practice in the long run to make the employee "eat humble pie." If you help employees save face, they may be considerate to you when the tables are turned. If you rub in the decision, you may irk them so much that they will be on the lookout for a confrontation they can't lose.

This shouldn't be interpreted to mean that you must be so downright nice as to appear sorry you were right. Try saying something like this: "I've checked your complaint from every angle, but it still looks like no to me. You made two comparisons when you stated that I was playing favorites. In each case the facts show that both employees you referred to outranked you in both output and quality of production. On my scorecard they deserve the better assignments. I'm far from glad that I had to say no to you. But I am glad that you brought your position out into the open. Perhaps now that I know how you feel, I can help you improve your performance so you can do some of the jobs requiring greater skill."

WHAT IS THE BEST WAY TO WIND UP A GRIEVANCE SETTLEMENT?

Carry out your part of the bargain and see that the employee carries out his or her part. Once an agreement has been made, follow through on corrective action promptly. You may lose all the goodwill you've built in settling the grievance if you delay in taking action.

IS THERE A STANDARD GRIEVANCE PROCEDURE SET DOWN BY LAW?

No. A company may choose to establish its own procedure voluntarily. If a union or other organization represents employees, however, the procedure will be based on an agreement between management and the labor union or employee association. This agreement will be written into your labor contract or whatever contractual document exists.

HOW IMPORTANT IS THE GRIEVANCE PROCEDURE AS SUCH? WOULDN'T IT BE SIMPLER IF EMPLOYEE GRIEVANCES WERE ALL HANDLED INFORMALLY?

Where a union is involved, the grievance procedure becomes a very important matter. The procedure may vary from company to company, but in any case your guide should be this: Know the authorized grievance procedure in your organization and stick to it. It's up to you, too, to see that the steward also observes the provisions of the grievance clause.

Take special notice of what may appear to be tiny technicalities, and be sure you observe them. For instance, some contracts call for the supervisor to give an answer within 24 hours after the complaint has been presented in writing. Be sure to do this so that you can't be accused of stalling or even lose the grievance entirely on such a technicality.

Of course, it would be desirable if grievances could all be settled in a casual, informal manner. But where a union is concerned, experience shows that it's best to be businesslike and to stick to the letter of the contract procedure. On the other hand, don't get so engrossed with the process itself that you overlook the original purpose of the grievance procedure—to settle grievances fairly and promptly.

WHAT HAPPENS TO GRIEVANCES THAT GO UNSETTLED?

They continue to fester. Frequently a supervisor feels that he or she has taken care of a complaint just by soft-soaping the aggrieved employee. This is a mistake. The grievance will continue to simmer in the employee's mind, even if nothing more is said about it to the supervisor. And dissatisfaction is contagious.

An unsettled grievance is like one rotten apple in a basket. It spoils the good ones—the good ones don't make a good apple of the rotten one. An offended or angry employee tends to make other employees lose confidence in the supervisor. The coworkers may encourage the dissatisfied employee to pursue the matter if it appears that you have been evasive.

WHEN DOES A GRIEVANCE GO TO ARBITRATION?

Most union-management contract agreements call for a grievance to go to arbitration if the grievance cannot be settled at any step of the authorized procedure. Once the complaint has been turned over to an impartial arbitrator, the arbitrator acts somewhat like a judge by listening to the arguments presented by both parties and then making a decision. The arbitrator does not mediate—that is, try to reopen the discussion between the company and the union. Both parties agree to abide by the arbitrator's decision. You should distinguish between arbitration and mediation. Arbitration focuses on grievances. Mediation, a form of guided negotiation, takes place during contract disputes.

WHERE ARE MOST GRIEVANCES MOST LIKELY TO OCCUR?

It's hard to pinpoint just which situations are most likely to breed grievances, but there are three important guidelines.

First, don't lose sight of the fact that grievances are symptoms of something wrong—with employees, with working conditions, or with supervision.

Second, employees are most likely to be worried about situations that threaten their security, such as: pay, promotions, transfers, work assignments, layoffs, performance appraisals, and elimination of—or impending changes in—their jobs because of automation, computerization, or organizational "downsizing."

Third, special care must be given to grievances that have serious legal implications, such as those arising from feelings of discrimination, denial of equal employment opportunity rights, or sexual harassment.

IT'S EASY TO SEE THAT IT WOULD BE BETTER TO PREVENT GRIEVANCES IN THE FIRST PLACE. HOW CAN YOU DO THAT?

The trick lies in detecting situations that breed grievances and then correcting these situations. Don't make the mistake of planting seeds of trouble where it doesn't exist, though. A perfectly happy worker may be able to find something to complain about if you ask directly, "What is there about your job that you don't like?" As a rule of thumb, however, you can reduce the number of grievances by applying common sense to your relationships with your staff. For example:

1. Give employees prompt and regular feedback about how well they are doing their jobs. Uncertainty in this area is a major source of employee dissatisfaction.

2. Remove, or try to ease, minor irritations as they arise. The presence of unnecessary aggravations tends to magnify the more serious complaints when they occur.

3. Listen to and encourage constructive suggestions. Take action whenever it is reasonable and nondisruptive.

4. Make certain of your authority before making commitments to employees. Then be sure to keep your promises.

5. When you make changes, take special care to explain the reasons— and as far in advance as possible.

6. Assign work impartially. Try to balance the distribution of attractive and disagreeable assignments so that employees share them equally.

7. Be consistent in your standards of performance and in the ways in which you reward those who comply or punish those who fail to measure up.

8. Render your decisions as soon as possible when responding to employee requests. A prompt no is often more welcome than a long-delayed yes.

9. If you must criticize or take disciplinary action, do not make a public display of it. Keep it a private matter between you and the employee.

GRIEVANCES ASIDE, IS THE PRESENCE OF BICKERING AND DISPUTES A SIGN OF POOR SUPERVISION?

Not necessarily. It is human to quarrel and complain. When many people must work together, conflict is inevitable. Accordingly, a small amount of conflict can be a good thing. It is when there is no end of quarreling and confrontation that supervisors should begin to worry about how well they are doing their jobs.

WHAT ARE THE MAIN SOURCES OF CONFLICT IN AN ORGANIZATION?

There are many. People with different ideas about what should be done and how to do it are a common source. Departments that are sometimes at cross-purposes—such as production and maintenance, production control and sales, sales and credit, accounting and retailing, purchasing and engineering—cause intergroup difficulties. But most of the causes of conflict in a supervisor's department are closely related to the work itself: how it is laid out and the way in which the supervisor manages the employees. In particular, a supervisor should be on guard against:

▸ *An appearance of an unfair allocation of tools, materials, supplies, and other resources.* There are few shops where there is always enough of everything to go around equally. The supervisor must often make the hard decisions about who will have what, how much, and when. When these decisions are made openly and fairly, employees are more likely to accept them without quarreling with one another. If allocations are made slyly or on the basis of favoritism, trouble will brew.

▸ *Expressed disagreements about what is important and what is not.* If these disagreements result from lack of information or misinformation, they should be cleared up right away. If the disagreements arise because individuals see things differently, the supervisor must try to get to the root of the problem. For example, a press operator may constantly push a benchmate for work to be processed, whereas the benchmate may insist that his or her work can't be released because its quality isn't good enough. The first individual sets priority on output, the other on quality. The supervisor must find an answer to this question: Are these priorities (or goals) merely a reflection of each individual's values, or are they related to the department's established goals and standards?

▶ *Changes in work flow or conditions that imply a change in status.* If in the past Anita handled incoming orders first before passing them on to Jack for posting, Anita may regard her work as more valued than Jack's. A change in the order of flow so that Jack handles the orders first may disturb Anita's sense of status, and she may begin finding fault with everything that Jack does. Experienced workers tend to develop "territorial rights." Hence, they feel that they should resist outside forces such as a new supervisor, new employees, or any changes in which they have not participated.

▶ *A growing sense of mistrust among employees.* This is liable to occur when things in the department are generally going wrong. If business is bad, or if the department has been criticized for mistakes or low productivity, employees may look around for others on whom to place the blame. For example, the production department may blame off-grade products on the maintenance people (the equipment was faulty), the floor salesperson may blame the cashier for a lost sale, or the nurse may blame the nurse's aide for upset patients.

▶ *Lack of stability in departmental operations.* Change is so threatening to many people that they will naturally take out their fears and anxieties in quibbling and complaints. Many times, change is something beyond the supervisor's control. But the supervisor can pour oil on troubled waters simply by maintaining an air of calm. He or she can, for example, talk with employees about the reasons for the change, how long it will last, and how it will affect—or not affect—normal operating conditions.

HOW DOES COMPETITION DIFFER FROM CONFLICT?

The former is usually productive; the latter is often counterproductive. The right kind of *competition* can stimulate a healthy, controlled battle between two individuals. Informal contests allow employees to try to excel at meeting departmental goals that are mutually beneficial. Carried too far, however, the contestants may lose sight of the common good and become antagonistic. *Conflict* tends to pit individuals and groups against one another in trying to control the department's resources in pursuit of their own goals. A lathe operator, for example, may insist on taking the only available tool in order to finish his or her *own* quota on time. He or she may not worry about whether or not this slows up another operator or the department in meeting its goals. Or a salesperson may demand the major portion of the section's travel expenses on the basis that his or her *own* customers are most important.

WHAT'S A GOOD WAY TO HANDLE
CONFLICT IN YOUR DEPARTMENT?

First, be alert to its presence. Next, seek out its causes. Then meet it head-on. A basic approach involves five steps:

1. ***Decide what it is that you want to have accomplished.*** Do you want peace and quiet at any price? Or do you want better quality? Greater productivity? A project finished on time? Fewer mistakes in transcribing? An end to delays caused by quarrels between the maintenance person and your production operator? Nothing will be resolved unless you first make up your mind what the desired outcome should be.

2. ***Call together the people who can best settle the issue.*** If the conflict is strictly between you and an individual, limit the confrontation to the two of you. If others are involved, invite them into the discussion. If a disinterested party, such as the quality-control department, can shed light on the subject, ask for its participation. If a referee or someone who can speak authoritatively about the company's viewpoint is needed, then get your boss into the act.

3. ***Be ready to bargain; don't hand out edicts.*** Conflicts are truly settled by negotiation. A short answer tends only to put off the problem, and it will keep recurring. If you keep your eye on the objective you have set, there are usually many ways to attain it. Remember that each individual has an objective, too. If the maintenance department, for example, can provide the necessary repairs while still keeping its costs in line—and dependable repairs are your objective—then let the maintenance people do it their way.

4. ***Don't be distracted by the red herring of personalities.*** Whereas many people rub one another the wrong way, most conflicts have a much more tangible basis. Herein lies the value of keeping the eyes of all concerned on the main objective. It tends to push personality conflicts into the background. Finally, try not to get emotionally involved yourself. Most importantly, don't choose sides.

5. ***Focus attention on mutually beneficial outcomes.*** Above all, don't make performance comparisons between individuals. This will only heighten competition and stress. Instead, hold up total organizational results as the criterion for success. If Kevin insists that Sharon takes up more than her share of the keyboard time, for example, try to reach a solution that makes the most effective use of the keyboard. That way, both Sharon and Kevin can contribute to departmental effectiveness, even though both may have to give in a little while doing so.

REVIEW ▼ 11 QUESTIONS

1. Contrast a real grievance with an imagined one.
2. Why is it a good idea to treat every complaint as if it were important?
3. Why should supervisors resist the temptation to "give in" on one grievance so that they can "win" on another?
4. How specific and conclusive should a supervisor's settlement of a grievance be?
5. To what extent are grievances handled differently when there is a formal grievance procedure prescribed by a labor contract?
6. From where might you expect most grievances to arise? Which kinds are likely to have the most serious implications?
7. Distinguish between conflict and competition within an organization.
8. Al and Agnes are quarreling over who should have use of a lift truck first while loading cartons into a truck for shipment. What steps would you take to settle this dispute?

A CASE IN POINT

The Passed-Over Pay Raise

Work in the word processing pool of the Cascade Underwriting Company is sporadic. Two or three days a week, the five word processing operators (or "processors") are under heavy pressure to produce. But rarely does a week go by when the slack is so great that the processors have to find ways to look busy. Janice, one of the newer processors, simply sits at her desk staring out the window when there is nothing to do. The other, more experienced processors, however, spend a great deal of their time in the employees' lounge or keep paper active in their printers whenever Ms. Tender, the office manager, comes by. In fact, one of the senior processors can do this so well that she can look busy while reading a magazine hidden in her desk drawer. Be this as it may, the last time annual merit reviews came around, Ms. Tender recommended all the processors but Janice for a pay raise.

When the other processors got their paychecks with increases and Janice found none in hers, she asked Ms. Tender for the reason. Ms. Tender said, "Because you waste too much time."

"I do not," said Janice. "The only time I'm not working hard is when I have nothing to do."

"When you run out of work," replied Ms. Tender, "It's your responsibility to let me know, and I'll find something for you to do."

"That's unfair," said Janice. "I'm as entitled to a good review and a raise as any of the other processors. If I don't get it, I'll ask to see Mr. Dunne, the head manager at this site."

"Go ahead," said Ms. Tender.

Later that week, Mr. Dunne invited Janice and Ms. Tender into his office to talk about Janice's grievance. Janice told her story to him very much as she had told it to Ms. Tender. Ms. Tender, however, insisted that Janice did not show the initiative in seeking work during slack periods that the other processors did. Furthermore, she said that she had to keep after Janice regularly to make sure that she kept busy.

After hearing both parties out, Mr. Dunne told Janice that he had to agree with Ms. Tender's decision, and that he considered the matter settled.

What do you think of the way this grievance was handled? Rank the following conclusions in the order in which they appeal to you (1 most valid, 5 least valid). If you wish to add another conclusion, write it in the space provided. In any event, be prepared to justify your ranking.

_____   A.   Mr. Dunne failed to ascertain properly the facts of the situation before making his decision. This was unfair to Janice.

_____   B.   Mr. Dunne gave Janice as fair a hearing as she deserved.

_____   C.   It was Janice's fault that she hadn't learned to follow practices in her department or to show initiative in seeking out work when she wasn't busy.

_____   D.   Ms. Tender's recommendation for no pay increase was correct, regardless of what the other processors may or may not have been doing.

_____   E.   Ms. Tender is not a very perceptive supervisor, and she certainly might have helped Janice get a better hearing if she had conscientiously reviewed the situation.

If you have another conclusion, write it here.

▶ _____

_____

_____

Complete the ACTION PLANNING CHECKLIST
for this chapter, which can be found on page 321.

COUNSELING EMPLOYEES WITH SPECIAL PROBLEMS

LEARNING OBJECTIVES

After studying this chapter, you should be able to:

1. Describe problem performance and distinguish between a neurotic person and a psychotic person.

2. Recognize the symptoms of an emotionally disturbed—or troubled—employee.

3. Explain the general approaches to employee counseling, discuss its limitations, and know when an emotionally disturbed employee should be referred to a professional counselor.

4. Identify various kinds of absenteeism and know the corrective action for each.

5. Recognize alcoholism and illegal substance abuse among employees and know the recommended remedial approaches for each.

OVERVIEW OF KEY CONCEPTS
IN THIS CHAPTER

▶ Supervisors have a legitimate concern regarding employee performance that either (1) does not measure up to established standards or (2) is disruptive to the normal conduct of operations. Troubled employees are not "crazy" or insane. Mostly, they suffer from temporary emotional problems stemming from an inability to adjust to the stresses of everyday life or the workplace.

▶ Troubled employees can be recognized by such disharmonious conduct as sudden changes in behavior, preoccupation, irritability, decreased productivity, increased accidents or absences, unusual fatigue, irrational anger or hostility, heavy drinking, or symptoms of drug abuse.

▶ Constructive counseling by a supervisor can help a great many troubled employees to improve their performance or control their behavior, provided that the degree of their maladjustment is slight and the underlying causes are not intense.

▶ Constructive counseling can also reduce absenteeism among chronic and occasional absentees. Other forms of absenteeism respond better to a three-part program involving (1) clear-cut rules, (2) consistent penalties, and (3) counseling to determine—and confront—the reasons for the absences.

▶ Alcoholism and drug abuse are found among special kinds of problem employees. Here, counseling by the supervisor is especially sensitive and should be accompanied by a reminder that performance standards must be met. In all but minor cases, professional assistance or advice should be sought.

HOW WOULD YOU DEFINE
PROBLEM PERFORMANCE?

Problem performance encompasses (1) job performance that does not measure up to established standards of output or quality and (2) behavior that is distracting or disruptive to the normal conduct of operations. The former problem is routinely dealt with during performance appraisals. The latter problem is far more difficult to identify and deal with, and often leads to the former. It is problem performance of the latter kind on which this chapter will focus.

WHAT KINDS OF EMPLOYEES
BECOME PROBLEM PERFORMERS?

They are mainly people who have a difficult time in adjusting to life—work life as well as home life. Most people encounter periods in their lives when adjustment is difficult. At such times, their performance at work may suffer. This is usually a temporary condition, and their performance soon returns to normal.

There are many other people who are especially susceptible to stress, and their resulting performance lapses are deep and prolonged. The chances are that they are troubled by deeply rooted personal problems or by conditions in their personal lives that make adjustment especially difficult. These people can be described as "troubled." When this troubled state persists, there is a good chance that the troubled person is suffering from a problem with an emotional, rather than a physical, cause. For this reason, we speak of a person in this troubled state as being "emotionally disturbed."

Supervisors must learn to deal with employees whose difficulty in adjusting to emotional problems is only temporary and with those whose adjustment problems are chronic.

WHERE ARE THESE TROUBLED PEOPLE
LIKELY TO BE FOUND AT WORK?

Just about everywhere and in every form. They may appear as the chronic absentee, the willful rule breaker, the boss hater, or the troublemaker. They may also appear in more sympathetic form as the psychosomatic employee, the person who has lost self-confidence, the alcoholic, the pill popper, or even the work-obsessed individual. Symptoms of emotional problems may even emerge unexpectedly in the most normal and stable individuals.

WHEN DO THE PERSONAL PROBLEMS OF TROUBLED EMPLOYEES BECOME A CONCERN OF THE SUPERVISOR?

When the *performance* of the troubled employee becomes unsatisfactory. (Note the emphasis on performance.) Employees under stress often function far below their capabilities, or they may disturb the work of others. When either condition occurs, these employees become problems to themselves and to their supervisors. Ultimately, many of these troubled employees become the subjects of grievances and discipline.

For many workers, the distinction between problems arising from their personal lives and those associated with their work becomes increasingly blurred. Sometimes, only the supervisor can sort these problems out. And, difficult as it may be, supervisors have a continuing responsibility to confront employee behavior that affects productivity.

ARE THESE EMOTIONALLY DISTURBED EMPLOYEES INSANE?

The overwhelming majority of troubled, or emotionally disturbed, employees are definitely not "crazy." Psychologists do, however, believe that one out of five workers is subject to emotional upsets that visibly disturb his or her work. The *behavior* of these employees is not normal. For example, when goaded by fear (instilled perhaps by a threat from a bill collector) or by anger (possibly the result of being refused a day off), they may act in a way that might be described as "crazy." But they are not (except for a very few) crazy, insane, or even abnormal.

WHAT ABOUT PSYCHOTIC AND NEUROTIC EMPLOYESS?

Both terms sound pretty ominous. But only the employee with a *psychosis* is seriously ill. The most common type of psychosis is schizophrenia, or split personality. Schizophrenics live partly in a world of imagination. When the world seems threatening to them, they withdraw. They may be able to adjust to life or even have successful careers, but when they lose their grip, their problems are beyond the scope of a layperson.

On the other hand, most people are neurotic to some degree. People who have exaggerated fears, who feel the need to prove themselves, or who are irritable, hostile, opinionated, timid, or aggressive (which somewhere along the line describes most of us) have the seeds of *neurosis* in them. It's when this condition becomes exaggerated that a neurotic employee becomes a problem to associates and to the supervisor.

Here are just a few examples of neurotic employees: the lift-truck operator who boasts about drinking and sexual prowess; the supervisor who gets pleasure from reprimanding an employee in front of others; the mechanic who visits the nurse every other day with some minor ailment; the records clerk who meticulously arranges the workplace in the same manner every day and can't begin the job unless everything is exactly right.

WHY MUST SO MUCH ATTENTION BE PAID TO TROUBLED EMPLOYEES?

Mainly because there are so many of them. Hardly a week goes by in which a supervisor does not deal with problems created by a troubled employee. Happily, most of these problems are minor. If left unattended, however, they can begin to demand a major portion of a supervisor's time and attention.

There are also many sociological and humanitarian reasons for being concerned about problem workers. One big reason is that a problem employee is probably also a problem husband, son, daughter, or wife. But industry's concern, admittedly, is primarily an economic one. Problem employees are expensive to have on the payroll because of their decreased productivity. They are characterized by excessive tardiness and absenteeism. They are difficult to supervise. And they have a tendency to upset the morale of the work group. Consequently, a supervisor should be concerned about (1) hiring problem employees in the first place, (2) handling them on the job so that they reach an acceptable level of productivity with the least disruption of the company's overall performance, and (3) determining whether troubled employees have become so seriously maladjusted that they need professional attention.

HOW CAN YOU RECOGNIZE AN EMPLOYEE WITH AN EMOTIONAL PROBLEM?

Be careful here. There are a vast number of employees whose problems are minor or temporary. With a little help and patience, they will be able to get themselves back on track. However, there are a few whose emotional problems are very deeply rooted. Their disturbances are very serious and are beyond the kind of relief a supervisor can be expected to offer. Unfortunately, it is often very difficult, even for a trained observer, to tell when an employee has crossed over the line into the more serious category. Generally speaking, the symptoms of employees with emotional problems are similar. These people tend to run away from reality. They do this by going on sick leave or by making too-frequent visits to the dispensary; they may believe that their supervisors are against them, or blame their failures on other people and other things rather than accepting any blame themselves.

Many problem employees fall into the following categories: They are given to sudden changes in behavior, tire easily, are suspicious, are sure that superiors withhold promotions, or believe their associates gossip maliciously about them. Some are characterized by excessive absenteeism, are given to drinking sprees and/or drug abuse, are insubordinate, or have ungovernable tempers.

Among themselves, problem employees differ widely, just as more normal people do. But within the framework of their symptoms, they are surprisingly alike in their reactions.

WHAT CAN YOU DO ABOUT YOUR TROUBLED WORKERS?

Let's make this clear. We are not talking here about psychotic persons or the ones with serious neurotic disorders. *They need professional help.* Nor are we talking about routine performance appraisals, where it can be assumed that criticism will be received and suggestions for improvement will be discussed rationally and objectively. What follows here applies mainly to counseling efforts with mildly troubled employees.

You can help troubled employees toward better adjustment only after establishing an empathic atmosphere. You must first reassure them that you are trying to help them keep their jobs or enjoy their work more. You are *not* looking for ways to punish them or for an excuse to get rid of them. No approach will do more harm to an emotionally disturbed person than adopting an attitude that says "Better get yourself straightened out or you'll lose your job." Emotionally disturbed people are fearful or angry enough without feeling additional pressure from their supervisors. You must genuinely want to help them, and you must project this conviction to them. With such empathy as a foundation, you must then give the troubled employees every opportunity to help themselves.

Employee counseling is essentially a problem-solving technique. It is task-oriented; that is, it deals with a specific, job-related condition. The supervisor's role is a facilitating one. You do not direct or control the session; the employee does. The counselor listens rather than talks. You do not criticize or argue. Nor do you offer "evaluative" opinions. You do not "judge" an employee's personal problems. Instead, you aim to act as a "sounding board" to help release the pressures that are adversely affecting the employee's performance. If the counseling is successful, the employee—not the supervisor—solves the problem.

It cannot be overemphasized, however, that supervisors have great limitations in their counseling roles. *They are not psychologists or social workers,* and they can do more harm than good if they attempt rehabilitation beyond their training and experience. They cannot be "fix-it persons" for employees' personal problems. Supervisors should be, of course, experts at recognizing these problems and be sympathetic toward them. Beyond that, their counseling roles should be restricted to providing "emotional first aid."

HOW IS EMPLOYEE COUNSELING APPROACHED?

The researchers in this field suggest that a supervisor can best counsel employees if the following six rules are followed for each interview:

1. Listen patiently to what the employee has to say before making any comment of your own.
2. Refrain from criticizing or offering hasty advice on the employee's problem.
3. Never argue with an employee while you are counseling.
4. Give your undivided attention to the employee.
5. Look beyond the mere words of what the employee says—listen to see if he or she is trying to tell you something deeper than what appears on the surface.
6. Allow the employee to control the direction of the session.

WHAT RESULTS SHOULD YOU EXPECT FROM COUNSELING AN EMPLOYEE?

Recognize what you are counseling an employee for, and don't look for immediate results. Never mix the counseling interview with some other action you may want to take, such as discipline.

Suppose Ruth has been late for the fourth time this month. The company rules say she must be suspended for three days. When talking to Ruth about the disciplinary penalty, try to keep the conversation impersonal. Your purpose at this point is to show her the connection between what she's done and what is happening to her.

Now in the long run you may wish to rehabilitate Ruth because she's potentially a good worker. This calls for a counseling interview. And it's better to hold the interview with Ruth at a separate time. (Of course, it would have been better to hold the interview before she had to be disciplined.)

Counseling interviews are aimed at helping employees to unburden themselves—to get worries off their chest. Whether or not the conversations are related to the problems the employees create for you at work is not important. The payoff comes when they gain confidence in you, and consequently don't vent their hostilities and frustrations on the job. Experience seems to show that this will happen if you are patient. It won't work with every troubled employee, of course, but it will with most of them.

HOW DO YOU START A COUNSELING SESSION?

Find a reasonably quiet place where you're sure you won't be interrupted or overheard. Try to put the employee at ease. Don't jump into a cross-examination. Saying absolutely nothing is better than that. If Ralph has become a problem because of spotty work, you can lead into the discussion by saying something like this: "Ralph, have you noticed the increase in the orders we're getting on the new model? This is going to mean a lot of work for the company for a long while ahead. I guess it has meant some changes, too. How is it affecting the operation of your machine? What sorts of problems has it created?"

Note how the supervisor talks only of performance problems. Only the employee—never the supervisor—should introduce anything whatsoever about personal problems.

HOW MANY COUNSELING INTERVIEWS SHOULD YOU HAVE WITH A PROBLEM EMPLOYEE? HOW LONG SHOULD A COUNSELING INTERVIEW LAST?

It is difficult to provide clear-cut answers to these questions. For a less serious case, one interview might clear the air for a long time. With employees whose emotional problems are more serious, it may take five or ten 15- to 30-minute conversations just to gain confidence. And with still others, the counseling will have to become a regular part of your supervisory routine.

You can readily see that counseling can be time-consuming. This is why it's so important to spot worried workers early and take corrective action while you can help them with the minimum drag on your time.

How long should an interview last? You can't accomplish much in 15 minutes, but if that's all you can spare, it's a lot better than nothing. At the very least, it shows the employee you're interested in the problem. Ideally, an interview should last between 45 minutes and one hour.

HOW CAN YOU RECOGNIZE WHEN AN EMPLOYEE NEEDS EMOTIONAL FIRST AID?

Dr. Harry Levinson, a nationally recognized authority and founder of the Levinson Institute, advises that the basic steps (Figure 12-1) for you to take in administering emotional first aid are as follows:

1.   Recognize the emotional disturbance.
2.   Relieve acute distress by listening (counseling).
3.   Refer cases beyond your limits to professional help.

To recognize the employee who needs counseling help, says Dr. Levinson, look for three major signs:

Extremes. The ordinarily shy person goes even deeper into a shell. The hail-fellow-well-met steps up social activities to a fever pitch.

Anxiety. If withdrawal or increased activity brings no relief, the employee may become panicky or jittery, show extreme tension, become flushed in the face, or perspire heavily.

Breakdown. If still unable to cope with the anxiety, the problem employee may break down altogether and be unable to control thoughts, feelings, or actions. Thinking becomes irrational. The person doesn't make sense to others. Emotions may become irrational. For instance, the tidy person may become slovenly, the quiet person noisy.

HOW CAN YOU PROVIDE RELIEF FOR THE EMOTIONALLY TROUBLED EMPLOYEE?

Dr. Levinson suggests you may be helpful simply by letting the emotionally disturbed employee know how much the current distress is affecting the job and how much of this the company will tolerate. Above all, a person under stress may become even more disturbed if plagued by fears of

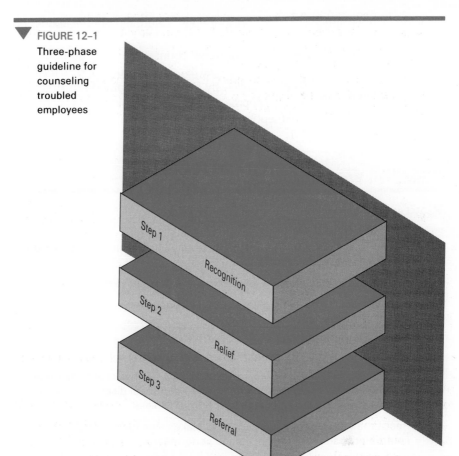

▼ FIGURE 12–1
Three-phase
guideline for
counseling
troubled
employees

Step 1
Recognition

Step 2
Relief

Step 3
Referral

what the company might do if and when it discovers the condition. If you can offer some rule of thumb, even if your comments are not entirely sympathetic, you at least provide something concrete to guide the employee's actions. (For example: "We appreciate the fact that you have something bothering you. And we're willing to go along with your present performance for a couple of weeks or so. But if it doesn't improve after that, we'll have to find a solution.")

If the employee voluntarily brings the problem to you, you can help most by listening, advises Dr. Levinson. This is more difficult than it appears, he cautions. Listening must mean truly *nonevaluative* listening, without interruptions, advice, prescriptions, solutions, pontifications, or preaching.

Nancy Hull, a former chemical-abuse counselor and an authority on the subject, also cautions about the legal aspects of counseling. In the film *The Troubled Employee,* produced by Dartnell Corporation of Chicago, Hull suggests a conservative approach to what an employee may consider a confrontation. Hull's perceptive guidelines have been adopted for supervisory use in Table 12-1.

TABLE 12-1 Rules of thumb for employee counseling

 1. Let the employee know that the company's concern is for job performance, not off-the-job behavior.

2. Be very specific about what the employee needs to do in order to perform up to the company's expectations.

3. Avoid making a diagnosis: supervisors are not expert in these matters.

4. Don't discuss personal problems during a counseling session unless unacceptable behavior occurs on the job.

5. Recognize, however, that, without professional help, personal problems generally get worse, not better.

6. If an emotionally troubled employee is seeking professional help, explain that this neither excludes the employee from normal disciplinary measures nor entitles the employee to special privileges.

7. Resist the temptation to moralize or to make value judgments; stick to confrontations that relate only to job performance.

8. Don't be swayed or distracted from your mission by emotional pleas, sympathy tactics, or "hard-luck" stories.

9. Emphasize—and maintain—the confidentiality of the discussion.

WHEN SHOULD YOU CALL FOR PROFESSIONAL HELP?

Dr. Levinson offers this rule of thumb: *If after two listening sessions you seem to be making little headway in establishing confidence, you should report the case (in confidence, of course) to the company nurse or the company physician.*

Dr. Levinson also advises that your approach in referral should be that of opening another door for additional help. Don't ever suggest by action or word that the employee is "crazy," hopeless, or unworthy of attention.

WHAT CAN PROFESSIONALS DO FOR TROUBLED EMPLOYEES THAT SUPERVISORS CAN'T DO?

Two kinds of industrial professionals usually work with mentally disturbed employees whose adjustment is beyond the limits of the supervisor's help:

▶ The *psychiatrist* is a fully qualified physician who has practiced medicine before qualifying for this specialty. An *industrial psychiatrist,* because of specialized training and experience, can diagnose more closely what an individual's trouble is and prescribe the proper kind of treatment. No supervisor should try to do either.

▶ The *counselor,* or *industrial psychologist,* works with the great majority of emotionally disturbed employees who do not need full-scale psychiatric treatment. Because of specialized training, the counselor's biggest asset is the ability to listen understandingly to an employee's account of his or her problems. The professional counselor has an advantage over the line supervisor in that the counselor doesn't have the authority to discipline, promote, or fire the employee and therefore has a greater chance of winning the employee's confidence.

ABSENTEES ARE A SPECIAL KIND OF PROBLEM PEOPLE. HOW LENIENT SHOULD YOU BE WITH THEM?

It depends on the reasons for absence. Professor P. J. Taylor of London University, who was formerly Medical Director of Shell (U.K.) Ltd., observes that 60 percent of all absentees have serious or chronic illnesses and 20 percent have acute, short-term illnesses such as the flu; 10 percent feel unwell because of minor illnesses such as colds, and they do or don't report to work according to their attitudes about their jobs; and the final 10 percent are completely well but feign illness to enjoy a day off.

It is the group of absentees who make up the bottom 20 percent who are suspect. Industrial psychologists call their "virus" *voluntary absence.* In many, this is deeply rooted. The Puritan ethic of work does not apply to them. There is an inevitable conflict between the desires for more leisure and more work. This tug is especially evident among younger workers. They often reflect an attitude of "entitlement." They feel that, somehow, the job is owed to them and that they have no responsibility for delivering a fair day's work in return.

Many authorities, however, still contend that employees who are chronically absent from work are mentally ill. They reason that the reality of work must be so unbearable to these emotionally disturbed employees that they literally escape from reality by staying away from work. Regardless of the reasons, you can help reduce absenteeism by:

▶   Firming up your rules about it.

▶   Being consistent in applying penalties.

▶   Trying to get at the reasons why an employee is frequently absent.

The last method requires the counseling technique. It is important that each individual case be followed up promptly. In your discussions of the problem with employees, be sure to permit them to explain their reactions to the job itself, the people they work with, the working conditions, their tools and equipment, and the kind of training they receive. You thereby avoid their feeling that you are placing all the blame on them. And if they are specific in their reactions, you then have specific complaints, rather than vague dissatisfactions, with which to deal.

Don't overlook, however, the power of job satisfaction in luring absence-prone workers back to the job. Surprisingly, however, physical working conditions seem to have little effect. In company after company, attendance figures show little variation between dirty, unpleasant areas and those that are clean and well lighted. Even most incentive schemes aimed at reducing absences are relatively ineffective. Closeness of the work team, its homogeneity, and the state of its morale seem to have the greatest effect.

HOW EFFECTIVE IS COUNSELING IN REDUCING ABSENTEEISM?

Success depends on the root causes of individual absences. See how the patterns and the motivations differ:

Chronic absentees. The people who have little capacity for pressure, either on the job or off, may be prime candidates for counseling. But first they must be made fully aware of the consequences of poor attendance. Theirs is a habit, usually of long standing, and correction requires pressure to attend as well as "hand holding."

Vacationing absentees. The people who work only so long as they need the cash and then treat themselves to a day or two off are difficult cases. These employees are often extremely capable on the job, but they feel no deep responsibility for it. Vacationers make a conscious choice to be absent and are rarely helped by counseling.

Directionless absentees. The younger employees who have as yet found no real purpose in work may simply follow the lead of the vacationer, who appears to lead a footloose, exciting life. A Dutch-uncle talk with the directionless absentee may be more effective than counseling.

Aggressive absentees. The persons who willfully stay away from work in the hope that their absences will cause an inconvenience for you are probably emotionally disturbed. Correction of this kind of behavior, however, requires professional counseling, not the kind of ordinary counseling that a supervisor can provide.

Moonlighters. The persons who hold more than one job are often either too tired to come to work or faced with conflicting schedules. Straight talk, rather than counseling, is prescribed. When attendance is affected, the moonlighter must be forced to make a choice between jobs.

Occasional absentees. The persons who seem to have slightly more absences than the rest of your staff are probably prime candidates for counseling. Their absences are legitimate. Their illnesses are real. Their problems are often temporarily insurmountable. These people deserve a mixture of sympathy, understanding, and sometimes outright advice. This might also be the time for you to take a look in the mirror. For example, are you contributing to the absenteeism by lack of support and training?

In summary, you can probably help people who are absent for the following reasons:

1. Getting to work is a problem, real or imagined.
2. Off-job pressures are so strong that they weaken the employee's resolve to get to work.
3. The employee is imitative, easily led or misled.
4. The work appears boring, disagreeable, or unattractive.
5. Working relationships are unpleasant.
6. There are in fact off-job problems—child care, serious illness, court appearances—that need immediate attention.
7. Absence or lateness has become a habit.

You will have difficulty, however, helping people who are absent because of these reasons:

1. The work or the pay associated with it holds no strong attraction.
2. Off-job pleasures have a greater appeal than work.
3. The employee is willfully absent in order to disrupt or inconvenience the organization.

HOW MUCH DISTINCTION SHOULD BE MADE BETWEEN ALCOHOL ABUSE AND DRUG ABUSE?

In principle, there may be very little difference. In practice, there are significant differences, especially legal ones. Many of the counseling approaches, however, are the same for both problems.

WHAT CAN YOU DO FOR ALCOHOLIC EMPLOYEES?

Whatever you attempt, proceed slowly and cautiously. Not all heavy drinkers are alcoholics. The more alcoholics drink, the less likely they are to admit to anyone (even themselves) that their ability to handle liquor has gotten out of their control.

An alcoholic employee is really just another kind of problem employee, but this problem is an aggravated one that may require the help of a professional. Nevertheless, many alcoholic workers have rescued themselves with the aid of Alcoholics Anonymous (AA), an association of ex-alcoholics who, because they don't preach and because they emphasize the individual's need to face weaknesses, have perfected the art of listening without being either sympathetic or critical.

Your best bet, however, is to recognize an alcoholic in the early stages. Then you can apply the same techniques to gain the person's confidence that you would use with any other problem employee. Your objectives are to provide security at work and to help with talking out problems. If these employees can be helped to recognize that excessive drinking is a problem they aren't handling, then you can refer them to the company doctor or nurse, who in turn may be able to persuade them to look into Alcoholics Anonymous or to visit a psychiatrist or a special clinic for alcoholics.

HOW CAN YOU TELL WHETHER OR NOT YOU'VE GOT AN ALCOHOLIC EMPLOYEE ON YOUR HANDS?

To guide you in recognizing alcoholic employees, Professor Harrison M. Trice of Cornell University advises that you look first to the employee's absence record. A sharp rise in the overall rate of absences almost always accompanies the development of drinking problems, he says. In a study of

200 cases of alcoholism in industry, Professor Trice also noted five differences from the normal conception of absences among problem drinkers:

> Absences are spread out through the week. Neither Monday nor Friday absences predominate (probably because the alcoholic is trying to be careful not to draw attention to the condition).

> Partial absenteeism is frequent. A worker often reports in the morning but leaves before the day is over.

> There may be frequent short absences from the workplace during the workday. Changes in behavior, especially a deterioration in performance, also may take place as the day progresses.

> Tardiness is not a marked feature of alcoholism in industry. The widespread notion that a problem drinker comes to work late was not substantiated.

HOW SHOULD YOU APPROACH COUNSELING AN EMPLOYEE YOU BELIEVE TO BE AN ALCOHOLIC?

Alcoholism requires a special form of counseling, say those who have coped with it most effectively. For example, the U.S. Department of Health, Education, and Welfare (HEW) in its *Supervisors' Guide on Alcohol Abuse* offers these hints to supervisors who are faced with this problem among their employees:

1. Don't apologize for confronting the troubled employee about the situation. Your responsibility is to maintain acceptable performance by all your employees.

2. Do encourage the employee to explain why work performance, behavior, or attendance is deteriorating. This can provide an opportunity to question the use of alcohol.

3. Don't discuss a person's right to drink. It is best not to make a moral issue of it. HEW views alcoholism as a progressive and debilitating illness, which, if untreated, can eventually lead to insanity, custodial care, or death.

4. Don't suggest that the employee use moderation or change his or her drinking habits. A person who is an alcoholic cannot, at the start, voluntarily control drinking habits.

5. Don't be distracted by the individual's excuses for drinking—a difficult spouse, problem children, financial troubles. The problem as far as you are concerned is the employee's drinking and how it affects work, behavior, and attendance on the job.

6. Don't be put off by the drinker's assertion that a physician or a psychologist is already being seen. The employee may claim that the physician or the psychologist doesn't consider the drinking a problem or thinks the use of alcohol will subside once the "problems" are worked out. Therapists probably wouldn't say that if they knew an employee's job was in jeopardy because of alcohol abuse; they would attach a new importance to the drinking habits.

7. Do remember that the alcoholic, like any other sick person, should be given the opportunity for treatment and rehabilitation.

8. Do emphasize that your major concern as a supervisor is the employee's poor work performance or behavior. You can firmly state that if there is no improvement, administrative action—such as suspension or discharge—will be taken.

9. Do state that the decision to accept rehabilitative assistance is the employee's responsibility.

Ann St. Louis, personnel counselor for Canada's Department of National Revenue, whose program maintains a 90 percent recovery rate among alcoholic government workers, adds this thought:

> An employer—far better than wife, mother, minister or social agency—can lead an alcoholic to treatment by "constructive coercion." Give an employee every chance to take treatment, but make it clear that he must cooperate or lose his job. This has proven to be more effective than loss of friends or family.

HOW WIDESPREAD IS DRUG ABUSE AMONG EMPLOYEES?

It is not so pervasive as you might think. Because regular drug use is incompatible with regular attendance, drug users tend not to select most regular or demanding kinds of employment. Attempts on a company's part to screen out hard-drug users before employment have not been particularly successful. Dismissal afterward can be difficult because drug users are good at hiding the tools of their habits even if they cannot conceal the symptoms.

Symptoms of drug use are well known. At work they manifest themselves objectively in terms of poor or erratic performance, tardiness, absenteeism, requests to leave early, forgetfulness, indifference to deadlines and safety, and in many instances theft of company property.

Treatment and rehabilitation for drug users are as difficult and complicated as for alcoholics, and the treatments are somewhat similar. Company policies against drug addiction, however, tend to be firmer than those against drinking and alcoholism. For one thing, the addict is different from the alcoholic because many addicts try to involve other people in drugs. The danger of an alcoholic's inducing another employee to become alcoholic is slight. Then, too, drug use is illegal; in most instances, use of alcohol is not.

Here again, a supervisor's responsibility should be limited to the detection of drug addiction, prevention of the use or sale of drugs on company property, and counseling of drug users, including referral—if indicated—to the appropriate company authority.

WHAT SORT OF RESPONSIBILITY DO SUPERVISORS HAVE FOR COUNSELING EMPLOYEES WITH TERMINAL ILLNESSES?

Much has to do with your own sense of compassion, as tempered by your company's policies. Increasingly, supervisors must cope with employees who are suffering from terminal illnesses, such as cancer and AIDS. The presence of these employees can be demoralizing to others on your staff as well. In general, the advice seems to run this way:

▶ Allow the affected employee to choose whether or not, and how, to tell other employees of her or his condition.

▶ Develop some sort of transitional role for the employee. It should be one that matches the individual's capacity for work and still reflects his or her value to the company.

▶ Within these limits, avoid special treatment and expect the employee to follow established rules, regulations, and standards of performance. This is what most terminally ill people who choose to keep working prefer. This enhances their sense of worth as adults who are still 100 percent alive and not 85 percent dead.

REVIEW ▼ 12 ▼ QUESTIONS

1. Why is it so important for supervisors to identify and attempt to help troubled employees in their work force?
2. When a supervisor is counseling an employee, should the emphasis be placed on behavior, performance, or attitude? Why?
3. Differentiate between a neurotic employee and a psychotic employee. Which of these should be referred to a professional counselor?
4. Describe the features of the counseling approach.
5. List the three phases of Dr. Levinson's approach to employee counseling. What symptoms characterize an extremely disturbed individual who ought to receive professional help without delay?
6. Discuss the difference between valid absences caused by bona fide illness and absences that psychologists describe as voluntary absences. What can a supervisor do to minimize the latter kind?
7. What should a supervisor stress when counseling an employee who has shown signs of alcoholism?
8. Why might a company have policies for confronting drug abuse that are different from those dealing with alcohol abuse?

A CASE IN POINT

The Popular Absentee

Gabriella is 23 years old and serves as a paralegal clerk in a large law firm. She has been employed there for six months. Gabby, as she is called, is charming and energetic and is very popular with the office staff and with the lawyers. Furthermore, Gabby's on-the-job performance is outstanding.

Gabby, however, is frequently late for work. She takes long lunch hours and has been absent from work an average of two days per month for the past three months. She apologizes when she saunters in late, but seems unconcerned about her tardiness and her absences. To her fellow paralegals, Gabby readily admits that she doesn't have a great deal of interest in her work. The best thing about the job, she says, is that it pays well enough for her to do some of the other things she likes to do in her off hours.

Gabby's supervisor, the office manager, observes: "She's a charmer and she has a lot of potential. I'd sure hate to lose her, but she's become a problem here."

If you were Gabby's supervisor, what would you do now? Five alternative courses of action are listed below. Rank them in the order in which they appeal to you (1 most effective, 5 least effective). You may add another approach in the space provided, if you wish. In any event, be prepared to justify your ranking.

_____ **A.** Encourage Gabby to improve her attendance. Sympathize with her lack of interest and try to make the job less boring for her.

_____ **B.** Have a shoulder-to-shoulder talk with Gabby, pointing out how damaging a poor attendance record will be to her career.

_____ **C.** Suggest that Gabby seek professional counseling for this problem so as to "get her head on straight."

_____ **D.** Tell Gabby that her job is on the line: either the lateness and absences stop, or she will be terminated.

_____ **E.** Because Gabby is well liked and does such good work when present, accept the minor disruptions caused by her tardiness and absences.

If you have another approach, write it here.

▶ _____

_____

_____

Complete the ACTION PLANNING CHECKLIST
for this chapter, which can be found on page 322.

13

APPRAISING EMPLOYEE PERFORMANCE

LEARNING OBJECTIVES

After studying this chapter, you should be able to:

1. Explain the purposes and benefits of performance appraisals and distinguish them from job evaluations.

2. Describe a graphic weighting scale, differentiate between objective and subjective evaluation factors, and suggest ways for minimizing bias.

3. Outline the main steps in an appraisal interview and discuss techniques for making it effective.

4. Discuss methods for handling sensitive problems that may arise during, or as a result of, an appraisal interview.

5. Explain the legal implications of a performance appraisal, recognize its limited relationship to financial rewards, and identify several extenuating circumstances that can contribute to poor performance.

OVERVIEW OF KEY CONCEPTS
IN THIS CHAPTER

▶ The objective of performance appraisals is to help employees improve the caliber of their job performance. When made aware of those areas in which they are already doing a good job and of those in which there is room for improvement, employees can be encouraged to develop strengths and to overcome weaknesses.

▶ The careful and fair application of both objective and subjective factors in appraisals will help assure employees that their ratings are based on facts and not on opinions. It is important to minimize the halo effect in making judgments, and it is essential that standards be clearly established for all factors that are evaluated.

▶ An appraisal interview should be carefully prepared so that it progresses systematically. The interview should first accentuate the positive by giving credit where credit is due. It may then shift to a discussion of areas where performance is not up to standard. The interview should conclude with an agreement concerning concrete action for improvement or further development.

▶ Supervisors must be prepared to deal with sensitive issues, such as accusations of bias, negative employee reactions to criticism, and the inability to assure good performers of immediate or tangible rewards.

▶ The appraisal of employee performance is an activity that is regulated by the Equal Employment Opportunity Commission. The EEOC advises that appraisals must be based on "critical work behaviors as revealed by a careful job analysis." Not only must evaluations be supportable by facts, but they must also be absolutely free from discrimination. Furthermore, supervisors must recognize that carelessness and lack of effort are not the only causes of inadequate performance. Mismatches between jobs and workers, physical or emotional stress, poor supervision, and indefinite procedures may all contribute to poor performance.

AT ITS ROOT, WHAT IS THE
TRUE PURPOSE OF AN APPRAISAL?

There are four basic reasons for making an appraisal of employee performance:

1. *To encourage good behavior or to correct and discourage below-standard performance.* Good performers expect a reward, even if it is only praise. Poor performers should recognize that continued substandard behavior will at the very least stand in the way of advancement. At the most drastic, it may lead to termination.

2. *To satisfy employees' curiosity about how well they are doing.* It is a fundamental drive in human nature for each of us to want to know how well we fit into the organization for which we work. An employee may dislike being judged, but the urge to know is very strong.

3. *To provide a firm foundation for later judgments that concern an employee's career.* Such matters as pay raises, promotions, transfers, or separation can be handled more smoothly if the employee is aware of the possibilities beforehand.

4. *To serve as a basis for an employee's training and development.* A good appraisal identifies performance weaknesses that often can be improved by specific training programs. It also highlights the presence of individual potential that can be developed through proper assignments and advanced training.

WON'T EMPLOYEES RESENT BEING EVALUATED?

The biggest fear in most supervisors' minds is that an employee will dislike being judged. Surprisingly, this fear is unfounded—if the appraisal is based on facts rather than on opinions and if you display a willingness to change ratings if an employee can show you that you're wrong. People want to know where they stand—even if what they hear isn't to their liking. But don't interpret this to mean that appraisal interviews are free from stress or that employees will make it easy for you. Chances are they won't.

Furthermore, do not let your discussion with the employee being rated take on the nature of an end-of-term school report. Mature adults resist this. Subordinates can easily regard the performance appraisal as just another way for the company to increase its control over them if this attitude prevails.

HOW OFTEN SHOULD YOU EVALUATE AN EMPLOYEE?

Twice a year for a formal appraisal is a happy medium. If you rate too often, you're likely to be too impressed by day-to-day occurrences. If you wait too long, you're likely to forget many of the incidents that ought to influence your appraisal. Even if your company has a plan that calls for rating only once a year, it's good practice to make appraisals of your own—informally, perhaps—more often. This does not mean that you should not observe employee performance routinely—and compliment or criticize it, as the case may be. You should do this, of course, regardless of formal appraisal sessions.

WHAT IS THE RELATION OF PERFORMANCE APPRAISALS TO JOB EVALUATION, COMPENSATION RATES, MERIT RATING, AND MERIT RAISES?

This is a sensitive question, often asked by employees. You should approach this issue carefully, because much depends on your company's policies toward it. *Job evaluation* is a systematic method for appraising the worth of a particular job, *not* the individual who performs it. The *compensation* set for a particular job is the result of a job-pricing decision based on the job's evaluation, which should have little or nothing to do with the person who ultimately performs the job. *Merit rating* is a term that is now obsolete. It once was synonymous with performance appraisal, and many employees still believe it is. The problem arises from its implication of *merit raises*—salary increases based on merit. Most organizations strive to separate the performance appraisal session from decisions regarding issuance of merit raises. The purpose is to keep the focus of the appraisal on performance, not on salary. This distinction is not always clear to employees.

It is a cardinal mistake, then, for a supervisor to stress the relationship of pay raises to performance during the appraisal interview. It is only human for persons who have been told that their work is good to expect an increase in pay to follow. If your company's compensation plan doesn't work that way, you may suffer a very red face when an employee tells you later on, "You told me my good work would bring a raise or a promotion."

HOW FORMAL WILL THE PERFORMANCE RATING PROCEDURE BE?

Because of legal implications, most organizations now carefully specify and monitor their performance appraisal programs. Most appraisal formats incorporate some form of "graphic weighting scale." A simple version is shown in Table 13-1. Typically, these formats provide a choice of ratings for each factor, ranging from "superior" or "outstanding" to "expected level" and on down to "unsatisfactory." Numerical weights often are attached to each rating so that a total score for the overall appraisal can be obtained.

A variation of the above is the "forced-choice" format. This provides a series of paired descriptive statements for each factor being rated. One statement is always more positive or less negative than its opposing member. Thus, in making judgments, a supervisor is forced to choose very carefully between two somewhat similar evaluations.

TABLE 13-1 Example of a graphic weighting scale

Factor	Rating*					Score
	A	B	C	D	E	
1. Quality of work	20	16	12	8	4	_____
2. Quantity of work	20	16	12	8	4	_____
3. Dependability	20	16	12	8	4	_____
4. Attitude	10	8	6	4	2	_____
5. Initiative	5	4	3	2	1	_____
6. Housekeeping	10	8	6	4	2	_____
7. Attendance	10	8	6	4	2	_____
8. Potential for advancement	5	4	3	2	1	_____
Total rating score						

*A, superior; B, very good; C, at expected level; D, below expected level; E, unsatisfactory.

WHAT FACTORS SHOULD YOU CONSIDER WHEN APPRAISING AN EMPLOYEE?

These can vary from plan to plan. What you are trying to answer about an employee's performance, however, are these questions:

What has the individual done since last being appraised? How well has it been done? How much better could it be?

▶ In what ways have strengths and weaknesses in the individual's job approach affected this performance? Are these factors ones that could be improved?

▶ What is the individual's potential? How well could the employee do if really given a chance?

Factors that are judged in appraisals tend to fall into two categories: objective factors and subjective factors. *Objective factors* focus on hard facts and measurable results—quantities, quality, attendance. *Subjective factors* tend to represent opinions, such as those about attitude, personality, and adaptability. Distinguish between the two. Be firmer about appraisal of objective factors than about those involving opinion only. But even subjective factors can be rated with confidence if they are supported by documented incidents. The sample performance rating form shown in Table 13-1 includes both objective and subjective factors.

HOW CAN YOU MAKE SURE YOUR RATINGS ARE CONSISTENT FROM EMPLOYEE TO EMPLOYEE?

Before we answer this question, it should be stressed that no employee's rating is ever measured against another's. Performance is always compared with the stated responsibilities and standards established for a particular job. If there is a variety of skills and experience among your employees, however, you may find it helpful to double-check your ratings to make sure that you are not favoring one employee or making an unsupported judgment about another. Accordingly, try this objective approach:

1. List the names of employees down one side of a sheet of paper and the factors to be rated across the top.
2. Look only at one factor at a time. Take quality, for instance. If you have rated Tom only "fair" and Pete and Vera "good," ask yourself if you are using the same standards for each. Perhaps upon reconsidering, you'll want to drop Pete's rating to "fair" because Pete and Tom produce the same quality of work, whereas Vera's quality is demonstrably better than either Pete's or Tom's.

You may also want to consider whether or not you're rating all employees either too high or too low. In most work forces there is some sort of variation in performance levels. Performance will be exceptionally high for some employees, exceptionally low for others, and somewhere in between for the remainder. Keep in mind, however, that every employee can rate near or at the top if she or he performs well against the stipulated responsibilities and standards.

DOESN'T AN EMPLOYEE'S RATING REPRESENT ONLY THE SUPERVISOR'S OPINION?

A good performance rating includes more than just a supervisor's opinion. It should be based on facts. In the consideration of quality of performance, what is the employee's error record? As to quantity, what do the production records show? And as for dependability, what is his or her absence and lateness record? Can you cite actual incidents in which you have had to discipline the employee or speak about the quality or quantity of output? Answering these questions makes your rating less opinionated and, consequently, more valid and worthwhile.

Such documented incidents become critical examples (often called *critical incidents*) of an employee's performance. These incidents should undeniably represent the quality—good or bad—of an employee's work. It is a good practice to make notes of such occurrences and place them in the employee's file. At appraisal time they serve to illustrate what you consider good or subpar performance and to support the ratings you make.

WHAT'S THE HALO EFFECT? HOW CAN YOU AVOID IT?

Nearly all of us have a tendency to let one favorable or unfavorable incident or trait overly influence our judgment of an individual as a whole. This is called the *halo effect.* It can introduce a wide range of biases, of which the most insidious are these:

▶ *Recency.* Remembering only what happened recently—yesterday, last week, or last month.

▶ *Overemphasis.* Placing too much weight on one outstandingly good or poor factor.

▶ *Unforgivingness.* Not allowing an employee's improved performance to overcome a poor record in the past.

▶ *Prejudice.* Allowing an individual's contrary personality to overshadow his or her good work.

▶ *Favoritism.* Being influenced by a person's likableness, despite poor job performance.

▶ *Grouping.* Tarring all employees in a substandard work group with the same brush.

▶ *Indiscrimination.* Being either too critical or too generous in regard to the entire group; giving no one, or everyone, a good rating.

▶ ***Stereotyping.*** Allowing judgments to be affected by preconceived notions about such things as race, sex, color, religion, age, or national origin.

One of the best ways to minimize the halo effect is to rate all your employees on a single factor before proceeding to ratings for the next factor. This approach helps to focus your attention on each individual's qualities one at a time, rather than lumping them together into one generalization.

WHAT IS THE BEST WAY TO HANDLE
THE APPRAISAL INTERVIEW ITSELF?

Whereas there are any number of approaches you might use, the following seven steps will form a pretty good path toward understanding and acceptance of the appraisal on the part of the employee.

Step 1. Prepare the employee, as well as yourself, to come to the meeting expecting to compare notes. This way, you will have your facts at hand and the employee will have had the opportunity to reflect on his or her performance during the previous period.

Step 2. Compare accomplishments with specific targets. Don't be vague or resort to generalizations. Be specific about what was expected and how close the employee has come to meeting those expectations.

Step 3. Be sure to give adequate credit for what *has* been accomplished. It is a temptation to take for granted those things that have been done well and to concentrate on the deficiencies.

Step 4. Review those things that have *not* been accomplished. Emphasize areas where improvement is needed. Explain why it is necessary for the employee to improve, and explore together with the employee how this can be done.

Step 5. Avoid giving the impression that you are sitting in judgment. If there is blame to be shared, acknowledge it. Don't talk in terms of mistakes, faults, or weaknesses. Never compare the employee with a third person. Stick to a mutual explanation of the facts and what they imply for both of you.

Step 6. Agree on targets to be met during the period ahead. Be specific about them. Relate them to what has not been accomplished during the current period. This will set the stage for a more objective appraisal discussion next time around.

Step 7. Review what *you* can do to be of greater help. Improvement is almost always a mutually dependent activity. An employee who feels that you share responsibility for the improvement will approach the task with greater confidence and enthusiasm.

WHERE SHOULD YOU CONDUCT PERFORMANCE RATING OR APPRAISAL INTERVIEWS?

Do it privately, in your own office or in a private room. You'll want to be able to give the interview your undivided attention. And you won't want to be in earshot of other employees. Allow yourself enough time—at the very least a half hour. Otherwise, the whole procedure will be too abrupt.

WHAT'S THE "SANDWICH" TECHNIQUE FOR TELLING EMPLOYEES ABOUT UNFAVORABLE ASPECTS OF THEIR WORK?

The sandwich technique means simply to sandwich unfavorable comments between favorable comments, as shown in Figure 13-1. For example, say: "I've been pleased with the way you've stepped up your output. You've made real improvement there. I am a little disappointed, however, by the quality of what you've produced. The records show that you're always near the bottom of the group on errors. So I hope you'll work as well to improve quality as you did quantity. I feel sure you will, since your attitude toward your work has been just fine."

The same technique is a helpful guide to the entire appraisal/review discussion. Use it by starting the talk off with a compliment. Then discuss the work that must be improved. Finish by finding something else good to say about the employee's work. Although some criticize this technique as "obvious," it is still an effective technique when constructive guidance is provided.

SHOULD YOU LEAVE ROOM FOR EMPLOYEES TO SAVE FACE?

Yes. Call it what you want, but you should give employees every chance to tell you what obstacles stand in the way of their making good. Don't interrupt or say, "That's just an excuse." Instead, take your time, and let the person talk. Often the first reason given isn't the real one. Only if you listen carefully will you discover underlying causes for poor attitude or effort.

▼ FIGURE 13-1
The
"sandwich"
technique

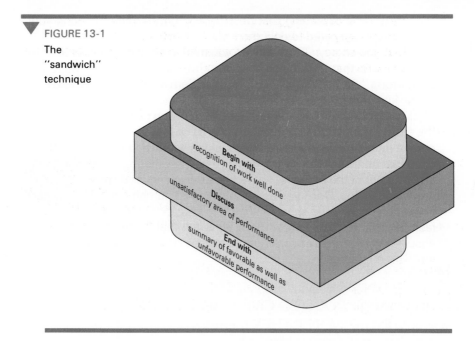

FIGURE 13-1
The "sandwich" technique

Begin with
recognition of work well done

Discuss
unsatisfactory area of performance

End with
summary of favorable as well as
unfavorable performance

Confidence in you as a supervisor and in the performance rating system is important. So don't be too anxious to prove that the employee is wrong. Above all, don't show anger, regardless of what kind of remark the employee makes. This advice still goes even if the employee becomes angry.

SHOULD YOU DISCUSS ONE EMPLOYEE'S RATING WITH ANOTHER EMPLOYEE?

Never! Always avoid comparisons. And be sure that each employee knows that you keep each rating confidential. Try to establish the entire procedure on the basis of confidentiality.

HOW DO YOU HANDLE CHARGES OF BIAS OR FAVORITISM?

Unfavorable criticism occasionally stings an employee so severely that the person reacts by charging bias or favoritism. Don't try to argue the employee out of it. Your direct denial probably won't be accepted anyway.

Instead, try acknowledging that possibly you have erred in making your rating. But be prepared to document your reasoning.

For instance, say: "Tony, why do you think I might be favoring Sam? If I've given you that impression, perhaps you can help me see where I've been wrong." So Tony says, "Well, you give Sam all the easy jobs, and I get all the junk that no one else wants."

Your reply ought to be along these lines: "I don't agree that I give Sam the easy jobs, but I do find that I ask him to do lots of jobs that need first-rate attention. He seems easier to get along with when I need something done in a hurry. On the other hand, I've been hesitating to ask you to do anything out of the ordinary. That's because you act as if I'm taking unfair advantage of you. Don't you agree that it's just human nature on my part to lean on people who show they want to cooperate? Maybe it's been my fault that you feel I've favored Sam. I'll watch that in the future. But how about your pitching in and taking your share of the load? Will you try it that way with me, Tony?"

ISN'T IT DANGEROUS TO GIVE EMPLOYEES HIGH RATINGS? WON'T THEY EXPECT TO GET IMMEDIATE RAISES OR PROMOTIONS AS A RESULT?

Knowledge of where an individual stands with the boss is every bit as important to a top-notch performer as it is to a mediocre employee— maybe even more so. If you fail to show your recognition of a good job, an employee is likely to feel, "What's the use of doing a good job if no one appreciates it?"

Good workers are hard to come by. They should know how you feel, even when you can't give them immediate rewards. Remember, people work for much more than what they get in their paychecks.

HOW CAN YOU TELL EMPLOYEES THAT THEIR WORK IS WAY BELOW PAR?

Don't be too harsh on poor performers. Be especially sure that your treatment has encouraged the best kind of performance. Otherwise, they may feel that their poor showings are more your fault than their own.

Your guides should be these: Be firm. Nothing is to be gained by being soft. If work has been bad, say so.

Be specific. For example: "We've been over this before. During the last six months I've made a point of showing you exactly where you have fallen down on the job. Remember the rejects we had on the X-56 job? And the complaints on the motor shafts? Only last week you put the whole shop in a bad light by the way you mishandled the shaft job again."

Don't rub it in, though. Allow the employee to maintain self-respect. End the discussion by summarizing what you have found satisfactory as well as the things that are unsatisfactory.

ISN'T IT TRUE THAT NO MATTER HOW WELL SOME EMPLOYEES DO THEIR JOBS, THERE'S LITTLE CHANCE OF THEIR GETTING BETTER JOBS?

Yes. It's especially hard on a good worker who is bucking a seniority sequence and who knows that, until the person ahead gets promoted or drops dead, there is little chance to move up. Suppose a number-two laboratory analyst said to you: "Each time I get reviewed, you tell me I'm doing a good job. But this hasn't done me any good. I'm getting top dollar for the job I'm on, and until the number-one analyst changes jobs, I'm stuck. All the performance review does to me is to rub salt in the wound!"

A good way for you to handle this complaint is to admit the situation exists, but don't oversympathize. Try saying something like this: "Sure, I agree that it's hard waiting for your chance. But some workers make the mistake of depending entirely on seniority for their advancement. I don't want you to fall into that trap. When the next better job opens, I hope both of us can say that you're fully qualified. That's one of the good things about performance ratings. You can find out where your weak spots may be and correct them. For a person who has your ability and does as well on the job as you do, there's no reason why you have to limit your ambitions to the number-one specialist's job here. Maybe you'll be able to jump from a number-two job here to a choice job in another department in the company."

HOW SHOULD THE SUPERVISOR FOLLOW UP AFTER THE PERFORMANCE APPRAISAL INTERVIEW?

An appraisal done today isn't finished for good. In order for an appraisal to be of lasting value to you and your employee, you should follow up the appraisal interview in the following ways.

Stick to Your Side of the Bargain. If you have promised to examine an employee's work more carefully to see if you've given a fair rating, do so.

Check the past record and show the employee any data that have been questioned. If you must change your rating, do it promptly and let the employee know that his or her point of view has been supported.

Provide Techniques for the Employee's Development. An employee will need your help to improve—especially skills. Give the worker the kind of training your review indicated would help. If the employee needs more versatility, broaden the assignments by giving different and challenging jobs. If workmanship is inferior, study what the worker is doing wrong and show how it can be done right.

Continue To Show Interest in the Employee's Work. Drop by the workplace occasionally with a view toward letting the employee know that he or she has improved—or gone downhill—since the interview. If progress is being made, give credit. If the employee is slipping, point out where you're dissatisfied.

HOW SOON SHOULD YOU APPRAISE A NEW EMPLOYEE?

Don't wait for the formal appraisal time. Constructively criticize new employees as soon as problems arise. Identify the causes of poor performance. Ask whether the unsatisfactory performance was due to forgetfulness, carelessness, lack of skill, or failure to understand the standards expected. Offer whatever assistance is needed. With new employees, you should document the conversations right away be sending them memos and placing copies in their personnel files. If a problem occurs a second time, immediately confront the employee and repeat the documentation. Otherwise, a poor start may deteriorate and leave you with an unsatisfactory, but permanent, employee.

WHAT ARE THE LEGAL IMPLICATIONS OF A PERFORMANCE APPRAISAL?

There are several. Most of them are related to the following legal doctrines:

▶ Equal pay for equal work.

▶ Absence of discrimination on the basis of age, sex, religion, color, or national origin.

▶ Accommodation of the physical and mental needs of the handicapped and of veterans of the Vietnam era.

▶ Equal employment opportunity.

Furthermore, performance appraisals are viewed by the courts as a form of employment test. As such, formal appraisals are subject to all the legislation applicable to selection and placement tests. Accordingly, to minimize accusations of noncompliance with legal requirements of any kind, supervisors should try to do the following:

1. Make certain that your appraisals are based on what the job actually requires employees to do, not on a comparison with other employees and not on what you'd *like* them to be able to do. This is the value of job analysis and a detailed job description.

2. Be especially cautious in making subjective judgments. Ask yourself, "Could I back them up if challenged?"

3. Stick to facts that can be documented. When in doubt, keep a record of an occurrence that might be disputed.

4. Never say anything, even in the spirit of "leveling" with an employee, that could possibly be interpreted as meaning that your appraisal was based on a favorable or unfavorable reaction to the individual's race, color, religion, age, sex, national origin, handicap, or veteran's status. It is difficult, of course, to be so neutral in your judgments, but you must do everything possible to avoid even the appearance of prejudice or discrimination. To do otherwise might bring you and your employer into court.

SHOULD A SUPERVISOR KEEP A WRITTEN RECORD OF WHAT TRANSPIRES DURING AN APPRAISAL INTERVIEW?

First ask your employer or personnel department for advice on this one. Then listen to our answers. We'll give you two:

No. If you have developed a rapport during the interview that promises that the two of you will go forward with mutual confidence, you may destroy this valued atmosphere by putting a summary of your interview in writing.

Yes. If your appraisal has been negative and you expect the improvement may not be forthcoming, it's wise to make a written record—

especially of what you expect from the employee in terms of improved performance in the future. If you do make such a record and place it in the employee's official file, you will be expected by law to give a copy to the employee. This is the problem. You'll have documentation if you need it later on, but you may make an enemy of the employee (or at least make him or her wary).

It is also a good idea to collect in an employee's official file some sort of documentation of critical incidents. These might include regularly kept reports that show the level and/or quality of output, written complaints or compliments from customers or internal staff members, and examples of very good or very poor work, such as a report filled with arithmetic or typing errors.

HOW ARE EMPLOYEE PERFORMANCE RATINGS RELATED TO PAY INCREASES?

This is strictly a matter of your company's policy. About the only generality that can be drawn is that employees whose ratings are less than satisfactory should not be recommended for pay increases. When a company has a rate range (maximum and minimum wage rates) for each job, many people believe that only workers who are rated "very good" or "exceptional" should advance to the maximum rate for the job.

IF YOU CAN'T GIVE AN EMPLOYEE A RAISE, WHY RATE THE EMPLOYEE AT ALL?

Performance rating is so often associated with money that supervisors and employees alike lose sight of the other important benefits. Periodic performance reviews help a supervisor to:

▶ Point out strengths and weaknesses to employees so that they can cultivate the former and correct the latter.

▶ Provide a fair and unbiased method for determining qualifications for promotions, transfers, and special assignments.

▶ Recognize those employees who have exceptional ability and deserve training for higher positions and responsibilities.

▶ Weed out those who aren't qualified for the work they are now doing and assign them to more suitable work or, if they are wholly unqualified, separate them from the company's payroll.

SOME EMPLOYEES TRY VERY HARD, BUT THEIR PERFORMANCE REMAINS BELOW PAR. WHAT IS THE REASON FOR THIS? WHAT CAN BE DONE ABOUT IT?

If there is a weakness in performance appraisal programs, it is that management assumes that employees have only to try harder in order to measure up to standards. This is often not the case. Many factors can contribute to substandard employee performance. For example:

1. *An individual may be assigned to work that does not match his or her capabilities.* The job may be too easy or too difficult. One solution is a transfer to a more suitable job. Or the job might be redesigned to give the employee a better fit. If an employee cannot handle the paperwork required, perhaps it can be done by someone else. If the job requires too little judgment for a highly intelligent person, perhaps it can be rearranged to provide options that use this person's analytic ability.

2. *An employee may not have received proper training.* In any case of continued poor performance, the supervisor should first reexamine the training program and find a way to review the job procedure with the employee from start to finish. A key operating point may have been missed.

3. *An individual may be the victim of pressures from the work group.* An employee may be trying to conform to your job standards, but coworkers may be giving him or her a hard time. To correct this situation, you may need to approach it from the group's point of view to change or modify the coworkers' position.

4. *A worker may not be up to the job requirements, physically or emotionally.* A checkup by the company nurse or doctor may be in order. If there are persistent family problems—divorce, death, severe illness—you may try gentle counseling. Your objective should be to show that you are sympathetic but that there is a limit to how long the related poor performance can be accepted.

5. *Your own supervision may be at fault.* It takes two to tango, and poor performance may be related to a supervisor's failure to provide

clear-cut standards, to train employees effectively, or to help with problems and changes as they arise.

6. *Mechanical or procedural problems may exist.* Possibly there is
some hitch in the operating process—improper tools, materials, or
equipment—or a conflict in prescribed paperwork procedures. You
may want to review these problems with your own boss or with the
appropriate staff departments.

REVIEW ▼ 13 QUESTIONS

1. What is it that employees expect to gain from a performance appraisal?

2. Distinguish between a job evaluation and a performance appraisal.

3. Explain the difference between an objective rating factor and a subjective one.

4. Cora complains that her supervisor keeps bringing up a mistake that she made months ago, something that rarely occurs anymore. What is the distortion that her supervisor is imposing on her performance? How might the supervisor lessen the tendency to make such distortions?

5. Should an employee accept full responsibility for his or her improvement as a result of a performance interview?

6. Why isn't it a good idea to wait until a formal appraisal session to correct the poor performance of an employee, especially a newly hired one?

7. What is meant by the statement that the performance appraisal is a legally protected activity? Who protects it?

8. What are some possible causes of poor performance other than carelessness or lack of effort?

A CASE IN POINT

You Never Made It Clear!

Vicki drums a pencil on her desk as she listens to Cesar's argument. Vicki is a shift supervisor for national reservations booking for a major motel chain. She is in the middle of a semiannual performance appraisal interview with Cesar, a reservation clerk, a man with a slight physical handicap. Vicki has just told Cesar that unless his work improves within the month, he will be discharged. This comes as a shock to Cesar. He loves this job and has assumed that it would be his forever. "What have I done wrong?" Cesar asks.

"Lots of things," says Vicki. "For one thing, your coffee breaks often extend to an hour or more. For another, our computer monitor shows that, on average, you handle only 20 customer contacts an hour, compared with the standard of 25. This can't be news to you, Cesar, I've spoken to you several times about it already."

"I remember your speaking to me about the coffee breaks, at my last performance review, but I thought I explained the reason to you."

"You reason wasn't satisfactory," says Vicki, "and I told you that it had to stop. Yet, only yesterday, you were away from your desk for nearly an hour. Other operators had to cover for you. That's one of the reasons that your call output is so low. Instead of improving since the last performance review, your productivity has gone down even further."

"Okay, Vicki, if you're really serious about these things, I'll try to do better in the future."

"I am serious, and you'd better do better within the month," advises Vicki. "If you don't, you'll be out of here by then."

"You mean that? Why didn't you warn me about it the last time? I thought our talk had been just a friendly discussion. In fact, you praised me for having a nice way with the customers. Besides, you never said anything about the standard of 25 customer contacts per hour. Now you're threatening me about them."

"Well, you know now," says Vicki, "and you've got only one more chance before being discharged."

"That's not fair," complains Cesar. "You never made this situation clear to me. You're discriminating against me, and I'm going to complain to the Equal Employment Opportunity Commission about it."

What might Vicki have done during Cesar's previous performance interview to avoid this outcome? Five alternative courses of action are listed below. Rank them in the order in which they appeal to you (1 most effective, 5 least effective). You may add another approach in the space provided, if you wish. In any event, be prepared to justify your ranking.

_____ A. Made sure that Cesar knew that he was expected to meet the standard of 25 customer contacts per hour and the penalty for not attaining it.

_____ B. Not have mentioned the coffee break problem, because that is just so much nitpicking.

_____ C. Helped Cesar save face by apologizing for criticizing his performance.

_____ D. Offered to show Cesar how to improve his productivity, provided he did his part by not wandering away from his work.

_____ E. Not have praised Cesar for his nice way with the customers.

If you have another approach, write it here.

▶ _____

_____

_____

Complete the ACTION PLANNING CHECKLIST
for this chapter, which can be found on page 323.

14

HOW AND WHEN
TO DISCIPLINE

After studying this chapter, you should be able to:

1. Explain the purposes of employee discipline and identify the most common types of offenses that require disciplinary action.

2. Discuss the range of employee responses to disciplinary action and describe those employees most likely to warrant such action.

3. Differentiate between positive and negative discipline, explain progressive discipline, and know the four elements of the "hot stove" rule.

4. Discuss the emphasis placed on behavior rather than personality, list the prescribed steps in the behavior modification approach, and know the limitations placed on supervisory authority in disciplinary matters.

5. Explain the two criteria for just cause, recognize common pitfalls in administering discipline, and discuss the importance of keeping proper support records.

OVERVIEW OF KEY CONCEPTS IN THIS CHAPTER

▶ Most employees exert the necessary self-control to keep themselves out of trouble. Only a relatively few employees find it difficult either (1) to meet work standards or (2) to conform to the rules and regulations imposed by an organized activity. Accordingly, effective discipline is aimed not so much at punishing as at encouraging good performance.

▶ When exerting discipline, supervisors are placed in the unenviable role of acting as both judge and jury. Employees will accept discipline from their supervisors, however, when it appears to be fair and just and consistently applied.

▶ Effective discipline should be an essentially positive effort. Its three hallmarks are (1) punishment suitable to the importance of the offense, (2) penalties that become progressively severe as offenses are repeated, and (3) disciplinary action applied only if there has been adequate warning, and applied immediately, consistently, and impartially.

▶ The supervisor's role in maintaining discipline requires unusual self-control, objectivity, and integrity. The supervisor not only must identify and apprehend transgressors, but she or he must also make judgments and impose penalties based on examination of mitigating circumstances, sensitivity to each individual's response to correction or encouragement, and consideration of past and improved performance.

▶ Disciplinary actions are increasingly subject to legal scrutiny for implications of prejudice or discrimination. In order to measure up to the test of just cause, two criteria must be met: prior notification of (1) what constitutes unacceptable behavior and (2) what the penalties for this behavior will be. Employees are entitled to, and expect, due process and are represented in this regard by labor unions and by the EEOC and other federal, state, and local agencies.

WHAT IS THE REAL PURPOSE OF DISCIPLINE?

The real purpose of discipline is quite simple. It is to encourage employees to meet established standards of job performance and to behave sensibly and safely at work. Supervisors should think of discipline as a form of training. Those employees who observe the rules and standards are rewarded by praise, by security, and often by advancement. Those who cannot stay in line or measure up to performance standards are penalized in such a way that they can clearly learn what acceptable performance and behavior are. Most employees recognize this system as a legitimate way to preserve order and safety and to keep everyone working toward the same organizational goals and standards. For most employees, self-discipline is the best discipline. As often as not, the need to impose penalties is a fault of management as well as of the individual worker. For this reason alone, a supervisor should resort to disciplinary action only after all else fails. Discipline should never be used as a show of authority or power on the supervisor's part.

WHAT SORTS OF INFRACTIONS MOST TYPICALLY TRIGGER THE NEED FOR DISCIPLINARY ACTION?

They vary all over the lot. It isn't so much the nature of the infraction as its degree. A small infraction of some standard or rule may often be tolerated. When the breach becomes large or persistent, however, the need for discipline becomes urgent and obvious.

In addition to poor performance—in terms of either output or quality—infractions that most commonly result in disciplinary action include absenteeism, insubordination, carelessness or negligence, horseplay or fighting, dishonesty or falsification of company records, slowdowns, abusive or obscene language, alcoholism, and drug use or possession.

WHY DO EMPLOYEES RESENT DISCIPLINE?

Employees don't object to the idea of rules and regulations, but they frequently object to the way a supervisor metes out discipline. In civil life, if a person breaks the law, the police officer only makes the arrest. The person is tried before a jury of peers who are guided by the rulings of an impartial judge, who in turn determines the punishment.

Now compare the civil procedure for handling lawbreakers with what happens in your organization. As supervisor, you're often called on not only to put the finger on the wrongdoer, but also to hear the case and decide the penalty. To many employees this seems unfair because you've acted as police officer, judge, and jury.

So don't take your job as disciplinarian lightly. It's a great responsibility and requires impartiality, good judgment, and courage on your part.

Incidentally, when the work group thinks the rules are reasonable, the group itself will impose discipline to keep its members in line.

WHY DO EMPLOYEES BREAK RULES?

As in most personnel problems, only a small percentage of workers cause disciplinary problems. People who break rules do so for a number of reasons—mostly because they are not well adjusted. Contributing personal characteristics include carelessness, lack of cooperation, laziness, dishonesty, lack of initiative, lateness, and lack of effort. The supervisor's job is to help employees to be better adjusted.

People break rules less often when the supervisor is a good leader and shows a sincere interest in employees and when employees get more enjoyment from their work. After all, if an employee finds the work uninteresting and the boss unpleasant, is it surprising that the employee will find reasons for being late or for staying away from work altogether?

If the supervisor gives employees little or no chance to show initiative on the job or to discuss ways in which the work should be done, the supervisor shouldn't be surprised that employees talk back or shirk their responsibilities. This is what some people do who can't express themselves in any other way.

Sometimes the real reason an employee breaks rules or seems lazy on the job has nothing to do with working conditions. The employee may be having worries at home—money problems or a nagging spouse—or may be physically sick. You might ask, "What concern is that of the supervisor?" It isn't—unless the supervisor wants that employee to be more cooperative and productive at work. If you're smart enough to see the connection, you can do much to improve this worker's performance. Don't snoop in personal affairs, but do offer a willing and uncritical ear. Let the employee know that you're an understanding person, that the boss is someone to talk to without getting a short answer or a lot of false advice.

So when an employee breaks a rule, make discipline your last resort. Instead, search hard for the reason the employee acts that way. Then try to see what you can do to remove the reason.

WHAT KIND OF HANDLING DO EMPLOYEES EXPECT FROM A SUPERVISOR IN THE WAY OF DISCIPLINE?

Justice and equal treatment. Being soft, overlooking nonstandard performance, or giving chance after chance to wrongdoers does not win popularity among most employees. In fact, it works the other way to destroy morale. This is because most people who work hard and stay in line are frustrated and disappointed when they see others get away with things. No one likes to be punished, but everyone likes to be assured that the punishment received is in line with the error. ("Let the punishment fit the crime" is the advice given in Gilbert and Sullivan's *Mikado.*) The treatment should be neither better nor worse than that given anyone else for the same fault.

SOME PEOPLE TALK ABOUT NEGATIVE DISCIPLINE AND SAY POSITIVE DISCIPLINE IS BETTER. WHAT DOES THIS MEAN?

Penalizing someone is negative discipline. Getting an employee to do what you wish through constructive criticism or discussion is positive discipline.

Supervisors, more than employees, understand that disciplining is an unpleasant task. All a supervisor wants is to run the department in peace and harmony, to see that things get done right, and to ensure that no one gets hurt. The supervisor who can establish discipline by good leadership won't have to exercise negative discipline through scoldings, suspensions, or discharges.

WHAT IS MEANT BY PROGRESSIVE DISCIPLINE?

This means that the penalties for substandard performance or broken rules get increasingly harsh as the condition continues or the infraction is repeated. (See Figure 14-1.) Typically, a first offense may be excused (but not overlooked!) or the worker may be given an oral warning. A second offense elicits a written warning. A third infraction may bring a temporary layoff or a suspension. The final step occurs when an employee is discharged for the fourth (or a very serious) infraction.

WHAT IS THE "HOT STOVE" RULE OF DISCIPLINE?

It is an allegory used to illustrate the four essentials of a good disciplinary policy. (See Figure 14-2.) If the stove is red-hot, you ought to be able to

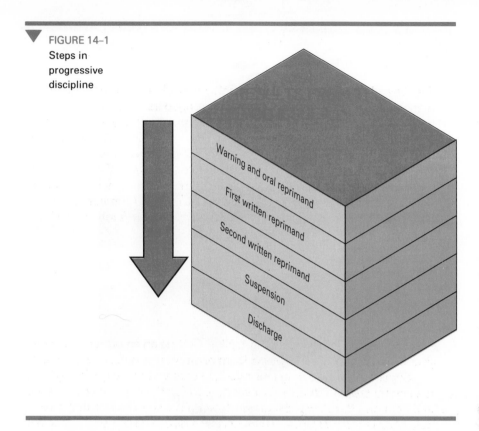

Warning and oral reprimand

First written reprimand

Second written reprimand

Suspension

Discharge

see it and to know that if you touch it, you will be burned; this is the principle of *advance warning.* If you touch the hot stove, you get burned (penalized) right away; this is the principle of *immediacy.* Every time you touch a hot stove, you will get burned; this is the principle of *consistency.* Everyone who touches a hot stove will get burned because it plays no favorites; this is the principle of *impartiality.*

CAN A SUPERVISOR ADMINISTER DISCIPLINE AND STILL REMAIN ON FRIENDLY TERMS WITH EMPLOYEES?

Yes, but only by focusing on performance, or behavior, not by focusing on personalities or attitudes. Make no mistake: disciplinary action can be an unpleasant experience for supervisor and employee alike. You cannot overlook poor performance or misconduct. Such problems rarely solve themselves. A supervisor must face up to them. Nevertheless, as with griev-

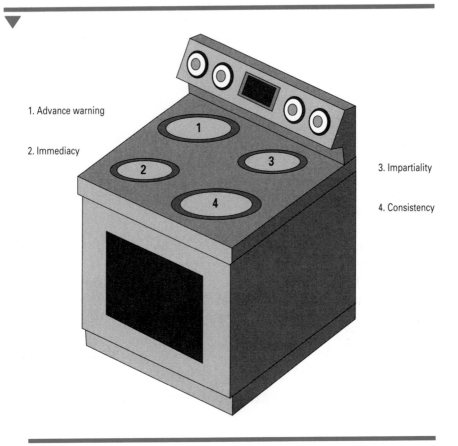

1. Advance warning

2. Immediacy

3. Impartiality

4. Consistency

FIGURE 14–2 The "hot stove" rule for discipline

ance handling, a supervisor must listen to an employee's explanation with the intent of understanding before evaluating that point of view. If criticism or action is indicated, make it clear that this is a response to unacceptable practice or conduct. It is not a condemnation of the employee as a person. Your objective is to instill self-control, not to embarrass an individual or to penalize for the sake of punishing.

PEOPLE SPEAK OF A BEHAVIOR MODIFICATION APPROACH TO DISCIPLINE. WHAT DOES THIS MEAN?

Behavior modification (BM) prescribes a step-by-step procedure for supervisors to follow in practicing positive discipline. It is based on proven

assumptions about what makes people most likely to respond constructively to criticism and requests for improvement. The six steps a supervisor should try to follow—in sequence—during a disciplinary interview with
an employee are listed below, along with an example of each:

1. *State the performance or disciplinary problem:* "Lester, you've
   damaged a lot of merchandise in the warehouse lately by driving the
   prongs of your lift truck into it."

2. *Ask the employee for his or her view of the problem:* "Can you tell
   me why this is happening?"

3. *Ask the employee for a solution to the problem:* "What can you
   suggest as a way of solving this problem of damage to merchandise?"

4. *Agree on a plan to solve the problem:* "Okay, we'll check the brakes
   on the lift truck, and you'll cut down on your speed and exercise special care so that damage to merchandise from that cause will be elimi-
   nated."

5. *Give the employee an oral or written warning:* "This time, I'll let
   this problem go with an oral warning. If the problem continues, however, I'll have to place a written warning in your personnel file."

6. *Set up a date for a review:* "Let's hope that the problem has been
   solved. We'll meet three weeks from now to see what kind of progress
   has been made."

Note the emphasis on performance as the problem, not attitude or
personality. Note, too, the involvement of the employee in analyzing the
problem and offering suggestions—including an improvement in his own
behavior—for its solution.

Should the damage continue, this will be reviewed at the next meeting.
Step 5 will then include, at the least, a written warning and possibly a more
severe penalty, such as notice of suspension or discharge if the condition
does not improve.

HOW FAR CAN A SUPERVISOR GO
IN HANDLING DISCIPLINE?

This depends on your company's management policy, and on the labor
agreement if your company has a union.

Legally, a supervisor can hire and fire. But firing is a costly action.
Breaking in a new employee can cost anywhere from $500 for an unskilled
laborer to several thousand dollars for a skilled mechanic. So most companies have tried to approach discipline from a positive direction. And
because discipline puts a supervisor in such a responsible position, many

companies have carefully spelled out just how far a supervisor can go before having to check with the boss.

Labor unions, in their desire to provide the maximum protection from injustice or unfair treatment, maintain that discipline shouldn't be handled by management alone. Unions contend that they, too, should help decide on an employee's punishment. How much say a particular union will have depends on how successful the union has been in writing this privilege into the contract or in establishing precedents for its participation.

So tread carefully in disciplinary matters. Find out from your company's policy-level management (your immediate superior or the personnel manager) just how far the company wants you to go, and how much involvement you must allow the union.

WHAT DETERMINES THE ACTION YOU SHOULD TAKE?

Facts rather than feelings. No one can make a decision without all the facts, or at least all that can be reasonably gathered. If a situation arises that looks as if it will require disciplinary action, look hard before you leap. Take time to investigate. Let the employee tell the full story, without interruptions. Check with witnesses for their observations. Look in the company record to see what other supervisors have done in the past. Speak to your boss or the personnel manager to get advice.

HOW EFFECTIVE ARE WARNINGS?

Warnings can do a lot of good—if you make them more than idle threats. Your warnings put employees on notice that their performance isn't up to standard. It gives you a chance to explain a rule that they may have taken only lightly before, and to make the penalty clear to them. When you warn employees, that's the perfect time for you to be constructive, to offer help, to practice positive discipline.

To make a warning a valuable piece of evidence in a union grievance, you should always make a written record of it. You'd be surprised how much weight arbitrators and the Equal Employment Opportunity Commission (EEOC) give to notations that you have written in your pocket notebook or the department logbook or have inserted in the employee's personnel file.

Some companies make this written notation a formal practice by requiring that supervisors fill out a form to be filed by the personnel department. These notations are called *written reprimands,* and copies of such reprimands are sent to the employee and the union.

UNDER WHAT CIRCUMSTANCES
CAN YOU FIRE AN EMPLOYEE?

As mentioned previously, the supervisor's authority is limited by the company's policy and by its agreements with the labor union, if one exists.

Speaking generally, however, some employee offenses are worse than others. Drinking or sleeping on the job, smoking in restricted areas, willfully destroying property, and falsifying time cards are often charges that result in discharge. It is also easier to generalize about offenses such as fighting on company property and gross insubordination. All these wrongdoings have one thing in common—they are single incidents rather than accumulations of minor offenses, and many of these single acts require immediate action by the supervisor.

To handle any of these serious offenses and still leave yourself free from reversal later on, there's an effective action you can take. It's short of discharge, but it certainly gets the culprit out of the company quickly and legally. This action is called *suspension.* It follows the advice arbitrators give employees: "Obey first—argue later."

To suspend an employee, you merely say something like this: "You've come to work with a load on. I think you're under the influence of liquor right now and are unfit to do your job. You could be subject to dismissal for being in this shape. I haven't made up my mind yet whether that's what I'll do. But in the meantime, you're suspended. Punch out your time card and don't come back to work until I call you. I'll try to let you know definitely tomorrow."

By suspending, you have demonstrated your willingness to enforce your authority when needed. And you have protected both yourself and the company from looking weak, foolish, or indecisive. If tomorrow, in the opinion of your boss, the personnel manager, or the company's lawyer, you can't make the discharge stick, you and the company are still in an effective position. It's when you cast the die—fire an employee and then have to take him or her back—that you have to "eat crow."

WHAT CONSIDERATION SHOULD BE GIVEN
TO AN EMPLOYEE'S GOOD WORK RECORD?

There's danger in carrying the rule book too far. Treating each offender equally does not mean that you should not weigh personal factors, too. For instance, what was the worker's attitude when the rule was broken? Was it done deliberately or accidentally? Was the worker emotionally upset by a circumstance beyond control (such as worrying about a sick child at home)? How long has the person worked for the company? What kind of work record has there been? Remember, it costs money to fire a good employee. Even civil courts put on probation a guilty person who has been considered a good citizen in the past.

In many instances, it is also good to wipe an employee's slate clean now and then. For example, if an employee who had a poor absence record two years ago has been nearly perfect since then, the employee should not have the past record brought up if at a later date there is another absence problem.

WHAT ARE THE UNDERLYING LEGAL REQUIREMENTS NEEDED TO DEMONSTRATE JUST CAUSE FOR DISCIPLINARY ACTION?

There are two requirements, and they apply to almost all situations. There must be:

1. *Prior notification of the types of performance or behavior that can lead to disciplinary action.* The notifications can be either oral or written. It is much better when they have been published and prominently displayed. Company rules and regulations do not cover everything, however. Neither do published standards. This is why it is so important for supervisors to communicate expressly to their employees exactly what the standards of performance and conduct are in their particular work areas.

2. *Prior notification of the penalties for unacceptable performance or behavior.* As with the first requirement, notifications of penalties are best when published and prominently displayed. Here again, supervisors should regularly make it clear to employees exactly what these penalties are and when they may be imposed. Where a progressive disciplinary policy is in effect, the steps in the progression should be communicated—in advance—to employees.

WHEN CAN'T YOU MAKE DISCIPLINARY ACTION STICK?

When the action has not been carefully planned and documentation gathered to support it. Actions must be based on genuine evidence, free from bias and discrimination. Impulsive, spiteful actions will backfire. Arbitrators, called in by labor unions to judge poorly conceived charges, are quick to spot weak cases and reject them. So are representatives of the EEOC. Dead beyond recall are the days when supervisors, or any other managers, could resort to discipline without being able to support their charges beyond a reasonable doubt.

As difficult as the disciplinary problem has become, however, most penalties and discharges can be made to stick—provided the supervisor makes none of the following mistakes:

No clear-cut breach of rule. In one company, a supervisor fired an employee for sleeping, only to see the decision reversed by the arbitrator. The union brought out the fact that the supervisor had made the observation from 60 feet away. The arbitrator ruled that at this distance the supervisor was "likely to see what he wanted to see."

Inadequate warning. Arbitrators frequently feel that workers are entitled to sufficient warning that their conduct won't be tolerated—even though the rules and penalties are in an employee manual. Typical is the case of an employee who has had a record of poor attendance for months without having been disciplined; suddenly the supervisor cracks down without warning and fires the employee.

Lack of positive evidence. Take this case of loafing—always a difficult charge to make stick: The company went along with the supervisor and fired a worker caught loafing. The arbitrator reversed the company's decision because (1) the supervisor had not been in the department continually but had popped in and out during one afternoon and (2) the person's job entailed occasional waits for material. Furthermore, the company could produce no time sheets that showed reduced output in black and white. The arbitrator ruled that the supervisor might have come into the department at the times the employee had been legitimately waiting for materials.

Prejudice. Real or imagined discrimination or favoritism weakens a disciplinary ruling. If a supervisor has shown that she has had it in for a worker and has just waited for an opportunity to enforce a penalty, an arbitration case may bring this out. If the supervisor has let some workers get away with the same offense for which she has punished another, she'll have a hard time justifying such unequal treatment.

Inadequate records. The value of written records of warnings and reprimands can't be overemphasized. Such records are especially valuable for documenting action taken to correct an accumulation of minor offenses. You may not want to discharge a person who's been late the first time—or even the fifth. But when it gets to be a frequent and costly habit, you'll want to take action. Unless you've built up a record of warnings and kept a file of them that can be shown to the union and an arbitrator if necessary, your case will be hard to prove.

Too-severe punishment. Many arbitrators recommend progressive punishment and look unfavorably on too-severe discipline—especially for first offenses. For instance, a supervisor in a can company noticed a worker away from his workstation ten minutes before the end of the shift. Later, a look at the employee's time card showed that he had punched out a half minute early. The man was fired because not long before that he had received a written reprimand for doing the same thing. He had been warned that the next time he'd be fired. An arbitrator ruled that a penalty was called for, but not such a severe one. Do it progressively, the arbitrator said—just a little tougher each time. A lighter penalty would keep an old (seven years' service) and valuable employee on the payroll.

Violation of policy or labor contract. Care should always be taken to ensure that infractions and discipline accurately reflect a company's established policies and/or, if a union is present, provisions of the labor contract.

HOW CAN YOU MAKE SURE THAT YOUR RECORDS WILL SUPPORT A DISCIPLINARY ACTION?

By taking care to make the proper records at each step of a progressive disciplinary action. Follow carefully your company's policies and procedures in this matter. The legal concept of *due process* is gradually taking hold in all areas of employment, especially those involving job security. This means that all employees, regardless of union representation, are entitled to fair and just hearing under adequate legal protection. Under such circumstances, a supervisor's opinions and recollections will not carry much weight. They will have to be supported by specific documentation. Records that help to provide this documentation include:

▸ **Regularly kept records,** such as time cards showing absences and latenesses, visits to the dispensary, production and quality-control tallies, and the like.

▸ **Written complaints** from customers or other contacts that can be identified without qualification with the individual who is to be disciplined.

▸ **Examples of unsatisfactory or careless work,** such as mistyped letters, incorrect tabulations on reports, or damaged goods—all tagged or marked in such a way as to identify the culpable individual.

▸ **Written summaries of appraisal and/or disciplinary conferences,** which should contain specific rather than general statements, including dates, figures, and clearly described incidents. The hard part here is that the law seems to say that copies of these reports (which are retained in personnel records) must be given to the individual at the time they are written.

REVIEW ▼ **14** QUESTIONS

1. Why might a well-behaved employee appreciate the presence of clear-cut disciplinary regulations in the workplace?
2. In what way does the enforcement of discipline at work differ from that in civil life?
3. Distinguish between negative discipline and positive discipline.
4. When Pedro saw Nelly sneaking out from work early again, he fired her on the spot, even though he hadn't given Nelly a previous warning. The discharge didn't stick, and Pedro was advised to use progressive discipline in future cases. How might he do that?
5. The "hot stove" rule is meant to help supervisors remember four important points about discipline. Briefly describe each.
6. What kinds of restraints may be placed on a supervisor's authority to handle disciplinary matters independently?
7. In order for disciplinary action to be supported by just cause, what two basic requirements must be met?
8. Why are written notations regarding warnings of possible, or actual, disciplinary action so important?

A CASE IN POINT

She Has Had It in for Me

Charley smirked. He had just returned from a session with the company's human resources director, and everything had gone his way. Charley's supervisor, Betty Silva, was not smiling. "Okay, Charley," Betty said, "we're back to ground zero, but next time, I'll make this penalty stick."

Here's what had happened. Charley, a press operator in a manufacturing plant that makes clasps for women's handbags, was a marginal producer. That is, his daily output regularly failed to get up to a level that Betty thought was suitable. Betty had not let this go unnoticed. More than once, Betty had told Charley that, in Betty's opinion, Charley's work was unsatisfactory. Charley's response was to say, "I'm doing my best." And Betty kept saying, "Your best isn't good enough." To which Charley replied, "Why don't you get off my case?" "I'll get off your case," said Betty, "when your attitude improves."

The situation became intolerable in Betty's eyes when a shipment of clasps had to be held up waiting for Charley to finish his press run. And, when the clasps were about to be packed, the inspector found that a significant number of them had not been struck squarely by the press and had to be discarded. Betty hit the roof when she heard of this development.

"That does it," said Betty to Charley. "Not only are you far too slow for this job, but what you do turn out isn't remotely up to scratch. Furthermore, your attitude toward your work here is entirely unsatisfactory. This will be your last day here. I'm preparing a separation notice right now. You can take it down to the human resources department. I'll call ahead so that they can start working on your last paycheck."

Charley had not been gone more than half an hour when the human resources director called Betty. "We can't make this separation stick," he said. "So far as we can see, there's nothing in the record to show that Charley's work is as bad as you say it is. And to make matters worse, he says you've had it in for him for a long while and are just looking for one bad day to try to fire him."

What should Betty do now to make sure that her disciplinary actions will be supported in the future—for Charley and her other employees? Five alternative courses of action are listed below. Rank them in the order in which they appeal to you (1 most effective, 5 least effective). You may add another approach in the space provided, if you wish. In any event, be prepared to justify your ranking.

_____ **A.** Maintain a record of Charley's performance, and of the performance of others who may be borderline, against standards.

_____ **B.** Move in quickly on Charley if his attitude doesn't show improvement.

_____ **C.** Crack down hard with a suspension the first time any employee's performance gets out of line.

_____ **D.** Take a more positive approach: Wait until a situation becomes truly critical before making it a disciplinary issue with an employee.

_____ **E.** Clearly communicate to all employees the standards of acceptable performance in the department—and the penalties for not meeting them.

If you have another approach, write it here.

▶ _____

_____

_____

Complete the ACTION PLANNING CHECKLIST
for this chapter, which can be found on page 324.

CHAPTER

15

ENSURING LEGAL COMPLIANCE IN THE WORKPLACE

LEARNING OBJECTIVES

After studying this chapter, you should be able to:

1. Identify and interpret the major equal employment opportunity laws and their impact on employment practices, especially as they pertain to discrimination toward minority, or "protected," groups.

2. Discuss the importance of women in the workplace and their difficulties in advancing from their traditional roles, including related subjects such as equal pay for equal work and sexual harassment.

3. Explain the legal and social aspects of an employee's right to privacy and the impact this has on a supervisor's right to manage.

4. Discuss the supervisor's legal and practical responsibilities in collective bargaining, labor-contract implementation, and relationships with union representatives.

5. Explain various facets of the Occupational Safety and Health Act and its enforcement at the department level.

OVERVIEW OF KEY CONCEPTS IN THIS CHAPTER

▶ A large body of equal employment opportunity (EEO) legislation has been enacted to protect and enhance the rights of minority groups, including blacks, women, Native Americans, Hispanics, Orientals, handicapped workers, older workers, and Vietnam era veterans. This places great responsibility upon supervisors to make sure that these laws are enforced in the workplace.

▶ Women are increasingly a major and valued portion of the work force. Nevertheless, the quality of their participation continues to need protection and enhancement. This is evident in the difference between women's pay and that of men. Most women ask only that their worth be judged on their merits and that they be given opportunities equal to those of men for higher-paying and higher-status jobs.

▶ Increasingly, the law—and society in general—demand that an employee's right to privacy be protected. This view has many ramifications in the areas of drug testing, lie-detector testing, and workplace monitoring, and in policies toward employees with terminal illnesses such as AIDS.

▶ In dealing with employees and labor unions, supervisors are viewed by the laws of the land as responsible agents of the organizations that employ them. Accordingly, it is important that supervisors refrain from interference during union representation elections and follow their prescribed roles during contract administration.

▶ The Occupational Safety and Health Act of 1970 created a large body of standards for safe working conditions, sanitation, and the handling of hazardous materials. This law places considerable responsibility upon supervisors for its enforcement. The law grants employees certain rights, but it also expects employees to participate actively in its implementation.

WHAT IS THE LEGAL BASIS FOR EQUAL EMPLOYMENT OPPORTUNITY PROGRAMS?

There is a great body of federal, state, and local laws. These have been reinforced by a number of significant rulings in the courts. The laws are further supported by guidelines laid down by the **Equal Employment Opportunity Commission (EEOC)**, the federal agency charged with enforcing the law.

There is no need for you to be bogged down with the details, which are extensive. A synopsis of the major federal laws, popularly referred to as the **equal employment opportunity (EEO) laws,** is provided for your review in Table 15-1. Most importantly, these laws specify that the great majority of business firms and public institutions cannot:

▶ Make any distinctions based on race, sex, or national origin in any condition of employment, including hiring, setting wages ("equal pay for equal work"), classifying, assigning or promoting, and allocating the use of facilities, and in training, retraining, and apprenticeship programs.

▶ Distinguish between married and single people of one sex and not of the other.

▶ Deny employment to women with young children unless the same policies apply to men with young children.

▶ Penalize women because they require time away from work for childbearing.

▶ Maintain seniority lists based solely on sex or race.

▶ Establish jobs as either men's or women's. The only exceptions allowed are jobs for which the employer can prove that there is a bona fide occupational qualification (BFOQ).

▶ Discriminate against workers 40 years of age or over in hiring, firing, promoting, classifying, paying, assigning, advertising, or eligibility for union membership.

▶ Similarly discriminate against qualified handicapped persons. The law defines handicapped, or disabled, persons as individuals who (1) have a physical or mental impairment (the term *impaired* is preferred by many) which substantially limits one or more major life activities, (2) have a record of such impairments, or (3) are regarded as having such impairment. You can see that the definition covers almost everything.

Obviously, EEO legislation was designed to protect minority groups of all definitions from discrimination. Its principal intent, however, has been to encourage more rapid utilization of blacks and women in the work

TABLE 15-1 Synopsis of major federal laws enacted since 1960 that affect equal employment opportunity

Law	Provision
Equal Pay Act (1963)	Amended the long-standing Fair Labor Standards Act of 1938 to require the same pay for men and women doing the same work and was extended in 1972 by Public Law 92-318.
Titles VI and VII, Civil Rights Act of 1964 as amended by Equal Employment Act of 1972	Prohibits job discrimination in all employment practices on the basis of race, color, sex, religion, or national origin. This includes recruiting, selecting, compensating, classifying, assigning, promoting, disciplining, and terminating, as well as eligibility for union membership. The EEOC administers these laws and monitors related affirmative action programs.
Executive Order 11246 of 1965 as amended by Executive Order 11375 of 1967	Prohibits discrimination in employment in organizations having contracts of $10,000 or more with the federal government. The orders require that these organizations institute affirmative action programs and recruit and promote women and minorities where necessary.
Age Discrimination in Employment Act (1967) as amended in 1975	Prohibits discrimination in hiring and employment of workers over 40 years of age unless BFOQ can be established.
Rehabilitation Act of 1973 and Executive Order 11914 of 1974	Prohibits discrimination of physically and mentally handicapped applicants and employees by federal contractors.
Vietnam Era Veteran's Readjustment Assistance Act of 1974	Prohibits discrimination—by federal contractors—in employment of disabled veterans and veterans of the Vietnam war; also specifies certain affirmative actions in the employment of veterans.

force. Note that the law is *not* a labor-management law: it is directed at employers, and they must comply without obstruction from labor unions.

IN THE EYES OF THE LAW, WHO IS A MINORITY EMPLOYEE?

Just about everyone who is not a middle-aged white male of European heritage and the beneficiary of a fairly adequate primary education. The generally more useful term applied to minorities today is *protected groups.* A protected group consists of people who, historically, have encountered discrimination in the American workplace. Most of the relevant laws specifically identify these people as ethnic and racial minorities (blacks, Hispanics, Asians, and Native Americans, in particular), women (white as well as black), disadvantaged young persons, handicapped workers, veterans of the Vietnam war era, and persons over 40 years of age.

The basic equal employment opportunity laws in the United States say that an employer cannot discriminate because of race, color, religion, sex, national origin, or age. In trying to make these laws work, various agencies of the U.S. government have interpreted them to apply to all victims of prejudice and discrimination. There has also been a special concern for those who are uneducated and have grown up in extreme poverty such as occurs in many urban ghettos and some rural areas.

WHAT HAS CAUSED THIS INTENSIFIED CONCERN FOR MINORITIES?

Great social forces at work in the past 40 years have altered the values of many people. What were once acceptable stereotypes of blacks and women, for example, are no longer tolerated—either by law or by society in general. Family life-styles and marriage patterns have radically changed. And with them have changed our notions of what are appropriate occupations and behavior for women—and for men. A great many people enjoy relatively affluent and privileged lives. This makes for harsh comparisons with those who do not have jobs or who are relegated to second-class work and often second-class pay. The power of television and instant communications intensified the awareness of these differences. People—especially those who believe that their second-class status is the result of discrimination (as it often is)—are impatient for improvement. The newer laws are a direct expression of the public's general dissatisfaction with these conditions and its wish to provide equal employment opportunities for all.

WHERE DOES AFFIRMATIVE ACTION APPLY?

In enforcing the provisions of the equal employment opportunity laws the EEOC has encouraged firms to engage in *affirmative action programs.* An affirmative action program consists of positive action taken to ensure nondiscriminatory treatment of all groups that are protected by legislation that forbids discrimination in employment because of race, religion, sex, age, handicap, Vietnam era war service, or national origin. The EEOC emphasizes that results count, not good intentions. If company statistics on pay and promotion, for example, show that the current status of minority groups is inferior to that of most other employees in that company or geographic area, the company may be directed to set up an affirmative action program. Companies with federal contracts over $50,000 and with more than 50 employees have no choice. They must have a written program in working order.

IN INVESTIGATING EEO DISCRIMINATION CHARGES, WHAT AREAS ARE MOST SENSITIVE?

The EEOC will look for three possibilities:

Differential treatment. This occurs when a member of a protected group is treated differently from a nonmember in the same situation.

Disparate effect. When a job requirement acts to exclude a protected group, it creates a disparate effect. The employer must demonstrate that the requirement is a "business necessity" and thus a BFOQ.

Evil intent. This is present, for instance, when an employer or supervisor is "out to get" a member of a protected group.

These infractions are most likely to occur in recruiting, interviewing, selecting, assigning, appraising, training, promoting, and disciplining of employees. Supervisors are intimately involved in all these areas. Accordingly, they bear a great deal of the responsibility for carrying out the spirit, as well as the requirements, of the law.

WHAT IS MEANT BY REVERSE DISCRIMINATION?

This is what many persons believe happens to men and also to members of the white race when preference in employment is shown to women, minorities, or both. In the *Bakke* case of 1978, the Supreme Court said in effect that it was wrong to use quotas designed to accommodate women and blacks in such a manner as to withhold employment from eligible men and whites. At the same time, however, the Supreme Court upheld the principle of affirmative action programs.

As you can infer, supervisors must tread a very unbiased line in this matter. They must be sure to support the principles of equal employment opportunity and affirmative action, and yet they must also be careful not to use these guidelines unfairly to discriminate against nonminorities.

IS IT TRUE THAT A DISADVANTAGED PERSON CAN BE "TESTED" OUT OF A JOB?

It was true to a great extent until 1971, when the United States Supreme Court (*Griggs v. Duke Power*) handed down a decision barring "discriminatory" job testing. Few tests, however, are intentionally discriminatory; it is just that most tests have been built around cultural models of white, middle-class people. As you can see by definition, privileged people are not typical of the hard-core unemployed, and tests—when used indiscriminately—screened out the latter. Nevertheless, as a result of the Supreme Court decision, testing for selection, placement, or training in industry has been modified to identify aptitudes and skills of disadvantaged persons rather than unwittingly separating out from the labor force people with untapped potential.

Federal guidelines for employment testing require that tests be validated (if adverse impact is present) so that a test really measures what it says it measures and does not exclude minorities or women in a discriminatory fashion. Tests must be validated on two counts:

Content validity. This means that the test content is truly related to the job requirements. It would be unfair to give a complex typing test requiring 100 words a minute when the job requires only the simplest sort of typing at 60 words a minute.

Construct validity. This means that the test is put together in such a way that it does not screen out applicants who could pass the content part if only they could understand the test questions themselves. For example, applicants might be able to demonstrate mechanical aptitude if they could read the questions. Perhaps the test should be administered orally rather than in writing.

It will be helpful to you if you also review the material on page 116 in Chapter 6 regarding the legal aspects of interviewing and testing of job applicants.

HOW FAR SHOULD YOU RELAX YOUR STANDARDS TO GIVE A BREAK TO WORKERS IN PROTECTED GROUPS?

The intention of the EEO laws is mainly that all workers, whether members of protected groups or not, be expected to meet the same job standards. This has not always been reflected in practice. In the absence of instructions from your organization to the contrary, however, avoidance of discrimination does not require that you lower your performance standards. The overriding factor is that job standards, benefits, and other aspects of employment be applied equally to all employees with neither favor nor discrimination.

WHERE DO WOMEN FIT INTO THIS PICTURE? HOW IMPORTANT ARE THEY TO NATIONAL PRODUCTIVITY?

They are absolutely essential. Out of every five persons working in the United States, two or more are women. And they perform work of increasing importance. Consider these two facts: Women now occupy more than 40 percent of all managerial and professional positions; and nearly two-thirds of all technical, sales, and administrative support jobs are filled by women. In fact, the increase in the number of women working has been nothing short of spectacular, as illustrated in Figure 15-1.

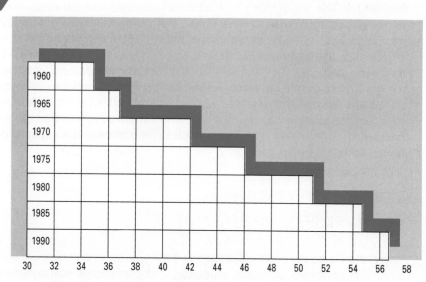

Percentage of all Women of Working Age Who Are in the Labor Force

Source: U.S. Department of Labor

FIGURE 15-1 **Growth in the percentage of women who work**

BUT WHAT ABOUT COMPENSATION FOR WOMEN?

Unfortunately, this is another story, and it is one that makes many women justifiably unhappy. Estimates vary, but it would appear that—on average—women receive only about two-thirds to three-quarters of the pay that men do in the labor market. How can this happen? Mainly because women have traditionally been shunted toward lower-paying, lower-status jobs and blocked from advancement into higher ones.

WHY DOESN'T JOB EVALUATION PUT AN END TO THIS DISCRIMINATION IN PAY?

It does, but only for work that is performed and compensated under a job-evaluation plan. Even then, it does not close all the possible loopholes. And of course it can do nothing to remedy the lack of opportunities, which is the role of the EEO legislation.

The relevant law of the land (the Fair Labor Standards Act as amended by the Equal Pay Act of 1963 and again by Public Law 92-318 of 1972) stipulates that all employees, regardless of sex or other discriminatory identification, should receive the same pay for the same kind and amount of work. *Job evaluation* is the basic means for making sure that this occurs. The "equal pay for equal work" standard, like job evaluation, requires scrutiny of the job as a whole. Its intention is that job titles be ignored and attention be focused on actual job requirements and performance. The law examines four factors in particular: equal skill, equal effort, equal responsibility, and similarity of working conditions. Whereas the law does acknowledge some exceptions, it will not permit the concepts of "women's jobs," "men's jobs," "job lists for nonwhites," and the like. On the other hand, the law does permit the use of merit pay plans that recognize, within a job pay range, different levels of performance among individuals or different levels of seniority.

HOW DIFFERENTLY FROM MEN SHOULD YOU TREAT WOMEN AT WORK?

There should be no basic difference in how you supervise women and men. The principles of sound, equitable, and considerate management should apply just as fully to the supervision of women as to the supervision of men. It probably can't be repeated often enough that a person is a person is a person. Regardless of sex—and color and national origin and religious preference—the starting point in good human relations is the recognition of each person's unique individuality and the conviction that she or he will respond most favorably when treated with respect and thoughtfulness.

BUT WHAT ABOUT CHARGES OF SEXUAL HARASSMENT?

The statistics often cited are shameful. Apparently, there are a great many men who purposely or inadvertently mix sexually oriented behavior or overtures with their work. Supervisors are the persons most notably (if not justifiably) charged with such harassment. Obviously, they are also the ones who must guard against any actions that give substance to the charge.

In a study of federal office workers, for example, a majority of women listed these types of occurrences that they found sexually oriented and particularly distasteful:

1.   Confrontation with letters, phone calls, or materials of a sexual nature.

2.   Pressure for sexual favors in return for preferred job assignments or job security.

3.   Touching, leaning over, cornering, or pinching—regardless of how nonsexually oriented the intentions might be.

4.   Pressure for dates off the job, for whatever reason.

5.   Sexually suggestive looks or gestures.

6.   Teasing, joking, remarks, or questions that have sexual overtones.

The message seems clear. Men, and women, who want to play games or seek favors with sexual implications must not do so at work. Supervisors have the responsibility for maintaining the proper levels of sexual decorum, even to the point of appearing stuffy and straightlaced as a consequence.

HOW ABOUT OLDER WORKERS?

Workers over 40 years of age are provided a protection against employment discrimination similar to that afforded all other protected groups. This means that it is legally dangerous to apply stereotypical judgments in employment-related matters involving older workers.

The Age Discrimination in Employment Act categorizes people over 40 as "older," but most authorities prefer to judge potential and competence by characteristics other than chronological age. Accordingly, take care when considering older people for employment or in evaluating their performance and/or potential for advancement. Keep in mind that age affects each person differently. Its effect depends on a large number of factors: heredity, durability, physical condition, exposure to weather, extreme living or working conditions, climate, indulgence in food or drink, drug abuse, and emotional and psychological stress. To paraphrase an old saying, "A person is only as old as he (or she) feels—*and performs on the job.*"

HOW STRONG ARE THE LAWS PROTECTING AN EMPLOYEE'S RIGHT TO PRIVACY?

The law regarding the crucial right to privacy at work is not as clear as it might be. It varies from state to state, too. In general, however, the law works in two ways: (1) employees are entitled to know what information is on file about them, and (2) supervisors are restricted in their efforts to find out confidential information about their employees or to pass on to others outside the company information that has been gathered about employees. Here are some examples of practices that are illegal or generally thought to be an invasion of employee privacy:

▶ Monitoring or recording telephone conversations without the employee's knowledge and consent.

▶ Using extraordinary means—such as calling a neighbor—to check on an employee's absences or off-job behavior.

▶ Random searches or "fishing expeditions" through an employee's locker or personal space at work. A search is acceptable only when a person in authority needs specific information for operations.

▶ Releasing information about an employee's performance to others outside the organization without the employee's permission.

WHAT ABOUT LIE DETECTORS AND DRUG TESTS?

The use of lie-detector tests is severely restricted to specified occupations (such as security guard) or for particular situations. Lie detectors can no longer be randomly used. In general, such tests (including testing for drug usage) are acceptable only if it can be clearly demonstrated that they are needed (1) to protect the business itself or its customers from damage or theft or (2) to protect employees from interference or harm. Most organizations adopt and publish a policy on these matters. It is the supervisor's responsibility to assist in the dissemination and enforcement of this policy.

DOES PRIVACY EXTEND TO
SENSITIVE ISSUES SUCH AS AIDS?

The legal view on this is also uncertain. In most instances, supervisors must rely upon policies adopted by their employers and comply with them. This must be done regardless of how other employees may view the matter. As with many issues that are, or were, controversial, a good guideline for supervisors is this: *Guard against being overzealous in taking positions whenever issues are still under debate. Support the letter of whatever law applies and your company's policy for implementing it.*

TO WHAT EXTENT DOES THIS CONCERN
FOR PROTECTED EMPLOYEES AND
FOR EMPLOYEE RIGHTS AFFECT A
SUPERVISOR'S RIGHT TO MANAGE?

It complicates a supervisor's life, for sure. But it can be handled if you follow these priorities:

1. First things should come first. It's a supervisor's job to deal promptly and firmly with subordinates whose performance is unsatisfactory, who act in an unsafe manner, or who are uncooperative or abusive. This is consistent with laws about management and labor relations. Furthermore, it matches what most employees expect of a boss.

2. Thereafter, full respect and attention should be given to equal employment opportunity laws and other legislation intended to protect the rights and welfare of people while at work. This should include an attitude of accommodation toward social concerns that are increasingly reflected in workplace practices, such as pregnancy leaves and child-care or parental-assistance programs.

WHAT IS THE LEGAL ROLE THAT FIRST-LINE
SUPERVISORS PLAY IN LABOR MATTERS?

In the eyes of the law, supervisors are the responsible agents of their companies. Your employers are held responsible for any action you take in dealing with employees or with labor unions, just as if they had taken the action themselves. For this reason, if for no other, it is essential that a supervisor be familiar with labor law on two particular points: (1) the way in which your actions affect labor unions in their attempts to gain or retain bargaining rights for employees, and (2) the labor contract that your company may have signed with a union and the impact this has on policies, practices, and procedures that make for amicable labor relations.

WHAT SHOULD BE YOUR ATTITUDE TOWARD AN EXISTING UNION?

Don't be antiunion. Adopt the attitude that once your company has made an agreement with a union, your best bet is to work as hard as you can to get along with that union. Don't waste your energy trying to undermine the union. Instead, put your efforts into making your department a better place in which to work.

It would also be a big mistake, however, to turn over to the union your interests in, and your responsibilities to, your employees. It's more important than ever, when your company has a union, to show employees that you still consider them your department's greatest asset. If you abandon their interests, you're likely to find employees looking to their union representatives, rather than to you, for leadership.

DURING A CONTEST FOR REPRESENTATION BY A LABOR UNION, WHAT SHOULD THE COMPANY'S SUPERVISORS DO?

You've pretty much got to take your instructions from the company, even if your personal inclination is to remain neutral or even to support the union's membership drive. Under these circumstances, most companies will expect supervisors to support the company's position. In that case you may be asked to:

▶ Represent the company to your employees in a positive way: "This is the company's record for fair treatment. I don't think you really need a union to get a good deal here."

▶ Raise questions about employees' relationships under union representation. "Have you been told what your strike benefits will be? Is it clear to you what the union will ask for in the way of dues?"

On the other hand, there are several things that your company cannot ask you to do, nor should you do them on your own. For example:

▶ Don't promise rewards for not joining the union.

▶ Don't make threats about what will happen if the union wins, such as saying that the plant will be closed or the union will call a strike.

▶ Don't pressure employees to commit themselves to the company. You can't, for example, ask what employees' attitudes are toward the union, whether or not they have signed a representation card, or whether they went to a union rally.

▶ Don't try to spy on employees' union activities. Don't stand near the door at a union meeting to see who is attending or even to count noses.

▶ Don't invite employees into your office to discuss the union. This, like most of the points already mentioned, is considered by the law to be intimidating and to imply an ultimate discrimination against employees who show an interest in union membership. When in doubt about what to do or say, ask your boss before doing or saying anything. Labor law is both expansive and complex; it takes an expert to interpret it properly.

HOW DOES THE SUPERVISOR'S DAY-TO-DAY ADMINISTRATION OF A LABOR CONTRACT INFLUENCE CONTRACT NEGOTIATIONS?

In many ways. If day by day a supervisor neglects or ignores grievances, assigns jobs unfairly, or neglects safety and other working conditions, collective bargaining will be made more difficult. Each time during the year that you throw your weight around thoughtlessly or take advantage of letter-of-the-law loopholes in the contract, you add to the store of incidents that the union representative will bring to bear in order to win their demands at contract time.

Take seniority as an example. Suppose you stand on your management right (and the absence of a specific contract clause to the contrary) to assign overtime only to the workers you favor, regardless of their seniority. Once or twice you defend your position by saying that the overtime requires the special skills of the two class A operators you held over. But the union observes that several times you've held over class A operators just as a convenience: the bulk of the work could have been done by laborers. When contract time rolls around, you can bet that the union negotiators will be in there pitching for a definite clause to spell out exactly how overtime will be distributed.

It's far better to handle your decisions reasonably and equitably during the year so that at contract time the union will accept more general provisions. This leaves the details to be worked out during the year on a mutual basis as the occasion arises. Experience seems to show that the more general type of contract is easier for all members of management to administer.

SUPERVISORS ARE SOMETIMES CHARGED WITH UNFAIR LABOR PRACTICES OF INTERFERENCE AND DISCRIMINATION. WHAT'S THIS ALL ABOUT?

Supervisors are most directly affected by the section of the Wagner Act (National Labor Relations Act) that prohibits unfair labor practices. Actually, there are five unfair labor practices, but the following two most frequently involve supervisors.

Interference. This would most likely take place during a union's organizing drive or an NLRB (National Labor Relations Board) representation election. Supervisors should be especially careful at such times to avoid (1) any actions that affect an employee's job or pay, (2) arguments that lead to a dispute over a union question, (3) threats to a union member through a third party, or (4) interactions without advice from top management with any of the organizing union's officers.

Discrimination. This term applies to any action (such as discharge of an employee, layoff, demotion, or assignment to more difficult or disagreeable work) taken by any member of management on account of the employee's union membership or activity. To be on safe ground, once a union has won recognition it's wise not to discuss union matters as such with employees or to express an opinion for or against a union or unionism. This is good practice off duty as well as on.

The simplest way to avoid charges of discrimination is to disregard completely an employee's union membership when you make decisions regarding job assignments, discipline, and promotions. Before you act, make sure in your own mind that you have separated ability, performance, and attitude toward the job from the employee's stand on unionism or zeal in supporting it.

WHAT ROLE DOES THE FEDERAL GOVERNMENT PLAY IN WORKPLACE SAFETY AND IN THE PREVENTION OF ACCIDENTS?

Since 1971, a major one. Until that time the safety of employees at work was largely the result of efforts on behalf of state governments, insurance companies, independent safety organizations such as the National Safety Council, and the employer. Passage of the Williams-Steiger Occupational Safety and Health Act of 1970 (effective April 1971) and the creation of the *Occupational Safety and Health Administration* (OSHA) have put the federal government and the Department of Health, Education, and Welfare (HEW) squarely into the safety act in every significant plant and office in the United States. The purpose of OSHA is to establish safety and health standards with which every employer and every employee must comply. And to make sure that there is compliance, OSHA makes more than 100,000 inspections annually.

HOW MUCH LEEWAY FOR VARIANCES DOES OSHA PERMIT?

Very little. The act minces no words. For example, the General Duty clause states that each employer:

1. Shall furnish to each employee employment and a place of employment that are free from recognized hazards causing or likely to cause death or serious harm to employees.
2. Shall comply with occupational safety and health standards promulgated by the act.

The poster that OSHA requires each employer to display in the area adds this.

> The act further requires that employers comply with specific safety and health standards issued by the Department of Labor.

The standards (called National Consensus Standards) are derived from the American National Standards Institute (ANSI) and the National Fire Protection Association (NFPA) and are supplemented by the Established Federal Standards, which were derived from previous acts. Set down in a tightly packed, 250-page volume called "Occupational Safety and Health Standards; National Consensus Standards and Established Federal Standards," published by the *Federal Register* (vol. 36, no. 105, part II),

May 29, 1971, the standards specify just about everything imaginable. They include specifications for guarding walks and walking surfaces, means of egress, powered platforms, environmental controls, noise, radiation, hazardous materials, sanitation, first-aid services, fire protection, compressed gases, material handling, machine guards, portable tools, welding, and electrical installations, and they pay particular attention to paper, textile, laundry, sawmill, and bakery operations.

The OSHA standards are regularly revised and updated and published in the *Federal Register.*

WHAT HAPPENS TO A COMPANY WHEN IT DOESN'T MEET OSHA STANDARDS?

It is given a citation. A severe penalty and fine will follow if the problem is not corrected. More specifically, the citation is issued to the manager in charge of the facility. It may even be issued, for example, to a supervisor who refused to make certain that a prescribed machine guard was in place. A company and an individual may seek a temporary variance from the standard, but in most instances the only recourse is to take corrective action as soon as possible. In many cases, heavy fines and even jail sentences have been imposed on companies and managers who failed to comply promptly with citations.

HOW FAR BEYOND SAFETY DOES OSHA EXTEND?

The Occupational Safety and Health Administration looks deep into the areas of employee health that may be affected by substances in, or conditions of, the process or working environment and into *general sanitation* on the premises. The sanitation standards are spelled out under the section "General Environmental Controls." An important area is housekeeping. For example, containers for waste disposal must be available and should be the kinds that don't leak and can be sanitized. Extermination programs must be in effect for vermin control. Food and beverage consumption on the premises is regulated.

Washrooms, toilet facilities, and water supplies are considered. Provision must be made for clear labeling of potable and nonpotable water. Toilet facilities are specified according to the number and sex of employees. Showers, change rooms, and clothes-drying facilities must be provided under certain circumstances.

OSHA pays notable attention, of course, to the presence of, and impact of, *hazardous materials.* Probably the most publicized material has been asbestos. Other particularly dangerous materials or conditions include vinyl chloride, which produces liver cancer; fumes from lead; coal dust; airborne textile fibers; and radiation. Even high noise levels can be injurious and must be guarded against.

HOW HAS OSHA AFFECTED SAFETY TRAINING?

It has made it mandatory. Supervisors are expected to make certain that safe procedures are taught not only to new employees but also as an ongoing program.

General safety training applies to the proper observance of safety regulations, routing for emergency egress in case of fire or other common danger, accident and injury treatment and reporting, and fire and explosion emergency activities.

Specific employee training required by OSHA applies to such areas as occupational health and environmental controls, hazardous materials, personal protective equipment, medical and first aid, fire protection, material handling and storage, machine guarding, and for welding, brazing, and torch cutting.

WHERE DO EMPLOYEES FIT INTO THE OSHA PICTURE?

The law insists that they, too, act safely within established standards—provided that employers live up to their responsibilities. In other words, an employee who refused to wear the safety glasses provided by the employer in prescribed areas could be cited. A bearded employee might be required to shave to make his respirator fit. Specifically, OSHA states:

> The Williams-Steiger Act also requires that each employee comply with safety and health standards, rules, and orders issued under the Act and applicable to his conduct.

Employees have several important rights under OSHA, however. For example, they may:

1. Request an inspection if they believe an imminent danger exists or a violation of a standard exists that threatens physical harm.

2. Have a representative (such as a union steward) accompany an OSHA compliance officer during the inspection of a workplace.

3. Advise an OSHA compliance officer of any violation of the act that they believe exists in the workplace, and question, and be questioned privately by, the compliance officer.

4.   Have regulations posted to inform them of protection afforded by the act.

5.   Have locations monitored in order to measure exposure to toxic or radioactive materials, have access to the records of such monitoring or measuring, and have records of their own personal exposure.

6.   Have medical examinations or other tests to determine whether their health is being affected by an exposure, and have the results of such tests furnished to their physicians.

7.   Have posted on the premises any citations issued against the employer by OSHA.

TO WHAT EXTENT DOES OSHA SPECIFY ACCIDENT RECORDKEEPING?

It insists that every company or separate establishment maintain a log of illnesses and accidents as they occur. Beyond that, the forms already used by your organization to monitor these matters and to investigate accidents are probably satisfactory.

The OSHA log (Form 200) is used to record each occupational injury or illness and identify whether it has caused a fatality, a lost workday, a permanent transfer to another job, or a termination of employment. In the area of *illness identification,* OSHA has expanded typical coverage; OSHA requires a report on occupational skin diseases or disorders, dust diseases of the lungs (pneumoconioses), respiratory conditions and poisoning due to workplace exposure to toxic materials, disorders due to other physical agents, and traumas (emotional shocks).

In addition, OSHA standards require that additional specialized records be maintained on such items as scaffolding, platforms, elevators and other personnel lifts, fire extinguishers, cranes, derricks, and power presses. These records should include maintenance and inspection dates. Still other records are required for radiation exposure, flammable and combustible liquids inventories, and the monitoring of toxic and hazardous substances.

Whereas your company will probably specify what records must be kept and who will maintain them, the supervisor—as in so many other areas—is a pivotal person in collecting the data.

REVIEW ▼ 15 ▼ QUESTIONS

1. What is meant by affirmative action, and how does it tie in with EEO legislation?
2. In seeking to ensure conformance to EEO laws, what evidence of discrimination does the EEOC look for? In which areas of management are these most likely to occur?
3. What is wrong with classifying a job as either a man's or a woman's, from both legal and practical standpoints?
4. The men in Jane's work group repeatedly—although jokingly and admiringly—address her as "Marilyn," an obvious reference to her physical resemblance to Marilyn Monroe. Jane doesn't particularly like this and complains to her supervisor. What should the supervisor do?
5. Why might an employee who works at a computer keyboard object to the number of her keystrokes being counted electronically as a measure of her performance? Do you believe that her employer has a right to make these measurements?
6. If, as a supervisor, you suspected an employee of drug dealing, would it be all right to inspect that employee's locker? Why?
7. Suggest two good reasons why a supervisor should know about labor-management relations laws.
8. What is the difference between unfair labor practices involving interference and those involving discrimination?
9. Distinguish between the Occupational Safety and Health Act and the Occupational Safety and Health Administration.
10. Can an employee refuse to conform to an OSHA standard? Why, or why not? What are an employee's rights under the act?

A CASE IN POINT

The Unwelcome Affirmative Action Program

In the southern office of the Century Credit Corporation, Millie was the first black woman ever hired. As a matter of fact, Millie's employment was initiated by the company only after it was directed by the EEOC to implement an affirmative action program. Millie turned out to be a good choice. She was neat, pleasant, and capable. By the end of her first year, she had received a raise and a promotion. Millie's progress continued into the second year, too, and she was given increasingly responsible assignments. Some of the employees applauded Millie's advancement. Others seemed not to care one way or the other. There was a general impression, however, that the affirmative action program was not particularly welcomed by the longer-service employees.

Century continued its affirmative action program by hiring three more black employees. These latest hires, although not as outstanding as Millie, performed their work satisfactorily. They did not advance as rapidly as Millie had, but they got normal merit increases after finishing their probationary periods. At the end of Millie's second year, she received still another well-deserved promotion. Coincidentally, one of the recently hired black employees also received a promotion at the same time.

This triggered an unpleasant confrontation one afternoon between Wanda Jane, a long-time Century employee, and Mr. Grant, the office manager. Wanda Jane had become increasingly irritated by Millie's progress, as well as by the employment and advancement of the other black women. When Wanda Jane cornered Mr. Grant, she said, "When are you going to show some spine and stop favoring these individuals just because they are black? There are half a dozen equally qualified white women who have been passed over just to give the blacks a break. It's got me and the rest of the staff plenty upset. If things don't change around here, we're going to call a meeting of the office employees at my home to see if we shouldn't organize our own little union to protect our rights."

If you were Mr. Grant, What would you do now? Five alternative courses of action are listed below. Rank them in the order in which they appeal to you (1 most effective, 5 least effective). You may add another approach in the space provided, if you wish. In any event, be prepared to justify your ranking.

_____ **A.**   Call a meeting of the employees to explain that you will continue to implement the Company's affirmative action program, but that you're sorry that it causes some incidents of reverse discrimination.

_____ **B.**   Assume that Wanda Jane's complaint is an isolated one and ignore the incident.

_____ **C.**   Postpone any further advancement for Millie until the white employees get more accustomed to working with blacks.

_____ **D.**   Tell Wanda Jane that the advancement of Millie and the other black employees has been entirely on merit and that you will not be coerced into changing the way you carry out the affirmative action program.

_____   **E.**   Make sure that the next few promotions go to white employees.

If you have another approach, write it here.

▶   _____

_____

_____

Complete the ACTION PLANNING CHECKLIST
for this chapter, which can be found on page 325.

Test your comprehension of the material in Chapters 11, 12, 13, 14, and 15. Correct answers are in the Appendix.

True-False

By writing T or F in the space provided, indicate whether each statement is true or false.

1. A grievance imagined by an employee doesn't need the immediate attention that a genuine grievance does.

1. _____

2. It is extremely important for a supervisor to be honest when settling a grievance, even if the supervisor has to admit a fault or mistake.

2. _____

3. When a union has been called into a dispute, it is part of the supervisor's responsibility to see that the union steward conforms to the established grievance procedure.

3. _____

4. A relatively healthy competition among groups or individuals within an organization, while striving to meet mutual goals, should be encouraged.

4. _____

5. A great many causes of conflict in a department are closely related to the work itself.

5. _____

6. An employee who develops a psychosis needs the help of a professional counselor, most probably a psychiatrist.

6. _____

7. Few people will experience emotional disturbances during their lives.

7. _____

8. The vast majority of people who show poor behavioral adjustment at work do not need psychiatric help.

8. _____

9. The best approach to improving the attendance of a young, directionless absentee is with sympathetic counseling.   9. _____

10. In counseling an employee whose work is affected by alcoholism, it is a good idea to stress the need to bring work performance up to standard.   10. _____

11. A meeting between a supervisor and an employee to discuss the employee's performance is called a *job evaluation.*   11. _____

12. If at all possible, it is a good idea to separate clearly a performance appraisal from any discussion of compensation.   12. _____

13. An important step in making a performance appraisal effective is for the supervisor and employee to discuss specific goals that are to be met in the future.   13. _____

14. The factors in a graphic weighting scale are usually tied to numerical values.   14. _____

15. Because a performance appraisal, in part, relies on opinions, it is not subject to legal scrutiny as stipulated, for example, by equal employment opportunity laws.   15. _____

16. Most employees regard a system of discipline as a legitimate way to preserve order and safety.   16. _____

17. To play no favorites when meting out discipline is an example of the principle of consistency.   17. _____

18. Discipline can be used to encourage and reward good behavior as well as to penalize and discourage undesirable conduct.   18. _____

19. The "hot stove" rule of discipline prescribes a sequence of increasingly more severe penalties.   19. _____

20. In justice to the individual and to the law, supervisors must be able to defend their disciplinary actions beyond a reasonable doubt.   20. _____

21. EEO legislation requires equal employment opportunities in regard to hiring, selection, placement, and training, but not to performance appraisals or promotions.   21. _____

22. Although their early progression in the workplace was slow, women are now rapidly catching up to, if not actually overtaking, men as far as pay and advancement go.   22. _____

23. Companies can do pretty much as they please with lie-detector and drug testing, but an employee's right to privacy is very clearly protected.   23. _____

24. *Discrimination* is the term applied to actions taken by management against an employee because of his or her union activity or membership.   24. _____

25. An employee may request that the Occupational Safety and Health Administration inspect and/or monitor her or his workplace and expect this request to be honored.   25. _____

Multiple Choice

For each item below, choose the response that best completes the statement or answers the question. Write the letter of the response in the space provided.

1. A complaint has received enough attention when:

   a. all the facts have been learned.
   b. the employee has been persuaded to return to his or her workplace.
   c. it has been removed as an obstacle to willing, productive work.
   d. the supervisor has evaluated its pros and cons.   1. _____

2. After becoming aware of a grievance, one of the first things a supervisor should do is to:

   a. give an immediate decision.
   b. check out its merits with the union steward.
   c. gather as much factual evidence as possible.
   d. report it to the human resources department.   2. _____

3. A good approach to avoiding grievances before they occur is:

   a. be sure employees know where they stand in regard to their performance.
   b. encourage employees to make suggestions and act on them favorably whenever possible.
   c. explain proposed changes carefully in advance.
   d. all of the above.   3. _____

4. In a typical department, the best way to manage the allocation of resources is to:

   a. give the most resources to the best producers.
   b. give the most resources to the worst producers.
   c. avoid revealing the basis on which resource allocations are made.
   d. make decisions about allocating resources openly and explain the reasons candidly.   4. _____

5. Employees who are in conflict are more willing to compromise when the supervisor:

   a. gives instructions about how to settle the conflict.
   b. makes it clear that no bickering will be tolerated.
   c. finds a course of action that will benefit both employees.
   d. refuses to get involved in what appears to be a private matter.   5. _____

6. Ted regularly upsets his coworkers with malicious gossip and unjustified suspicions. This is an a example of:

   a. schizophrenic behavior.
   b. psychotic behavior.
   c. neurotic behavior.
   d. a workaholic.   6._____

7. In a counseling interview, the supervisor must remember to:

   a. help the employee to unburden herself or himself.
   b. emphasize that work is more important than the employee.
   c. keep the conversation impersonal.
   d. stress the possibility of disciplinary action.   7. _____

8. Which of the following is not a good idea when counseling an emotionally troubled employee?

   a. Listening patiently for what's beneath the surface.
   b. Refraining from arguing and offering advice.
   c. Allowing the employee to speak without criticism.
   d. Controlling the direction of the interview.   8. _____

9. Jill has heard that one of her employees is having marital problems. Jill should:

   a. warn the employee that personal problems cannot
      be allowed to interfere with work.
   b. ask the employee is there is something that Jill can
      do to help.
   c. offer to refer the employee to a marriage counselor.
   d. do nothing until the employee's behavior affects his
      job performance.   9. _____

10. Employees who are most likely to require professional
    counseling for excessive absenteeism are:

    a. chronic absentees.
    b. aggressive absentees.
    c. moonlighters.
    d. vacationing absentees.   10. _____

11. On an employee performance rating form, the factor
    "potential ability to lead and teach others" is an exam-
    ple of:

    a. a subjective factor.
    b. an objective factor.
    c. a job standard.
    d. a legal requirement.   11. _____

12. An occurrence that is chosen as characteristic of an
    employee's general character or performance is:

    a. a halo effect.
    b. an objective factor.
    c. a subjective factor.
    d. a critical incident.   12. _____

13. The overriding objective of performance appraisals is to:

    a. improve departmental morale.
    b. comply with federal regulations.
    c. make sure that supervisors keep on top of their employees' performance.
    d. aid employees in improving the quality of their job performance.   13. _____

14. Becky wants to make sure that her performance ratings are fair to each employee, and so she plans to rate each person on a given factor before moving on to the next factor. This is:

    a. illegal; you cannot make this kind of employee comparison.
    b. ineffective; it is too cumbersome to accomplish her goal.
    c. a good idea that can help her reach the goal of fairness.
    d. only possible if all employees agree to that system.   14. _____

15. A written record of what was discussed during a performance appraisal interview is a good idea:

    a. never.
    b. always.
    c. especially if your appraisal has been negative.
    d. only if you and the employee are in complete agreement.   15. _____

16. A supervisor who uses progressive discipline:

    a. never issues penalties.
    b. avoids negative discipline.
    c. gives decreasingly harsh penalties according to an employee's seniority.
    d. gives increasingly harsh penalties as the offense is repeated.   16. _____

17. If a supervisor excuses a habitual rule breaker, it will probably:

    a. improve that person's behavior in the future.
    b. be something they can keep between the two of them.
    c. harm the general state of discipline in the department.
    d. improve the overall state of morale in the department.   17. _____

18. When a supervisor can rely mostly on positive discipline, there is likely to be:

    a. a lower incidence of disciplinary cases.
    b. a loss of respect for the supervisor.
    c. a deterioration in the quality of work.
    d. a general laxness in departmental morale.   18. _____

19. If a good employee breaks a minor rule, the best thing for a supervisor to do is to:

    a. look the other way and forget it.
    b. make an indelible impression by cracking down hard and fast with a really stiff penalty.
    c. take action immediately with the appropriate penalty.
    d. make a note to discuss this with the employee at the next scheduled appraisal interview.   19. _____

20. Especially when challenged by a labor union or by legal action, it is difficult for a supervisor to make a penalty stick if:

    a. the employee is the main support of a family.
    b. the employee has been issued previous warnings.
    c. the rest of the work force disagrees with the action taken.
    d. there has been no clear-cut infraction of a rule or regulation.   20. _____

21. It is illegal to refuse to hire a Hispanic person who is otherwise qualified for the job, because it is prohibited by:

    a. Title VII of the Civil Rights Act of 1964.
    b. the National Labor Relations Act.
    c. the Rehabilitation Act of 1973.
    d. Executive Orders 11246 and 11375.   21. _____

22. Which of the following statements about women is true?

    a. Sexual harassment is no longer a serious work-related problem.
    b. Women do not usually receive pay equal to men for equal work.
    c. Women now occupy more than two-thirds of all managerial and professional positions.
    d. None of the above.   22. _____

23. Which of the following is or are generally considered to constitute invasion of an employee's privacy?

    a. Monitoring or recording telephone conversations without the employee's knowledge or consent.
    b. Random searches of an employee's locker or personal work space.
    c. Releasing information about an employee's performance to others outside the organization without the employee's permission.
    d. All of the above.   23. _____

24. Carmen, a supervisor in a textile mill, has strong personal feelings against labor unions. During an organizing drive she could be found guilty of interference if she:

    a. expressed her personal views to her employees.
    b. assigned an employee who is an active unionist to particularly unpleasant work.
    c. defended the company's current labor relations record.
    d. refused to discuss the pros and cons of the drive with the organizing union's officers.   24. _____

25. OSHA has most importantly affected safety training by:

    a. creating the National Consensus Standards.
    b. making safety training mandatory.
    c. empowering employees to report hazardous conditions.
    d. requiring the display of the OSHA poster.   25. _____

ACTION PLANNING CHECKLISTS, AND KEYS TO SELF-CHECKS

1. Made a commitment to stop doing "hands on" work and to embrace fully the management viewpoint.	2. Determined to maintain good health, work hard, set a good example for your employees, and continue to learn.	3. Identified individuals/groups to whom you owe responsibility: higher management (your boss), staff departments, associate supervisors, union representative, and most of all your work group.
Action Needed Yes No — Completed _____	Action Needed Yes No — Completed _____	Action Needed Yes No — Completed _____
4. Checked the resources that enable you to carry out your job responsibilities: facilities, equipment, tools, power, utilities, materials, supplies, and information (dollar value of all this).	5. Obtained the personnel particulars about your work force: personal data on each employee, such as age, length of service, work history, present job title and description, and pay rate.	6. Learned about current and upcoming production schedules and other output requirements and project deadlines.
Action Needed Yes No — Completed _____	Action Needed Yes No — Completed _____	Action Needed Yes No — Completed _____
7. Found out exactly what the quality requirements or specifications of your product or service are.	8. Pinned down the cost and expense limitations under which you will be expected to operate.	9. Accepted the fact that pressures on you will be many and varied, with changing worker attitudes being the most pressing of all.
Action Needed Yes No — Completed _____	Action Needed Yes No — Completed _____	Action Needed Yes No — Completed _____
10. Gave thought to how well your present abilities measure up to the demands for technical, administrative, and human relations skills—and what you might do to improve them.	11. Prepared to balance your supervisory efforts between task-centered and employee-centered concerns.	12. Reviewed the managerial process so that you can anticipate problems and decisions that require planning, organizing, staffing, directing, and controlling.
Action Needed Yes No — Completed _____	Action Needed Yes No — Completed _____	Action Needed Yes No — Completed _____
13. Accepted that your role often will be ambiguous and will put you between higher management and your employees; hours will be long; rewards will come mainly from a sense of accomplishment.	14. Guarded against pitfalls for new supervisors: poor relationships, failure to plan ahead, confusion about your role, lack of initiative, discouragement, and inability to meet changing conditions.	15. Retained an attitude of doing the best you can today with a plan for developing your knowledge and skills so that you can do even better tomorrow.
Action Needed Yes No — Completed _____	Action Needed Yes No — Completed _____	Action Needed Yes No — Completed _____

1. Time set aside for planning: 5 minutes daily/15 minutes weekly/1 hour monthly.	2. Nothing new nor any changes attempted without prior planning.	3. Goals based on a realistic look at departmental strengths and weaknesses and company-imposed restrictions.
Action Needed Yes No Completed _____	Action Needed Yes No Completed _____	Action Needed Yes No Completed _____
4. Goals quantified, explicit, and time-oriented.	5. Departmental goals arranged in order of priority.	6. Plans, procedures, and regulations that fit into chosen goals.
Action Needed Yes No Completed _____	Action Needed Yes No Completed _____	Action Needed Yes No Completed _____
7. Plans flexible enough to permit change when needed.	8. Control limits and control procedures established to enable you to monitor departmental progress toward goals.	9. Knowledge of your company's general policies, especially as they relate to personnel matters.
Action Needed Yes No Completed _____	Action Needed Yes No Completed _____	Action Needed Yes No Completed _____
10. Up-to-date knowledge of procedures that affect operating practices.	11. Provision for feedback to your superiors about difficulties in policy implementation or the need for policy change.	12. Acceptance of company policies as your policies so far as employees are concerned.
Action Needed Yes No Completed _____	Action Needed Yes No Completed _____	Action Needed Yes No Completed _____
13. Prudence in checking company policy implications before taking trend-setting action at the departmental level.	14. Willingness to explain and interpret policies, procedures, and regulations to employees in language they understand.	15. Commitment to goals that the company has set and to those you have set for your own operations.
Action Needed Yes No Completed _____	Action Needed Yes No Completed _____	Action Needed Yes No Completed _____

1. Your work force's organization focused on departmental responsibilities and objectives.

Action Needed Yes No	Completed _____

2. Each employee knows what his or her job is and how it relates to others in the department.

Action Needed Yes No	Completed _____

3. An organization chart constructed for your department.

Action Needed Yes No	Completed _____

4. Your awareness of, but not conflict with, the informal organization in your department.

Action Needed Yes No	Completed _____

5. Identification of both line and staff responsibilities in your department and with other company departments.

Action Needed Yes No	Completed _____

6. Knowledge of where and how your department fits into your company's overall organizational structure.

Action Needed Yes No	Completed _____

7. Identification of your company's and your department's organizational form: functional, divisional or product, geographic, customer, and/or project or task force.

Action Needed Yes No	Completed _____

8. Estimate of the degree of centralization and decentralization in your company and in your department. Satisfaction with the extent of your own span of control, neither too narrow nor too broad.

Action Needed Yes No	Completed _____

9. Clear understanding of your own responsibilities and their related authorities according to the classifications in the text.

Action Needed Yes No	Completed _____

10. Full development and utilization of your personal sources of authority.

Action Needed Yes No	Completed _____

11. Regular use of delegation within your department to relieve yourself of unnecessary work and to develop the skills and confidence of subordinates.

Action Needed Yes No	Completed _____

12. Willing acceptance of responsibilities delegated from above with an eye toward using them for your own development.

Action Needed Yes No	Completed _____

13. Knowledge of the chain of command in your company and general conformance to it.

Action Needed Yes No	Completed _____

14. Cooperation with, and use of, company staff departments.

Action Needed Yes No	Completed _____

15. Regular review of departmental structure to optimize communications, clarify responsibilities and duties, and retain flexibility for contingencies, or use OD techniques to build a stronger team.

Action Needed Yes No	Completed _____

313

1. Departmental standards and controls related to departmental plans and goals.	2. Departmental controls established to cover employee performance, machine operations, materials usage, product or service quality, cost, and job assignment.	3. Control standards clearly written, numerically expressed where possible, and based on either historical records or systematic analysis.
Action Needed **Completed** Yes No _____	**Action Needed** **Completed** Yes No _____	**Action Needed** **Completed** Yes No _____
4. Standards set for employees' personal time to include attendance and tardiness, rest periods, and quitting time.	5. Standards set for quantity of production or output—for the department as a whole and for individual operations.	6. Standards set for quality of workmanship, product, and service—for the department's output and for each operation.
Action Needed **Completed** Yes No _____	**Action Needed** **Completed** Yes No _____	**Action Needed** **Completed** Yes No _____
7. Standards set for materials and supplies usage—yield, waste, storage, and inventory accumulation.	8. Standards set for all pertinent time factors, including job times, schedule fulfillment, and project completions.	9. Regular check to make sure that control measurements are accurate and relevant to the person or process being controlled.
Action Needed **Completed** Yes No _____	**Action Needed** **Completed** Yes No _____	**Action Needed** **Completed** Yes No _____
10. Corrective action directed toward causes of variances rather than symptoms.	11. Understanding of intent of budgetary controls received and the degree to which you must conform to them.	12. Willingness to make the necessary cost-benefit decisions when setting, interpreting, or applying controls.
Action Needed **Completed** Yes No _____	**Action Needed** **Completed** Yes No _____	**Action Needed** **Completed** Yes No _____
13. Application of the exception principle as often as possible.	14. Sensitivity to the people problem in exercising controls; emphasis on motivation rather than punishment.	15. Encouragement of employees' self-control whenever feasible.
Action Needed **Completed** Yes No _____	**Action Needed** **Completed** Yes No _____	**Action Needed** **Completed** Yes No _____

1. Acceptance of a personal responsibility to seek out problem situations in your department and try to solve them.	2. Regular check on actual results in your department to see if there is a gap between them and what you had expected to happen.	3. Focus on a search for causes rather than quick or easy conclusions when attacking problems.
Action Needed Yes No / Completed _____	Action Needed Yes No / Completed _____	Action Needed Yes No / Completed _____
4. Understanding that solutions to problems require that you make firm decisions and carry them out.	5. Maintenance of good records, or knowledge of where they are kept, so that you can find adequate information when handling problems or decisions.	6. Careful evaluation of all alternative courses of action before committing yourself to a decision.
Action Needed Yes No / Completed _____	Action Needed Yes No / Completed _____	Action Needed Yes No / Completed _____
7. Keeping an eye and an ear to what might occur now or in the future to create problems in the weeks or months ahead.	8. Strong curb on your instincts and hunches until you've made a systematic analysis of a situation.	9. When possible, an effort made to place a numerical or dollar value on the expenses of implementing a decision as well as the cost associated with the problem.
Action Needed Yes No / Completed _____	Action Needed Yes No / Completed _____	Action Needed Yes No / Completed _____
10. Goal to have the benefits of an action outweigh the cost or effort of putting the action into effect.	11. Neither too much haste nor too much delay in making decisions.	12. Guard against wishful or biased thinking when making choices.
Action Needed Yes No / Completed _____	Action Needed Yes No / Completed _____	Action Needed Yes No / Completed _____
13. Application of your available problem-solving time to those vital few areas where the payoff is likely to be large, as opposed to chasing after the trivial many.	14. Willingness to seek advice and counsel when you are faced with difficult problems and decisions.	15. An awareness of the value of the information that may be available through the organization's management information system.
Action Needed Yes No / Completed _____	Action Needed Yes No / Completed _____	Action Needed Yes No / Completed _____

315

1. An understanding of the five-step staffing process and the supervisor's role in it.	2. Acknowledgment of the supervisor's responsibility in having the right workers on the right jobs in sufficient numbers at the right time.	3. Knowledge of how a job analysis is prepared and the way it relates to a job description and a job specification.
Action Needed Yes No Completed _____	Action Needed Yes No Completed _____	Action Needed Yes No Completed _____
4. The ability to describe a job accurately and to specify the qualifications of the person who might fill it.	5. The ability to make a reasonably accurate estimate of work-force size requirements.	6. Care taken to neither understaff nor overstaff.
Action Needed Yes No Completed _____	Action Needed Yes No Completed _____	Action Needed Yes No Completed _____
7. Periodic review of peaks and valleys in departmental work loads so as to maintain an even balance between size of staff and the work to be done.	8. Knowledge of the normal table of organization (TO) for your department.	9. The ability to interview job candidates objectively, using open-ended questions to probe the suitability of their education, experience, and skills for the open position.
Action Needed Yes No Completed _____	Action Needed Yes No Completed _____	Action Needed Yes No Completed _____
10. Knowledge of legal (especially EEOC) guidelines that must be observed in conducting employment interviews and in selecting and placing employees.	11. Improvement of your interviewing skills such as questioning, listening, and evaluation.	12. Periodic review to assess the applicability of performance tests as aids in selection of applicants for jobs in your department.
Action Needed Yes No Completed _____	Action Needed Yes No Completed _____	Action Needed Yes No Completed _____
13. Knowledge of, and an ability to calculate, your department's turnover rate.	14. Knowledge of, and an ability to calculate, your department's absenteeism rate.	15. A plan for keeping turnover and absenteeism rates within standards acceptable to your parent organization.
Action Needed Yes No Completed _____	Action Needed Yes No Completed _____	Action Needed Yes No Completed _____

1. Continual alert for symptoms of training needs—such as lowered output, off-standard quality, higher costs, accidents, or poor morale.	2. Care in orienting each new employee to your department by using the checklist for the induction talk recommended earlier in this chapter.	3. A systematic rather than a hit-or-miss approach to each and all training programs in your department.
Action Needed Yes No **Completed** _____	**Action Needed** Yes No **Completed** _____	**Action Needed** Yes No **Completed** _____
4. Preparation of a simple job breakdown sheet with key points identified before you begin the training on a particular job.	5. Proper employee preparation and motivation provided before you begin the demonstration of a job.	6. Training demonstrations that emphasize both telling and showing.
Action Needed Yes No **Completed** _____	**Action Needed** Yes No **Completed** _____	**Action Needed** Yes No **Completed** _____
7. Emphasis on identification and demonstration of key points that make or break a job.	8. Breaking the training material into easily learned pieces, not attempting too much during any one session.	9. Arranging the training sequence so that the learner begins with the least difficult and progresses to the most difficult phases.
Action Needed Yes No **Completed** _____	**Action Needed** Yes No **Completed** _____	**Action Needed** Yes No **Completed** _____
10. Allowing trainees to try out the job under your watchful eye before turning them loose on their own.	11. Regular feedback to the trainee regarding how well—or how incorrectly—the employee is learning the job.	12. Encouragement of questions throughout the entire training process.
Action Needed Yes No **Completed** _____	**Action Needed** Yes No **Completed** _____	**Action Needed** Yes No **Completed** _____
13. Remaining available to trainees for help and guidance after they have been put on their own.	14. Training in your department based on an analysis of skills needed (Figure 7–2) and a planned timetable for completion.	15. Training approaches tailored to needs and learning capabilities of each individual, drawing on available resources (visual aids, manuals) and the advice and assistance of the training department.
Action Needed Yes No **Completed** _____	**Action Needed** Yes No **Completed** _____	**Action Needed** Yes No **Completed** _____

1. Concern for human interactions as well as production problems.	2. An awareness of differences—and diversity—in motivation, values and goals, and performance among your employees.	3. Assessment of each employee as to which levels of Maslow's hierarchy of needs are most important.
Action Needed Yes No Completed _____	Action Needed Yes No Completed _____	Action Needed Yes No Completed _____
4. In trying to motivate employees, searching always for the unsatisfied need.	5. Provision of challenging assignments to satisfy the needs of employees who wish to use more fully their knowledge and skills.	6. Opportunities offered to employees to maintain their own self-discipline.
Action Needed Yes No Completed _____	Action Needed Yes No Completed _____	Action Needed Yes No Completed _____
7. Provision of conditions at work that can create satisfaction for those employees who respond to positive motivation.	8. Feedback to higher management on the need for "hygiene" factors to prevent dissatisfaction among employees.	9. A gradual shift of your role from an authority-oriented supervisor toward more of a goal-oriented facilitator.
Action Needed Yes No Completed _____	Action Needed Yes No Completed _____	Action Needed Yes No Completed _____
10. Efforts made to arrange work or design jobs so that the "work itself" can provide motivation.	11. Sensitivity to the dynamics of group relationships in your department.	12. Willingness to share employees' loyalties with their work group(s), whether formal or informal.
Action Needed Yes No Completed _____	Action Needed Yes No Completed _____	Action Needed Yes No Completed _____
13. An attempt to integrate individual and group goals with the goals of the department.	14. Alert to the need for protection of individuals from unreasonable group pressures to conform to group norms.	15. Provisions for employees, individually and collectively, to participate in solving work-related problems.
Action Needed Yes No Completed _____	Action Needed Yes No Completed _____	Action Needed Yes No Completed _____

1. A minimum of "noise" blocking your communication process; employees ready to listen, absence of conflicting instructions and other distractions.	2. Emphasis on the free flow of information up, down, and across your department.	3. Willingness to track down and retrieve information for employees who request it.
Action Needed Yes No **Completed** ____	**Action Needed** Yes No **Completed** ____	**Action Needed** Yes No **Completed** ____
4. A guard against overcommunicating and talking about sensitive subjects.	5. Your boss kept regularly informed of controversial matters, attitudes and morale, and progress toward goals.	6. Development of your skill as an active listener, using your responses to establish empathy and rapport.
Action Needed Yes No **Completed** ____	**Action Needed** Yes No **Completed** ____	**Action Needed** Yes No **Completed** ____
7. Recognition that words mean different things to different people; use of hard facts rather than vague generalities.	8. Knowledge of, but avoidance of, the grapevine as a method of supervisory communication; rumors spiked as soon as possible.	9. Development of your person-to-person skills, both spoken and written.
Action Needed Yes No **Completed** ____	**Action Needed** Yes No **Completed** ____	**Action Needed** Yes No **Completed** ____
10. Development of your group communication skills for use in informal staff meetings and planned conferences and with bulletin boards, posters, displays, and visual aids.	11. Regular and candid assessment of whether your orders and instructions are being communicated effectively.	12. A willingness to repeat an instruction to make sure that it is clearly understood.
Action Needed Yes No **Completed** ____	**Action Needed** Yes No **Completed** ____	**Action Needed** Yes No **Completed** ____
13. Care that your tone of voice is appropriate for the situation; rephrasing your orders as "requests" as often as possible.	14. Commands reserved for emergencies or for situations where a high degree of immediate coordination is needed.	15. Written orders and instructions used mainly to amend those already in writing or for work that is especially complex and/or varies from normal sequence, timing, quantities, or quality.
Action Needed Yes No **Completed** ____	**Action Needed** Yes No **Completed** ____	**Action Needed** Yes No **Completed** ____

1. An awareness of the importance of leadership skills (persuasion, influence, rapport) as contrasted with so-called "inborn" leadership traits.	2. An acknowledgment that effective leadership depends on providing motivation rather than on manipulation.	3. A determination, through self-analysis, of whether your assumptions about employees represent a Theory X or Theory Y viewpoint.
Action Needed **Completed** Yes No _____	**Action Needed** **Completed** Yes No _____	**Action Needed** **Completed** Yes No _____
4. An attempt to help employees discover personal goals consistent with those of the organization.	5. Development of skills in applying all three kinds of traditional leadership approaches: autocratic, democratic, and participative.	6. Differentiation between results-centered and situational leadership approaches.
Action Needed **Completed** Yes No _____	**Action Needed** **Completed** Yes No _____	**Action Needed** **Completed** Yes No _____
7. A balanced application of leadership techniques contingent on the particulars of each situation.	8. A concern for people (people-centered leadership) equal to your concern for results (task-centered leadership.)	9. Demonstrated personal progress toward point 9,9 on the Managerial Grid©.
Action Needed **Completed** Yes No _____	**Action Needed** **Completed** Yes No _____	**Action Needed** **Completed** Yes No _____
10. Recognition of the choices that can be made by a supervisor along the continuum of leadership styles.	11. Willingness to apply autocratic leadership in emergencies and participative leadership when suitable.	12. An attempt to match your leadership style to the followership inclinations of each employee.
Action Needed **Completed** Yes No _____	**Action Needed** **Completed** Yes No _____	**Action Needed** **Completed** Yes No _____
13. Consistency in the nature of your relationships with others: superiors, subordinates, and peers alike.	14. Maintenance of good examples of personal commitment and a willingness to make sacrifices to help your employees meet department objectives.	15. A conscious effort to treat employees equitably in similar situations; neither to play favorites nor to pick on those you dislike.
Action Needed **Completed** Yes No _____	**Action Needed** **Completed** Yes No _____	**Action Needed** **Completed** Yes No _____

1. Respect for, and attention given to, all grievances, real or imagined.	2. Decisions based on facts that have been thoroughly gathered and carefully examined.	3. Unwavering standard of fairness in judging the merits of complaints and grievances.
Action Needed Yes No / **Completed** _____	**Action Needed** Yes No / **Completed** _____	**Action Needed** Yes No / **Completed** _____
4. Candidness and the absence of trickery when discussing grievances with employees.	5. All discussions with employees or union representatives conducted in a businesslike manner and a civil tone, with personalities set aside.	6. Decisions carefully explored beforehand, but made as quickly as possible.
Action Needed Yes No / **Completed** _____	**Action Needed** Yes No / **Completed** _____	**Action Needed** Yes No / **Completed** _____
7. Willingness to pass along and support as your own the rulings on grievances made by higher authorities.	8. Decisions rendered in clear-cut terms along with full explanations of your reasoning.	9. Opportunities for employees to save face when rulings on grievances go against them.
Action Needed Yes No / **Completed** _____	**Action Needed** Yes No / **Completed** _____	**Action Needed** Yes No / **Completed** _____
10. Follow-up on decisions to make sure that promised corrective action actually takes place.	11. Strict adherence to your company's grievance procedure, if one has been established.	12. Insofar as possible, handling each grievance as a confidential matter between you and the employee involved.
Action Needed Yes No / **Completed** _____	**Action Needed** Yes No / **Completed** _____	**Action Needed** Yes No / **Completed** _____
13. Acceptance of a limited amount of conflict or competition as normal so long as it is not intense or disruptive.	14. Awareness of sources of conflict and competition: unequal resource distribution, disagreements on priorities, work-flow changes, territorial infringements, mutual mistrust, and constant change.	15. Resolution of conflict by establishing settlement objectives, calling on people who can help, bargaining rather than issuing edicts, avoiding personalities, and focusing on mutually beneficial outcomes.
Action Needed Yes No / **Completed** _____	**Action Needed** Yes No / **Completed** _____	**Action Needed** Yes No / **Completed** _____

321

1. An awareness of and sensitivity to employees who display emotional problems, without overreaction to them.	2. Recognition that all people have soft spots in their emotional armor, and that this does not mean they are crazy.	3. An ability to distinguish between neurotic behavior (which may be tolerated) and psychotic behavior (which is bizarre and may become threatening to the individual or to others in the workplace).
Action Needed — Yes No — Completed _____	Action Needed — Yes No — Completed _____	Action Needed — Yes No — Completed _____
4. A willingness to work along with and to offer encouragement to employees whose emotional problems are temporary.	5. Recognition of the signs of poor emotional adjustment—sudden changes in behavior, preoccupation, irritability, increased absences, fatigue, accidents, waste, excessive drinking, and substance abuse.	6. A desire to help employees adjust to their emotional problems—rather than to ridicule them for these problems or to minimize their importance to the individual.
Action Needed — Yes No — Completed _____	Action Needed — Yes No — Completed _____	Action Needed — Yes No — Completed _____
7. Time set aside in your schedule to counsel employees who need attention.	8. Conduct of your counseling sessions in a nonthreatening manner, with emphasis on nondirective interviewing.	9. Development of your listening skills so as to become a non-evaluative listener—a person who does not comment or pass judgment on what is said.
Action Needed — Yes No — Completed _____	Action Needed — Yes No — Completed _____	Action Needed — Yes No — Completed _____
10. Readiness to refer an emotionally disturbed person to your company nurse, doctor, or psychologist for professional advice and treatment whenever your own efforts are not fruitful.	11. A combination of firmness and empathy when counseling employees with problems of absenteeism, alcoholism, or substance abuse.	12. Selective use of different counseling approaches for willful absentees (vacationers, the directionless, moonlighters, and the aggressive) and chronic and occasional absentees.
Action Needed — Yes No — Completed _____	Action Needed — Yes No — Completed _____	Action Needed — Yes No — Completed _____
13. An alertness for early-warning signs of alcoholism and substance abuse in an employee.	14. A willingness to confront an alcoholic employee—or a substance abuser—with the choice between abstinence or the loss of his or her job.	15. A sensitivity, along with an expectancy of useful performance, in dealing with employees who have terminal illnesses.
Action Needed — Yes No — Completed _____	Action Needed — Yes No — Completed _____	Action Needed — Yes No — Completed _____

1. An attitude toward appraisals that focuses on the major goal of improvement of the individual's performance so as to match the job's requirements.	2. Care in separating the discussion of an employee's appraisal rating from any talk, or consideration, of money.	3. Knowledge of the distinctions between objective and subjective rating factors.
Action Needed Yes No · Completed _____	Action Needed Yes No · Completed _____	Action Needed Yes No · Completed _____
4. A conscious effort to apply the same standards to all, so that your ratings are consistent from employee to employee.	5. Maintenance of a file of critical incidents, or specific and representative examples, of each employee's performance and behavior so as to support the appraisal you make.	6. Your guard up against the halo effect, which discriminates for or against a person based on a single incident or trait.
Action Needed Yes No · Completed _____	Action Needed Yes No · Completed _____	Action Needed Yes No · Completed _____
7. Proper appraisal interview: privacy, enough time, emphasis on job standards, credit where due, mutual examination of facts, focus on the future, and sharing of responsibility for performance.	8. Establishment of a positive, constructive atmosphere during the appraisal interview so that employees do not feel that they sit in the judgment of one who believes himself or herself infallible.	9. Willingness to listen to an employee's rebuttal of your rating and to change that rating if the argument is sound.
Action Needed Yes No · Completed _____	Action Needed Yes No · Completed _____	Action Needed Yes No · Completed _____
10. Treatment of an individual's appraisal as confidential, with respect to his or her associates or peers.	11. Strict observance of legal (especially EEOC) regulations as they affect the performance appraisal and the interview.	12. Maintenance of the proper records of the appraisal interview and of the discussions that take place during it.
Action Needed Yes No · Completed _____	Action Needed Yes No · Completed _____	Action Needed Yes No · Completed _____
13. A continuing interest in, and appraisal of, the individual's performance, so that your judgment isn't a one-time decision.	14. Your active assistance in helping the employee overcome specific weaknesses or develop desirable skills.	15. Thoughtful reexamination of conditions that may detract from performance: poor skills-job match, inadequate training, physical or emotional problems, insensitive supervision, and technical problems.
Action Needed Yes No · Completed _____	Action Needed Yes No · Completed _____	Action Needed Yes No · Completed _____

1. Discipline considered as an ongoing training program to encourage desired performance and to discourage undesirable behavior.		2. Discipline used only for corrective purposes and never as a display of authority.		3. Establishment of rules that are reasonable and generally regarded by the work group as mutually beneficial to them and the company.	
Action Needed Yes No	Completed _____	Action Needed Yes No	Completed _____	Action Needed Yes No	Completed _____
4. Understanding of the reasons why employees break rules— willfully by frustrated or disturbed employees and unthinkingly by untrained or misinformed employees.		5. Standards of performance and departmental rules enforced fairly—neither too leniently nor vindictively.		6. Discipline that stresses the positive rather than the negative, improvement rather than punishment.	
Action Needed Yes No	Completed _____	Action Needed Yes No	Completed _____	Action Needed Yes No	Completed _____
7. An approach to meting out corrective discipline that is progressive, with increasingly severe penalties for successive infractions.		8. Advance warnings of possible disciplinary action communicated to employees through training sessions and general information media such as bulletin boards, manuals, and face-to-face discussions.		9. Corrective discipline exercised without undue delay: the principle of immediacy.	
Action Needed Yes No	Completed _____	Action Needed Yes No	Completed _____	Action Needed Yes No	Completed _____
10. Disciplinary action that is consistently applied in like situations and for similar failures to meet standards or to conform to established rules and regulations.		11. Use of behavior modification techniques when conducting disciplinary interviews so as to (a) emphasize performance and (b) involve the employee in the corrective solution.		12. Knowledge of company policies, procedures, and regulations (and influence of labor contract if a union is present) as they affect enforcement of performance standards and organizational discipline.	
Action Needed Yes No	Completed _____	Action Needed Yes No	Completed _____	Action Needed Yes No	Completed _____
13. Enforcement of discipline that meets the legal requirements of prior notice of (a) what constitutes unacceptable performance or behavior and (b) the corresponding penalties.		14. Care in noting oral or written warnings in your records; maintenance of production, quality, safety, and absence records for early detection and correction of off-standard performance.		15. Precheck for priority of corrective disciplinary action: clear-cut violation, adequate warning, concrete evidence, impartiality, credible backup records, and appropriate penalties.	
Action Needed Yes No	Completed _____	Action Needed Yes No	Completed _____	Action Needed Yes No	Completed _____

324

1. Acceptance of a broad definition of "minorities" as "protected groups" under the law: blacks, women, ethnic minorities, the disadvantaged, the handicapped, and workers over 40 years old.	2. Knowledge of, and respect for, the basic legal protections against discrimination in all aspects of employment because of race, religion, national origin, age, or sex.	3. Understanding of the legal and practical implications of an affirmative action program.

Action Needed Yes No	Completed _____	Action Needed Yes No	Completed _____	Action Needed Yes No	Completed _____

4. Understanding of EEOC's three culpable variations of discrimination: differential treatment, disparate effect, and evil intent.	5. Expectation of satisfactory performance, however, from all minorities and/or members of protected groups once they have become integral parts of your work force.	6. Avoidance of stereotyped thinking about why women work—as well as their interest in, and capability to perform, various types of work.

Action Needed Yes No	Completed _____	Action Needed Yes No	Completed _____	Action Needed Yes No	Completed _____

7. Strict avoidance of any form or implication of sexual harassment, either by you or by any member of your staff.	8. Respect for the capabilities of workers over age 40 and for their equal treatment under the law.	9. Observance of an employee's right to privacy and the restrictions affecting drug and lie-detector tests.

Action Needed Yes No	Completed _____	Action Needed Yes No	Completed _____	Action Needed Yes No	Completed _____

10. Full recognition that in the eyes of the law a supervisor acts as a representative of the company in labor relations matters involving its employees.	11. Care not to interfere with or discriminate against union activities, as proscribed by the Wagner Act, at any time—but especially during an organizing drive.	12. Diligence and precision in interpreting and applying labor contract matters during the life of the contract.

Action Needed Yes No	Completed _____	Action Needed Yes No	Completed _____	Action Needed Yes No	Completed _____

13. Knowledge of OSHA standards as they apply to safety and health conditions in your areas of responsibility.	14. Respect for employees' rights under OSHA and enforcement of their responsibilities.	15. Prompt reporting of occupational injuries and illnesses that occur in your department so that they may be entered in the company's OSHA log.

Action Needed Yes No	Completed _____	Action Needed Yes No	Completed _____	Action Needed Yes No	Completed _____

KEYS TO SELF-CHECKS

Note that Self-Check items are arranged in chapter sequence in blocks of five each. That is, for Part 1, the questions (either true-false or multiple choice) follow this pattern: Chapter 1, items 1 to 5; Chapter 2, items 6 to 10; Chapter 3, items 11 to 15; Chapter 4, items 16 to 20; and Chapter 5, items 21 to 25. For Part 2: Chapter 6, items 1 to 5; Chapter 7, items 6 to 10; Chapter 8, items 11 to 15; Chapter 9, items 16 to 20; and Chapter 10, items 21 to 25. For Part 3: Chapter 11, items 1 to 5; Chapter 12, items 6 to 10; Chapter 13, items 11 to 15; Chapter 14, items 16 to 20; and Chapter 15, items 21 to 25.

KEY TO SELF-CHECK FOR PART 1

True-False

1. F	6. T	11. T	16. F	21. T
2. F	7. F	12. T	17. T	22. F
3. T	8. F	13. T	18. T	23. T
4. F	9. F	14. T	19. T	24. T
5. T	10. T	15. F	20. F	25. F

Multiple Choice

1. c	6. a	11. b	16. c	21. b
2. b	7. c	12. c	17. a	22. a
3. a	8. c	13. a	18. d	23. d
4. d	9. d	14. c	19. c	24. d
5. c	10. b	15. b	20. d	25. c

KEY TO SELF-CHECK FOR PART 2

True-False

1. T	6. F	11. T	16. F	21. T
2. T	7. T	12. T	17. T	22. T
3. F	8. F	13. F	18. F	23. F
4. F	9. F	14. T	19. T	24. F
5. F	10. T	15. F	20. F	25. T

Multiple Choice

1. a	6. a	11. c	16. b	21. b
2. d	7. c	12. a	17. c	22. c
3. b	8. d	13. d	18. d	23. c
4. c	9. b	14. a	19. b	24. a
5. d	10. c	15. c	20. d	25. b

KEY TO SELF-CHECK FOR PART 3

True-False

1. F	6. T	11. F	16. T	21. F
2. T	7. F	12. T	17. F	22. F
3. T	8. T	13. T	18. T	23. F
4. T	9. F	14. T	19. F	24. T
5. T	10. T	15. F	20. T	25. T

Multiple Choice

1. c	6. c	11. a	16. d	21. a
2. c	7. a	12. d	17. c	22. b
3. d	8. d	13. d	18. a	23. d
4. d	9. d	14. c	19. c	24. b
5. c	10. b	15. c	20. d	25. b

INDEX

PHOTO CREDITS